HE WHO
IS MADE
LORD

The ISEAS – Yusof Ishak Institute (formerly Institute of Southeast Asian Studies) is an autonomous organization established in 1968. It is a regional centre dedicated to the study of socio-political, security, and economic trends and developments in Southeast Asia and its wider geostrategic and economic environment. The Institute's research programmes are grouped under Regional Economic Studies (RES), Regional Strategic and Political Studies (RSPS), and Regional Social and Cultural Studies (RSCS). The Institute is also home to the ASEAN Studies Centre (ASC), the Singapore APEC Study Centre, and the Temasek History Research Centre (THRC).

ISEAS Publishing, an established academic press, has issued more than 2,000 books and journals. It is the largest scholarly publisher of research about Southeast Asia from within the region. ISEAS Publishing works with many other academic and trade publishers and distributors to disseminate important research and analyses from and about Southeast Asia to the rest of the world.

HE WHO IS MADE LORD

*Empire, class and race
in postwar Singapore*

MUHAMMAD SUHAIL MOHAMED YAZID

ISEAS YUSOF ISHAK
INSTITUTE

First published in Singapore in 2023 by
ISEAS Publishing
30 Heng Mui Keng Terrace
Singapore 119614

E-mail: publish@iseas.edu.sg
Website: <http://bookshop.iseas.edu.sg>

This book is the result of a co-publication between ISEAS – Yusof Ishak Institute and University of Hawai'i Press. University of Hawai'i Press has the right for exclusive distribution of the printed copies in North America.

The responsibility for facts and opinions in this publication rests exclusively with the author and his interpretations do not necessarily reflect the views or the policy of the publisher or its supporters.

ISEAS Library Cataloguing-in-Publication Data

Name(s): Muhammad Suhail Mohamed Yazid, author.
Title: He Who is Made Lord : empire, class and race in postwar Singapore / by Muhammad Suhail Mohamed Yazid.
Description: Singapore : ISEAS-Yusof Ishak Institute, 2023. | Includes bibliographical references and index.
Identifiers: ISBN 978-981-5104-30-1 (soft cover) | ISBN 978-981-5104-31-8 (e-book PDF) | ISBN 978-981-5104-32-5 (epub)
Subjects: LCSH: Heads of state—Singapore. | Singapore—Colonial influence. | Singapore—Social conditions—History.
Classification: LCC JF251 M95

Cover photo: Ministry of Information and the Arts Collection, courtesy of National Archives of Singapore
Cover design by Lee Meng Hui
Index compiled by Raffaie Bin Nahar
Typesetting by Stallion Press (S) Pte Ltd
Printed in Singapore by Mainland Press Pte Ltd

CONTENTS

LIST OF ABBREVIATIONS

AMCJA	All-Malaya Council of Joint Action
ARTIS	*Angkatan Revolusi Tentera Islam Singapura*, or the Revolutionary Muslim Army of Singapore
COI	Commission of Inquiry
FMS	Federated Malay States
ISC	Internal Security Council
J.M.N.	*Johan Mangku Negara*
KMS	*Kesatuan Melayu Singapura*, or Singapore Malay Union
MBE	Member of the Order of the British Empire
MCP	Malayan Communist Party
PAP	People's Action Party
PMIP	Pan-Malayan Islamic Party
PUTERA	Pusat Tenaga Rakyat, or Centre of People's Power
S.M.N.	*Seri Maharaja Mangku Negara*
SLAD	Singapore Legislative Assembly Debates
SPA	Singapore People's Alliance
SS	Straits Settlements
UMNO	United Malays National Organisation
WWII	Second World War

PREFACE

The study of Malay political culture has always fascinated me. This is somewhat an awkward situation: the rajas, along with their attendant pomp and pageantry, kindle and tickle the imagination of this individual of middle-class background who has spent almost his entire life in a republic. As I have come to comprehend, the notion of hierarchy, subordination and deference occurs everywhere and subjects everyone, from the family institution to the grandest platforms of international politics. Such is the condition of human society.

When I was a student in the Departments of History and Malay Studies at the National University of Singapore (NUS), I had the opportunity to critically explore this human condition. I delved into research on the political culture in Singapore and Malaysia, unpacking the creative efforts to resurrect precolonial *kerajaan* elements to serve the interests of imperial and post-imperial regimes. This led to an earlier iteration of this book in the form of my Master of Arts thesis in 2019. That year also coincided with two milestone anniversaries in Singapore: the bicentennial commemoration of the island's "founding" by Sir Stamford Raffles and the 60-year mark of the PAP's rise to power. Officials urged Singaporeans to treat 2019 as an opportune moment to assess the nation's journey and contemplate on its future. The thesis was a response to those calls.

Since then, the thesis has been augmented, enhanced and refined into this monograph, having benefitted from further research undertaken during my time as a PhD candidate in History at the University of Cambridge. Recent historiographical debates on decolonization and the Commonwealth have also enriched this project. With these additions, this book has become more than just an account of Singapore's national history—it is a critical analysis of international hierarchies, class divisions and racial inequalities during the global age of decolonization. These issues continue to haunt contemporary life today, and thus this book contains the reflections of one historian about his own present.

ACKNOWLEDGEMENTS

This book is an outcome of half a decade's worth of conceptualization, research and writing. It has had various incarnations as I encountered different institutional contexts, research communities and ways of looking at the world.

I would like to express my deepest appreciation, first and foremost, to my master's thesis supervisor, A/P Sher Banu A.L. Khan from the NUS Department of Malay Studies. This project is only possible thanks to her solemn dedication to excellence, the scholarly profession and responsibilities as an academic confidante. She is just—quite simply—a fantastic human being. For that, I owe her a debt of kindness which can never be repaid.

I too owe as much to Dr Kelvin Lawrence from the NUS Department of History. Till today, he remains my greatest intellectual influence. The meagre skills I hone as a historian are made better because of his guidance and critique. His artfulness, honesty and humane sensibilities are qualities which I aspire to have. I am happy that our professional ties have transformed into a friendship which I hope will endure. Thanks to him, I can now only see shades of grey.

This book came to see the light of day because of scholarship funding offered by the Tun Dato' Cheng-Lock Tan Fund and by the NUS Department of Malay Studies. My stint as a Research Associate in the ISEAS – Yusof Ishak Institute has indeed been formative for my worldview as a Singaporean academic. I truly enjoyed the institute's homely environment, but I would like to mention by name Mr Choi Shing-Kwok, Director and Chief Executive Officer, and Dr Benjamin Loh, my former supervisor. The team at ISEAS Publishing, particularly Mr Ng Kok Kiong, has shown excellence, commitment and professionalism in assisting me with the publication and review process. Due to the team's tireless labour, the entire experience of publishing this monograph has been nothing but smooth.

Furthermore, I value the steadfast support from the University of Hawai'i Press under the headship of Dr Clem Guthro. Comments from two anonymous reviewers have also been helpful during revision process. And finally, my heartfelt appreciation goes to Dr Terence Chong, Director, Research Division and Deputy Chief Executive Officer of the ISEAS – Yusof Ishak Institute, who has backed this project since day one and whose sharp intellect and mentorship have made a lasting impression on me.

My time as a student in NUS has been crucial to my intellectual journey. I would like to thank the professors whose classes have nurtured my curiosity over the years: A/P Masuda Hajimu, A/P Timothy Barnard, Dr Donna Brunero, Dr Sharon Low, A/P Bruce Lockhart, Prof Brian Farrell, Dr Akiko Masuda, Dr Noorman Abdullah, Dr Imran Tajudeen, Dr Suriani Suratman, A/P Noor Aisha Abdul Rahman, A/P Khairudin Aljunied, Prof Farid Alatas and A/P Maznah Mohamad. Also, I am indebted to A/P Joey Long for his kind advice on this book project.

I must specifically mention A/P Albert Lau, whom I consider to be the greatest Singaporean historian of all time. His undergraduate classes were the reason I developed a research interest in Singaporean and Malaysian history in the first place. His precision, persuasive ability and calibre as a scholar command my eternal admiration—not to mention the fact that he is a generous person of the most pleasant demeanour. Thank you, Prof.

I am truly fortunate to have met outstanding scholars who have challenged me intellectually during my time as a PhD candidate at the University of Cambridge. They include Dr Michael Edwards, Dr Nicole CuUnjieng Aboitiz, Dr Malika Leuzinger, Nicholas Sy and Veronica

Sison, the members of the South Asian Studies Reading Group. I am also grateful to have had erudite interactions with Dr Rachel Leow, my PhD advisor. Above all, I would like to thank my PhD supervisor, A/P Iza Hussin, who has guided me through the COVID-19 pandemic with her graciousness and has pushed me beyond my intellectual comfort zone.

My gratitude extends to members of the graduate community during my time in NUS: Mu'izz Khalid, Syed Hafiz and Afra Alatas. In Cambridge, I am in the wonderful company of my peers who have provided a warm, merry and uplifting fellowship for both intellectual and noble pursuits: Jihan Zaki, Ching Ching Lam, Kun Liang, Rui Li, Yinuo Han, Ashton Ng and Quah Say Jye. Julia Roberts deserves a particularly special mention because she believed in me and this project since very early on and gave me a push at a time when I needed it most. All of them have become more than just associates—they are now friends.

I dearly hold the intimate bonds of brotherhood offered by Rashid Ja'afar, Kok Chun Hong and Liew Zhen Hao, all of whom provided an unconditional listening ear as I went on rambling about my uncanny ideas, strange schemes and convoluted strategies. Allan Pang and Benjamin Khoo set a gold standard of friendship because they tirelessly read drafts and gave me precious feedback, while Joel Chong never failed to give the right advice at the right time. Sandy Wang, Syafiqah Ja'afar, Dr Ho Chi Tim and Kevin Zhang were all obliging in their encouragement. I cannot thank them enough.

My family, especially my parents, has been everything to me. Without them and my beloved Rachel Lee, I am nothing.

1

YANG DI-PERTUAN NEGARA OF SINGAPORE

On the morning of 3 December 1959, Yusof bin Ishak, smartly dressed in a beige *Baju Melayu*, arrived at the centre of Singapore town in a Rolls-Royce. Prime Minister Lee Kuan Yew greeted Yusof and ushered him into a chamber at the heart of the City Hall building. Dozens of politicians, officials and foreign dignitaries were already waiting for Yusof. Following his entry, the magisterial melody of *God Save the Queen* reverberated off the chamber's walls, followed by the confident tune of the new state anthem, *Majulah Singapura*.[1]

All present were standing. Ahmad Ibrahim, the advocate-general, then read out the Commission of Appointment from Queen Elizabeth II, recognizing Yusof as Her Majesty's representative in Singapore. Yusof recited his oath of allegiance in Malay:

> I, Yusof Bin Ishak, do swear that I will well and truly serve Her Majesty Queen Elizabeth II, her heirs and successors, in the office of Yang di-Pertuan Negara. So, help me God.[2]

Prime Minister Lee and the chief justice, Sir Alan Rose, witnessed the oath. After the signing of all official documents, both anthems echoed once more, but this time, *Majulah Singapura* took precedence. Yusof was now Singapore's first Malayan-born Yang di-Pertuan Negara ("he who is made lord").[3] Even though he represented the sovereign power of the British monarch on the island state, the Queen's portraits were nowhere to be seen in the chamber.

After the solemn procedures, the newly appointed Yang di-Pertuan Negara and his entourage emerged from City Hall to much fanfare. Fleets of buses and lorries had ferried schoolchildren and youths to the grand ceremony. In spite of the light drizzle, the 10,000-strong exuberant crowd greeted the Yang di-Pertuan Negara with shouts of "*merdeka*", which was by now a familiar rallying cry meaning "freedom" or "independence" in Malay.[4] City Hall's grandiose structure and its colossal Corinthian columns towered over the crowd and had for many decades projected the might of British imperium. During official events, Singapore's colonial rulers often stood at the very top of the perron, lifting their visual presence over crowds assembled at the grassy forecourt of the Padang. This spatial arrangement projected the hierarchical realities of the relationship between rulers and subjects.[5] The Padang itself has a deeper history. As a "colonial civic space", it was the site of commemorative events to display the might of the reigning imperial power, whether it was the British or the Japanese.[6]

That particular day, however, the crowd at the Padang was not there to marvel at the building or gaze at the colonial officials who lorded over them. Their eyes were fixed on a group of men—fellow compatriots in a new era of representative politics. As these men took their designated seats, there was the grand thundering of a 17-gun salute followed by the tune of *Majulah Singapura*. This time, there was no *God Save the Queen*.[7] Besides the new state anthem, the ceremony also marked the officiation of another significant emblem: the state flag. Forming the mammoth backdrop of the podium, the flag—its colours of red and white, its crescent moon and five stars—was unmissable.[8] Organizers and spectators draped the flag over skyscrapers encircling the Padang, and many in the crowd were dressed in its pristine colours. Culture Minister S. Rajaratnam hailed the flag and the state anthem as "symbols of self-respect", propounding that they carried the "hopes and ideals" of the people of Singapore.[9]

Amid the arresting sights and sounds, the prime minister was first to step onto the elevated platform on the steps of City Hall. Like the Yang di-Pertuan Negara, he was also relatively new to his office. In June

1959, the political party under his leadership, the People's Action Party (PAP), secured a decisive win in the Legislative Assembly elections. It was the first election under a new constitution which granted Singapore full self-government after more than a century of British colonial rule. With Yusof's elevation to the highest office in the land, the aspirations of this constitution were finally met. Sir William Goode, the interim Yang di-Pertuan Negara and last colonial governor of Singapore, had received his farewell send-off a day earlier to mark his departure from both the office and the island.[10] Lee declared that the "cock-hats with white plumes", the symbol of British overlordship, had now been set aside with the electoral triumph of the PAP's "collective leadership". Although Governor Goode's pontifical imperial persona was transformed into the more humbling image of the Yang di-Pertuan Negara, he did not leave Singapore. Only now, with the appointment of a Malayan-born person to succeed him, the cock-hats were sealed forever. Speaking directly to the panoply of faces before him and to the thousands listening on the radio, Lee heralded Yusof as "the personification of State of which you and I are members … he symbolises all of us. To him devotion and loyalty are due".[11]

The adoption of new symbols like the flag, national anthem and the Yang di-Pertuan Negara was meant to facilitate a sense of common loyalty to the city-state. Lee pointed out that nation-building in Singapore was different from "older" nations because the residents of the island had barely any collective sense of nationhood. The prime minister added, "whilst we are searching for that vital sense of oneness in a common destiny, let us not forget that what we have always inculcated is a sense of belonging to Singapore as part of a larger Malayan whole".[12] This crucial caveat predicated the concept of a Singapore free from British rule on the island's future as part of Malaya. The Federation of Malaya, however, had already attained independence from Britain in 1957 without Singapore. After the Second World War, the city-state was constitutionally partitioned from the eleven constituent states of the Federation as a result of the realignment of British plans in the region. Political leaders of Singapore saw the island's new self-governing status as a progressive constitutional milestone towards the eventual reunification of both territories. Lee then concluded his stirring speech by further sanctifying the Yang di-Pertuan Negara, calling on the people of Singapore to offer their "loyalty and affection" to Yusof.

After Lee descended from the podium, it was the Yang di-Pertuan Negara's turn to address the people. Yusof proclaimed:

> Henceforth, Singapore will determine her own destiny. The future of Singapore will depend on the unity and loyalty of her people and on their readiness and determination to carry out honestly and sincerely the principles of which the new State of Singapore is founded.[13]

Yusof went on to elaborate these principles. He urged the people of Singapore to forgo communal sentiments and to embrace a "national consciousness" based on loyalty to the State. He then drew attention to the critical role of youth in establishing a united Singapore, perhaps in recognition of the dominant demographic position of young people.[14] Indeed, the youthfulness of Singapore's population signalled the dextrous potential of a newly awakened nation emerging from the archaic order of colonial rule. After the Yang di-Pertuan Negara's uplifting speech, there was a jubilant marchpast of contingents made up of participants from unions, businesses and political organizations, all saluting the freshly coronated Yang di-Pertuan Negara. Twenty thousand balloons were released into the sky, while ships anchored nearby blew their sirens.[15]

News of Yusof's appointment also circulated throughout the world. In the coming hours, messages of goodwill poured in from within and outside of the Commonwealth of Nations, congratulating Singapore on its constitutional development.[16] The most important message of them all was perhaps from the prime minister of the Federation of Malaya, Tunku Abdul Rahman, who mentioned a rather intimate detail to reflect the fraternal links which bonded Singapore and the Federation. The Tunku revealed that he had sent Aziz Ishak, a minister of his cabinet who was also Yusof's younger brother, to lead an official delegation from the Federation to attend the ceremony in Singapore.[17]

But the swearing-in ceremony, the grand marchpast and goodwill messages only marked the start of a longer series of extravagant celebrations as part of "Loyalty Week". The Singaporean government poured in over $150,000 for this week-long carnivalesque event, organizing exhibitions, processions and performances in Singapore's many languages. Rajaratnam asserted that Loyalty Week was "both a celebration and an affirmation"; it was a celebration of Singapore's aspirations for self-determination and an affirmation of its successes in achieving those aspirations.[18]

The swearing-in of the first Malayan-born Yang di-Pertuan Negara was clearly pregnant with symbolic meaning. On the one hand, the intricate displays of ceremonial grandeur and the infusion of national symbols indicated that Singapore was disentangling itself from the shackles of colonial rule. On the other hand, there were traces of the island's continued emplacement within the British Empire—fragments of the colonial order were renewed, repurposed and reinterpreted. Besides the faithful broadcast of *God Save the Queen* and Yusof's oath of loyalty to the Crown, the event's immersion in pomp and circumstance preserved the rituals of imperial political culture.[19] But the order of things seemed different from the days of colonial rule. There were no pompous White governors, portraits of the British sovereign or the flying of the Union Jack. The new flag and anthem were the more prominent features of the ceremony, adding a distinct nationalist flavour to the entire spectacle.

In their speeches, Lee and Yusof invoked a sense of emancipation from colonial rule and a charted path towards a shared future with Malaya. Both men further signalled a desire to foster a transcendental sense of common loyalty among the people—but loyalty to what or to whom? Was it to Singapore, the Federation of Malaya, to the Yang di-Pertuan Negara or the "collective leadership" of the PAP? In a Singapore working towards eventual independence from British rule, Lee also appealed to a sense of common destiny to be reunited as part of a "Malayan whole". Was loyalty to Singapore simply interchangeable with loyalty to Malaya? The questions here animate the historical efforts to make the office of Yang di-Pertuan Negara meaningful. While the installation of a Malayan-born appointee was meant to communicate a shared sense of unity in a society aspiring for self-determination, underlying tensions continued to bedevil the symbolic projections of the office. *He Who is Made Lord* brings the story and significance of the Yang di-Pertuan Negara into greater clarity.

In the midst of the global era of decolonization and the Cold War, complex negotiations between the British, Singaporean leaders and other stakeholders in the Commonwealth were taking place, shaping the political landscape of the city-state. On the surface, the Yang di-Pertuan Negara can be appreciated as a sign of Singapore's freedom from the fetters of the colonial order. The office represented the nation of intent in the city-state and was enshrined as a symbol which embodied the character, values and aspirations of the people of Singapore. The historical situation, however, was not so straightforward. While the Yang di-Pertuan Negara was ostensibly above party politics, the office, as a state institution, came to be bound up in prevailing power struggles.

Singaporean leaders pushed for a wide range of programmes with the aim of seeking union with the Federation and a tenable path for independence from Britain. The British, in the meantime, refused to relinquish Singapore as part of their imperial domain, while Federation leaders had other plans following their separate attainment of national sovereignty. The Yang di-Pertuan Negara was an outcome of the entangled tensions between these concurrent political projects—a tapestry made of multiple imaginings of Singapore's post-imperial future. *He Who is Made Lord* bares the shifting nature of power relations that shaped these competing ambitions and divergent aspirations. By looking into the creation and execution of the office of Yang di-Pertuan Negara, Singapore's decolonization presents itself as a multifaceted process of struggle, ambiguity and contingency.

The analytical core of the story approximately begins in 1956. This was the year when official talks on Singapore's constitutional status first began between the British government and political representatives from the city-state. Its end point is set in mid-1963 when Singapore was on the cusp of entering the Federation following the passing of the Malaysia Agreement, the basis of a political union entailing the merger of British North Borneo, Sarawak and Singapore with the Federation of Malaya. This new nation-state, or "Malaysia", was to be inaugurated only on 16 September 1963 and could be taken as the fulfilment of the nationalist dream to be reunited, according to Prime Minister Lee, "as part of a larger Malayan whole".

But before the formal establishment of Malaysia, the realization of this dream was not a foregone conclusion. This brief period between 1956 and 1963 was an unsettling time for Singapore, offering a vibrant sense of possibility but also a gnawing atmosphere of political restlessness. The office of Yang di-Pertuan Negara was born in this historical context. Even though this book looks closely at this brief period, it nevertheless traverses greater temporal depth to demonstrate how the office was an artefact that was actively shaped by the many layers of Singapore's past. The following sections serve as a theoretical chart to help navigate the narrative in the subsequent chapters. Some readers may find the following sections helpful in critically engaging with the story of the Yang di-Pertuan Negara, while others might find Chapter 2 a better starting point for their reading experience.

Yang di-Pertuan Negara in Context

The Yang di-Pertuan Negara emerged during "the Malayan trajectory of Singapore's history".[20] This was a period which spans a century prior to the Second World War and follows the island's placement within the wider context of British Malaya. Reaching its zenith on the eve of the First World War, British Malaya was a loose conglomeration of British imperial dependents centred on the Malay Peninsula and tenuously consolidated as part of the wider empire. Historians have advanced many ways of understanding empires. Some consider the two related concepts of "imperialism" and "colonialism" as interchangeable when referring to the European empires from the second half of the nineteenth century.[21] But to think about empires in the broadest way possible, one can see them as "agglomerations, often untidy and unwieldy" involving many types of cross-territorial structures of governance under the economic, cultural and political dominance of an imperial state over the world system.[22] Imperialism is then the drive to preserve and expand empires, while colonialism could be understood as a specific manifestation of imperialism.

Through administrators seconded from the metropole, colonialism involved a multi-dimensional system of domination which entailed the governance of a foreign territory known as the colony. This class of alien administrators—along with a supporting cast of military officers, technical experts and businesspeople—typically form a small minority in the colony. Under the colonial regime, the socio-political order was defined by what Partha Chatterjee has instructively called the "rule of colonial difference", a principle which sustained the separateness of these White elites from the colonized peoples.[23] Singapore could be described as a specific type of colony called a "maritime enclave", similar to British Hong Kong.[24] For much of the nineteenth century up to the early decades of the twentieth century, the island was the base of the highest-ranking colonial official in British Malaya. Singapore's economy thrived on entrepot trade and had developed into an important economic and intellectual node; it was the nucleus of the British Empire in Southeast Asia.

This base of imperial power played a pivotal role as a hub for Malay nationalism. Historians like William Roff and Anthony Milner have shown how the island served as a conduit for ideas of modernism and self-determination within global intellectual networks.[25] These ideas were channelled from the region and from rest of the world and recalibrated within specific local spaces to ferment the idea of a *"bangsa Melayu"* (Malay race or nation). From the second half of the nineteenth century, the scale of imperialism intensified due to improved technologies of travel, industry and communication. These developments stimulated radical shifts in British Malaya that were marked by the increasing connectivity with the wider world, a more exploitative capitalistic economy and drastic demographic changes arising from immigrant labour primarily from India and China. Responding to colonial modernity, elites from among the "indigenous" Malays articulated the conceptual basis of a modern political community based on the *bangsa*. Yusof himself rose to prominence within this intellectual milieu. The future Yang di-Pertuan Negara was the founder and managing editor of the *Utusan Melayu*, a paragon newspaper which became a platform to deliberate the composition of the *bangsa* and to transmit ideas on modernization.

While the concept of *bangsa* gained currency among a growing class of local intelligentsia, historians have largely portrayed immigrant communities, owing to the transient nature of their labour, as being intimately intertwined with the nationalist fervour back in their lands of origin.[26] This racialization of nationalism intertwines with the well-known "divide and rule" policy of British colonialism. This policy could be characterized by the lack of enthusiasm among colonial administrators to foster a post-racial society rooted to the locality, choosing instead to govern the colonial population in an expedient manner along ethnic or tribal lines. There were nevertheless local-born Chinese like Tan Cheng Lock who envisioned a Chinese community committed to Malaya.[27] Most political organizations established before the Second World War, however, hardly took a cross-communal orientation, with one exception being the Malayan Communist Party (MCP).[28] A few segments of the Straits Chinese community even saw the empire as the basis of their national loyalty.[29] During the inauguration of Yusof as Yang di-Pertuan Negara, Lee was truthful in claiming the novelty of nation-building in Singapore considering these disparate expressions of loyalty among the many communities in British Malaya.

The singular event that shattered the status quo in British Malaya was the Japanese invasion during the Second World War. Historians largely hold onto the view that the coming of Japanese imperial rule was a watershed for Southeast Asia. The occupation of Japanese forces in the region displaced the previously impenetrable class of European colonial rulers propped up by the "Whites-only" colour bar, notwithstanding the co-option of a few, selected members from the indigenous ruling class. This interruption provided the opportunity for another handful of local elites to lead their compatriots through Japanese patronage, allowing a new class of non-European leaders to build their prestige and influence.[30] After the war, things could not go back to the way they used to be. The global geopolitical landscape had been radically altered, setting the stage for a new age of decolonization.

If empire was the formation of a British dominated world system, then one way to approach the decolonization of the British Empire is to see it as the decline of that system.[31] Other Western empires shared this experience of imperial decay. The immense wealth and influence of these imperial powers nevertheless ensured that the world system remained unequal despite the transformation of imperial dependents into independent nation-states. More specifically to the British Empire, ties of dependency were given a new lease of life in the form of the Commonwealth of

Nations, with former imperial masters exercising influence in ex-colonial states through ties of culture, defence and capital.[32]

These asymmetries in the global order did not go unchallenged. In this postwar age of global decolonization, self-determination became a dominant concept through which modern communities negotiated their right to exist and govern themselves. Accompanying this was the rise of the world system of nation-states, a global hegemonic structure which presumably upheld the sovereign equality of all nation-states. This postwar international system is best exemplified by the entrenchment of United Nations (UN).[33] In a concerted push for a more equal global order, Afro-Asian states actively used international platforms like the UN to stake their positions as nation-states which were equal in status to the former imperial powers. The efforts of these Afro-Asian states eventually led to the institutionalization of self-determination as a right.[34]

Even as the British Empire made way for the rise of new nation-states, the island state of Singapore seemed to be trapped as a colonial dependent after being constitutionally severed from the peninsular states up north. Historians of Singapore have understandably seen the initial postwar decades as a time of considerable interest as Singaporean nationalists rode on these decolonizing currents to push the British out and undo separation from Malaya. The Yang di-Pertuan Negara was a product of this historical context. Although scholars have acknowledged the establishment of the office as an important symbolic juncture in the history of Singapore's decolonization, the Yang di-Pertuan Negara has been relegated to the role of a prop in the background of a larger socio-political stage. Perhaps adhering to an ironic historical fate, the presence of the Yang di-Pertuan Negara in the academic literature conforms to the office's desired purpose—a dignified umpire insulated from the ugliness of political battles.

The conspicuous absence of the Yang di-Pertuan Negara is obvious in the representative works on Singapore's political history. Through careful scholarly labour, scholars have portrayed the 1950s as a period of intense political contestations in the city-state. For instance, John Drysdale's work has for decades been a staple reference for those interested in the vibrant constitutional politics of postwar Singapore.[35] Other historical works surveying a longer timeframe of the island's history, like Mary

Turnbull's *A History of Modern Singapore*, also feature the postwar decades as a politically febrile time that offered many possibilities.[36] In recent years, however, there has also been conscious effort amongst scholars to recover the legacies of other "forgotten" historical actors operating in this context of political pluralism. Student movements like the University of Malaya Socialist Club, trade unions and other activist organizations launched their specific struggles to define this new postwar political order. The recovery of these stories of political activism patently present a picture of a competitive socio-political landscape.[37] Despite the renewed interest in the climate of Singapore's postwar politics, Yusof has only received a few passing mentions for his contributions to Malay journalism, or a simple acknowledgement of his appointment as Yang di-Pertuan Negara.[38]

This glaring lack of scholarly attention on the Yang di-Pertuan Negara is not surprising. When it comes to "ceremonial" head of states in the Commonwealth realms, scholars of decolonization often overlook the occupants of these offices, treating them as distant, non-political actors.[39] This assumption isolates the Yang di-Pertuan Negara as well as its appointee from the prevailing contestations for power in postwar Singapore. While the office was meant to be apolitical, its origins, establishment and operation were political. Readers will discover that the embeddedness of the Yang di-Pertuan Negara in the historical context made the office inseparable from the power struggles in postwar Singapore. In fact, the office had intensified tensions between nationalist leaders and other political stakeholders.

Among the many stakeholders in postwar Singapore, the British were perhaps the most important because they remained paramount power. Despite a deteriorating capacity to maintain their moribund empire, they still saw themselves as a dominant player in global affairs at least through the 1950s and tightly clutched onto the vestiges of their imperial dominance.[40] Indeed, the British did not stand idly as innocent facilitators to the political activities of Singaporean leaders who became increasingly brazen in pushing for the nationalist cause. The colonial state came to be the arena of struggle between the colonial power and nationalist leaders. The British, however, did not control everything in Singapore, even if they acted like they could. If examined from a global perspective, multiple interlocking circumstances of global dimensions circumscribed Britain's position as paramount power in the national unit.

Two works in particular have been critical placing the political developments in Singapore into larger cross-territorial frames, showing how the unfolding of local events both facilitated and challenged British imperial aims in Singapore, Southeast Asia and the world. Tim Harper's detailed study on the late colonial state in British Malaya explores the dynamic interactions between the economic and social forces of decolonization.[41] He has recovered the radical shifts in social and economic relations following the Second World War which led to the counterinsurgency measures against the MCP and the subsequent reordering of the colonial state. Meanwhile, Karl Hack's work on the decolonization process in Southeast Asia elucidates British defence concerns amid the geopolitical conflict of the Cold War.[42] Strategic considerations were pivotal in deciding which colonies to decolonize and which to recolonize. The Yang di-Pertuan Negara was therefore a particular outcome of calculations (and miscalculations) of developments which stretched across national and international realms.

Yang di-Pertuan Negara and Singapore's Decolonization

Convulsions in global power relations mark the era of decolonization. But how can one conceptualize this dramatic phenomenon? Karl Hack has argued that decolonization is an ongoing process that can be traced to the period before the Second World War and remains in motion today. He further advocates for better attempts at integrating factors such as state-building, geopolitics and nation-building into studies of decolonization.[43] Hack's conceptual sketches resonate with Jan Jansen and Jürgen Osterhammel's more precise understanding of decolonization. They see decolonization not only as a specific historical moment when multiple empires disintegrated during the initial decades after the Second World War, but also as a "many-faceted process" attendant to the end of colonial rule over a subordinate territory.[44] The transfer of power from imperial overlords to local leaders was but one facet of decolonization. The rise of nation-states which are equal to one another (at least in principle) marked structural reform in the international system, and this became concomitant with a change to the socio-political norms previously entrenched by empires.[45] Due to the complicated processes which stretched across multiple contexts, Hack, Jansen and Osterhammel all agree that decolonization is characterized by "vagueness and ambiguity".[46] In response to this theoretical murkiness, Hack has even suggested a typology of different kinds of decolonization.[47] Just as imperialism was a complicated process of domination and transformation over the many aspects of human life, decolonization was its counter-process, covering cultural, political and environmental dimensions.

While it might be productive to embrace a more definite take on decolonization, it might be as fruitful to consider a more basic approach to the concept. At the heart of decolonization and across all the planes of its existence lies a critical animating force: the struggle for power. No single factor or party was solely responsible for decolonization because it was a historically contingent phenomenon which entailed fluctuations in power relations on a global scale.[48] When talking about the nature of power, Friedrich Nietzsche offers a gripping perspective. Power can be identified by its plasticity and is characterized by the capacity to remake, "to transform and to incorporate into oneself what is past and foreign".[49]

The story of the Yang di-Pertuan Negara is a tale about ingenuity. It is a story of simultaneous struggles for power between different historical actors—whether it was the colonial secretary in London or the chief minister in Singapore, the Tunku or Lee Kuan Yew—all of whom came into conflict and at times moved in concert with one another to overcome challenges and secure their dominance in the socio-political order. They embraced a selective appropriation of novelty, engineered new interpretations to existing features in the status quo and even adapted elements drawn from an imagined past. Through the imaginative blending of these materials and practices, historical actors replenished their political capital. They adapted the Yang di-Pertuan Negara for different political projects in their pursuit of privileges and power, thereby turning the office into a contested site.

Singaporean leaders toiled, persevered and competed with one another to change the prevailing socio-political order. Contending with global power relations, they seized the prevailing political currency of self-determination to establish themselves as "genuine" anti-colonial nationalists. In doing so, they distinguished themselves as effective political leaders in the age of decolonization. Since the British had ruled out the viability of the city-state being an independent nation-state, most Singaporean leaders saw reunification with the Federation as the only feasible measure to achieve complete emancipation from colonial rule. In other words, merger would ensure their political survival as nationalist heroes while meeting security interests of Britain and other Commonwealth partners.

No other historical episode has exemplified these competing struggles for power better than the "Battle for Merger", which has become a part of the "foundation myth" of PAP-dominated Singapore.[50] From 1961, the PAP government began to see its long-awaited catharsis for merger within reach in the form of the "Malaysia Plan", which was intended to bring about the political union of Singapore with the Federation of Malaya. This "Battle for Merger" has largely been portrayed as a battle of wills between the PAP and its splinter party, the Barisan Sosialis (hereinafter, the Barisan). The latter openly opposed the Malaysia Plan, arguing that merger would put Singapore on unequal terms in the larger Federation. In recent years, both academic and public discourses have been fixated on the justifiability of Operation Coldstore, a crackdown by security forces a few months before merger which resulted in the detention of over a hundred suspected communists, including leaders from the Barisan.[51] This controversial episode is emblematic of the intertwinement of Singapore's local politics with the larger geopolitical forces of the Cold War.

The controversy of Operation Coldstore has led to an overemphasis on a defining event at the expense of adequately representing other circumstances at play during the historical moment. Singapore's pursuit of political unification with the Federation was more than Operation Coldstore. There were complicated diplomatic negotiations between Britain, the Federation, Singapore and the Bornean states as well as other Commonwealth countries, which also played out on international platforms like the UN and Afro-Asian summits.[52] Both Tan Tai Yong and Nordin Sopiee have shown that the establishment of Malaysia did not come about because of a heroic fulfilment of a grand political vision but was a result of a precarious dealings among diverse players with differing interests, and as both authors rightly point out, these differences were not necessarily resolved upon Malaysia's formation.[53] Within this political and diplomatic fray, it may be challenging to precisely locate the salience of the enigmatic Yang di-Pertuan Negara.

To foreground the significance of the Yang di-Pertuan Negara, one needs to look within the political tussles and diplomatic manoeuvres to identify another concurrent battle—namely on the cultural front. The symbolic dimension of culture was one terrain on which historical actors attempted to rework the entrenched norms of the colonial order during decolonization. Benedict Anderson's canonical work, *Imagined Communities*, has brought the idea of nationalism as a cultural artefact to the forefront of studies on nationalism.[54] Still, fashioning "national culture" is tricky, especially in a multi-ethnic colonial society like Singapore. The expedient nature of these cultural projects to define a cohesive national community has the potential to engender a sense of dislocation; while it may be inclusive to some, it might also be exclusive or foreign to others.[55]

During the campaign for merger, the PAP government came up with its own cultural schematics to prepare Singapore for independence from colonial rule and to make headway for merger with the Federation.[56] Irene Ng's biography of Singapore's Minister of Culture, S. Rajaratnam, captures the herculean task undertaken by his ministry—which was effectively the state's propaganda department—to foster a common "Malayan" identity for the people of Singapore during this period.[57] Edwin Lee's *Singapore: The Unexpected Nation* also speaks to these nation-building efforts.[58] Both authors have discussed the promotion of Malay language, the creation of national symbols and the launch of media campaigns as part of the campaign for merger, but the office of Yang di-Pertuan Negara itself has never been the subject of focus. As a state institution meant to cultivate a shared sense of a community and inspire a spirit of self-determination, the office is a particularly unique historical artefact, one that needs to be studied as a dyad of *both* political and cultural dimensions. Furthermore, the appointee was his own man, a historical actor in his own right.

Sir William Goode, the last governor of colonial Singapore, assumed the office of Yang di-Pertuan Negara in June 1959, and Yusof bin Ishak became his Malayan-born successor six months later. The latter held the office until its reconstitution into a presidency following Singapore's independence as a republic and separation from Malaysia in 1965. Since Yusof was Yang di-Pertuan Negara for most of the office's constitutional life, he played a defining role in shaping what it stood for. Yusof did not leave behind any personal memoirs, and thus publications on him written by biographers are critical sources for assessing the historical significance of the office. To date, Melanie Chew has written the most comprehensive biography of the late president.[59] She has extensively traced Yusof's life, including his delicate position as Yang di-Pertuan Negara during Singapore's brief yet tumultuous stint in Malaysia.[60] The greatest weakness in Chew's work is also its greatest strength. The author has gravitated towards hagiographical tendencies, but in doing so, she has reproduced excerpts from glowing interviews with Yusof's contemporaries, all of which are primary material for critical analysis.[61]

Besides Chew, Norshahril Saat has authored a biographical publication on Yusof to commemorate Singapore fiftieth anniversary of independence as a sovereign republic, an event remembered in popular discourse as "SG50". He tells a story of a man who was a champion of modernism, meritocracy and multiculturalism.[62] Relying on a mix of official sources and oral history interviews, Norshahril's work can be appreciated as a revealing piece of social memory focused on Yusof's years as president of the independent Republic of Singapore.[63] But this publication, like other shorter publications on Yusof, largely neglect his tenure as Yang di-Pertuan Negara.[64] Kevin Tan's biography of Puan Noor Aisha, Yusof's widow and Singapore's former first lady, nevertheless provides invaluable insight into the life of her late husband. Puan Aisha's personal anecdotes are intimate glimpses into the circumstances behind Yusof's acceptance of public office.[65] This collection of biographies, however, are largely concerned about Yusof's personality, contributions and ideas, rather than on the office of Yang di-Pertuan Negara itself. To subject the office as well as the execution of Yusof's official duties to a sustained critical examination, the Yang di-Pertuan Negara needs to be historicized within the prevailing struggles for power.

Existing works on Singapore's constitutional history further perpetuate the dominant memory of Yusof as president of the independent republic post-1965 rather than Yusof as the Yang di-Pertuan Negara. Little consideration is made of the Yang di-Pertuan Negara's cultural significance and the office's role during the historical moment; it has mainly been treated as a mere forerunner to the office of president, as a relic from a bygone age.[66] The point here is that no scholarly appraisal of the Yang di-Pertuan Negara and its role in Singapore's decolonization exists. This book is a direct response to this dearth. In order to distance the memory of Singapore's current status as a sovereign nation-state, the Yang di-Pertuan Negara must be seen on its own terms and within the historical circumstances in which it was established, free from predestination as the office of president. It was meant to signal the coming of a new age for Singapore, making the office an *exceptional* institution with a rich political-symbolic structure. In this respect, the Yang di-Pertuan Negara serves as a valuable historical artefact to examine the representations of the nation of intent in Singapore during a distinct juncture of the island's history.

Yang di-Pertuan Negara as Representation of the Nation

To understand what the Yang di-Pertuan Negara represented, some theoretical scaffolding on nation and nationalism may be helpful. Key theorists generally agree that there is no nation before nationalism and that the nation can be understood as a form of community unique to the modern era, having emerged in the nineteenth century.[67] This thesis, labelled as the "modernist theory" of the origins of nations, argues that the nationalist agenda ("nationalism") has been driven by elites to persuade other individuals of their shared interests to establish a social collective or to apply Anderson's well-worn description, an "imagined community".[68] The establishment and preservation of this social collective through the world system of nation-states is the goal of nationalism. Ernest Gellner has furthered this understanding by arguing that nationalism is the effort to make the very concrete, material realities of the state consistent with the nation, hence the idea of the "nation-state".[69] With mass participation as its modus operandi, nationalism has been facilitated by the economic, technological and socio-political changes brought about by modernity.

But the nation of intent in Singapore was not just a simple outcome of modernity. The island was colonized by a European power, and this has had important implications. Partha Chatterjee has been critical of theorists of nationalism (specifically Anderson) for imposing a universalized "modular" understanding about nationalism onto formerly colonized societies based on the experience in Europe and the Americas, thereby denying the autonomy of colonized elites to think of their own ideas of the nation.[70] These "anti-colonial" nationalisms are thus seen as an imitation of preceding models.[71] Anderson's approach takes the idea of nationalism as a political movement "too seriously"; according to Chatterjee, the battle for sovereignty had taken place long before political battles for independence, when the colonized first defended their "spiritual" domain—that of language, customs and family—from the interference of the colonial powers.[72] Building on Chatterjee's theoretical position, scholars like Anthony Reid have attempted to identify typologies of Asian nationalisms which differed from the nationalisms in the West.[73]

The point that needs to be emphasized is that the nation, rather than being a universal phenomenon or innate entity, is a historically bounded entity delimited by its embeddedness within particular circumstances. In *Represented Communities*, John Kelly and Martha Kaplan postulate that the nation should not be treated as a transcendental or idealistic entity à la Anderson because the nation can only exist in representation, both in the institutional and semiotic sense.[74] In the same vein, Craig Calhoun argues that a nation is made of accepted ways of thinking and speaking, all of which form a structure of knowledge that shapes consciousness. It is "constituted largely by the claims themselves, by ways of talking and thinking and acting that relies on these sorts of claims to produce collective identity".[75] In general agreement with Calhoun, Alan Finlayson asserts that while nationalisms are shaped by specificities of different contexts, they "operate as a certain kind of ideological discourse" through the universalization of values propagated by nationalists for all members of the nation.[76] Nationalists interpret and rearticulate the concrete realities of any action, entity or event to make it significant for others.[77] In short, the nation *needs* to be represented in order to exist.

To represent the nation of intent, Singaporean leaders competed among themselves to invest symbolic meaning in the Yang di-Pertuan

Negara, turning it into a national symbol. Michael Geisler has theorized that national symbols operate as a "mass media system"; together, they form a communicative structure to signify the nation's existence.[78] As evident during Yusof's swearing-in ceremony, the Yang di-Pertuan Negara appeared alongside slogans and other emblems to represent a nation of intent for Singapore—a Singapore that was free from colonial rule and reunited with an independent Malaya. A nationalist discourse invests symbolic meaning in these otherwise meaningless "objects", and as national symbols, they in turn become "subjects" that express the nation. As sociologist Karen Cerulo points out, national symbols are both receptacles and projections of the nation:

> They function as modern totems that merge the mythical, sacred substance of the nation with a specified, manifest form, one that is grounded in everyday experience of sight, sound, or touch. By blending subject and object, national symbols move beyond simple representation of nation. In a very real sense, national symbols *become* the nation.[79]

The Yang di-Pertuan Negara did not contain meaning in and of itself. Singaporean leaders circulated ideas, messages and values in order to represent the nation of intent through the office. As Lee himself declared, Yusof as Yang di-Pertuan Negara became the very "personification" of Singapore.

But even as Lee and other PAP leaders attempted to seize the initiative to represent the nation of intent through the office, the Yang di-Pertuan Negara's meanings were open-ended and far from definite. Borrowing Philip Gorski's theoretical observations, individuals and social groups negotiated the office in two social spaces: on the one hand, there is a "space of nation" and on the other, a "space of nation-ization".[80] The former is "objective", concrete, specifically rooted in territoriality and the social interactions between human beings, while the space of nation-ization is "symbolic", where "real and possible nations are or can be imagined and enacted" in which one may find "symbolic resources which nations are made and unmade".[81] The space of nation-ization is discursive as it centres on narratives, sacralization of symbols and commemorative rituals:

> In a nation-ization struggle, social and cultural actors propose and oppose various conflicting visions of the nation and of the sense of being a group more generally. They struggle both over how the nation should be defined and about its relative salience as a principle of group identity and action. This struggle is simultaneously symbolic and practical, and inextricably so.[82]

During Singapore's decolonization, different historical actors—from the blue-collar worker to the politician in the halls of power—invested meaning in the Yang di-Pertuan Negara as a means to actively negotiate their interests in an emergent post-imperial Singapore. The Yang di-Pertuan Negara was a bricolage of multiple competing visions for Singapore. As the office operated in "objective" space, a concurrent "symbolic" struggle was taking place to define what Singapore represented and what it could be. In other words, the office, when operating in its historical context, signified different things to different people.

A useful analytical frame to penetrate the instability of the Yang di-Pertuan Negara's meanings is to consider Gayatri Spivak's reflections on the interplay of two types of representation—that of "portrait" and "proxy".[83] As a "portrait", the Yang di-Pertuan Negara was meant to "re-present" the character and values of the nation of intent which was emerging out of colonialism and moving towards merger with the Federation. The logic involved here is akin to that of a portrait, a tangible depiction of a figurative entity, idea or concept. But perhaps ironically, in the performance of his constitutional duties, the Yang di-Pertuan Negara was the "proxy" of the British Crown. As the Queen's representative in Singapore, he also represented Britain's continued dominion over the island state. The Yang di-Pertuan Negara exercised sovereign powers on behalf of the Queen, spoke for Her Majesty and was the lasting link to a larger imperial hierarchy. The Yang di-Pertuan Negara's slipperiness as a symbol was thus premised on the office's design *both* as a representation of a nation of intent and as a representation of British overlordship. The indivisible nature of its symbolic and political structure constituted the tension at the heart of the office's historical existence.

The Yang di-Pertuan Negara was a peculiar construction. Even as Singaporean leaders explicitly sanctified the office as the symbolic representation of the nation of intent, it did not change the fact that the Yang di-Pertuan Negara was an element of colonial statecraft. The legal basis of the office was the State of Singapore Act. Passed by the British Parliament to enact a new charter for self-governing Singapore, this edict officiated the 1958 Singapore Order-in-Council (hereinafter "the Constitution"). The constitutional predication of the office meant that the Yang di-Pertuan Negara was an institution of the modern (colonial) state with the appointee wielding authority similar to other heads of state in the Westminster system. The duties and responsibilities of these titular figures include the prerogative to dissolve the legislature, appoint the head of government, or dispense pardons to criminals. Some of these powers have to be exercised in accordance with advice from elected ministers, but others remain under the personal discretion of the head of state.

Yang di-Pertuan Negara as Representation of the Crown

The political-symbolic structure of the Yang di-Pertuan Negara was made concrete through its human form. Overlaps of biography and history are therefore crucial in imagining the possible meanings of the Yang di-Pertuan Negara. Moreover, the Constitution offered no comprehensive guidance on the demeanour or temperament required for eligible candidates, suggesting that the appointee had some room to perform what he thought should be proper conduct for someone of that high office. The story which this book tells comes with an occasional conflation of appointee with the office of Yang di-Pertuan Negara. This is not meant to equate the totality of the individual with the entirety of the office but rather to emphasize the interplay of agency in projecting the office's meanings. The very impossibility to separate both appointee and office in embodied performance sets another field of semiotic contentions which must be interrogated. At times, the Yang di-Pertuan Negara was relatable as a fallible human being, while on other occasions, he remained distant, magnificent and elusive, cloaked with the shrouds of state power.

Thinking about the human element of the Yang di-Pertuan Negara prompts comparison with monarchs. The close relationship between royalty and the building of the nation-state is a much-discussed issue within the scholarly literature on nationalism.[84] This perpetuates a persistent, long-drawn tendency to personify a community of belonging. Post-Enlightenment ideas of the individual have often been inscribed onto the nation, treating it like an entity that is autonomous and equal to others yet peculiar by itself.[85] Monarchies themselves have been harmonized into modern conceptions of sovereignty. As historian Eric Hobsbawm argues, monarchs have been used to strengthen political regimes in both autocratic and parliamentary states, making the "royal person" the focal point of national unity and sovereignty. The generational transitions between occupants of the throne further conjure a sense of continuity that links the nation's long history with its present.[86] More relevant to Singapore, the Malay rulers of the pre-colonial political order embodied this concept through the *kerajaan*.[87] Leaders from the United Malays National Organisation (UMNO) later moulded the rulers into corporeal symbols for the party's vision of a postcolonial state centred on Malay dominance.[88]

The office of Yang di-Pertuan Negara derived its authority from the British Crown. It is therefore important to set its historical existence within a larger British imperial landscape during the age of decolonization. Among many studies on the British Crown, Philip Murphy's work is perhaps the most convincing in showing how the royal family had shaped ideas of British authority not just at home, but also in the imperial and Commonwealth realms.[89] Members of the royal family negotiated their agency and authority with officials from the metropole, colonies and ex-colonies in different historical contexts, projecting shifting meanings of the Crown. Through their individual dispositions, the British monarchs have played different roles at different historical junctures.

The similarities between the Yang di-Pertuan Negara and monarchs, however, must not come at the expense of identifying dissimilarities. The office was not a seat of royalty. Unlike the thrones of royal houses in the Malay Peninsula, the Yang di-Pertuan Negara had no claims of longstanding precolonial historicity—it was established as a result of the 1958 Constitution. The nominee had to be appointed by the British sovereign, and as the representative of the Crown in Singapore, he served at the sovereign's pleasure. In this sense, the Yang di-Pertuan Negara was instead much closer to the governor-generals of the Commonwealth, both in form and substance. In fact, the office was initially conceived as a "Malayan governor-general". In the countries of the Commonwealth, governor-generals—along with other ceremonial heads of state such as presidents in the case of republican countries—perform constitutional functions expected of the British monarch in the United Kingdom.[90] As viceregal officers of the Crown, they act as umpires, serving the "dignified" aspect of power and transcending the vicious battles of party politics. These posts often do not have a consistent manual, making them pliable to the changing personalities of their appointees and shifting customs specific to their contexts.[91] The Yang di-Pertuan Negara was therefore a specific incarnation of the office of governor-general which was tailored to the political situation in Singapore during the final years of colonial rule.

The Yang di-Pertuan Negara and the governor-generals share a burdened history, serving as the constitutional connection between a (formerly) dependent state and the Crown. When these viceregal offices were first established in the White settler colonies of the British empire-Commonwealth (known as the "old dominions"), the appointment of governor-generals became occasional episodes of political tension between local governments and London. To some, the governor-generals represented the overlordship of Britain over a particular territory.[92] But depending on circumstances, Crown representatives were at times embraced as a proud testament of a society's Britannic heritage.[93] This ambivalent relationship endured after the Second World War. In the global age of decolonization, there has been a trend within the Commonwealth towards formally shaving off constitutional linkages with the Crown. In 2021, Barbados became the latest country to establish itself as a republic by abolishing the British sovereign as its head of state, even though the Caribbean state remains a member of the Commonwealth.[94]

As the world enters a post-Elizabethan era following the recent death of the Queen, who was a relatively beloved figure in the Commonwealth, one can reasonably expect this trend to continue. There is also a richer history at play here. This precedent of transitioning into a republic while retaining Commonwealth membership is based on India's case when it transitioned from a sovereign dominion into a republic in 1949. As opposed to the situation before the Second World War, loyalty to the Crown was no longer necessary to qualify for membership of this international fraternity—a move which the British stomached to extend the viability of the Commonwealth in the postwar world.

Understanding the governor-generals of the Commonwealth therefore helps to situate the Yang di-Pertuan Negara within a shared historical terrain with former dependents of the British Empire. In *Viceregalism*, H. Kumarasingham and other scholars recognize viceregal officers in the Westminster system or "parliamentary heads of state" as political actors in their own right.[95] The authors have chosen to work with the term "viceregalism", which is derived from the word "viceroy". This term is evocative of the heritage of the British Raj in colonial India where the viceroy, as representative of the Crown, had almost absolute authority in governing the colony.[96] "Viceregalism" grounds the parliamentary heads of state as particular incarnations modelled after the constitutional monarchy in Britain and is used to conceptualize the latitude available to them during exceptional moments of political crises. Responding to the lack of academic attention on the parliamentary heads of state as political actors, the authors have sought to dispel the assumption that these titular figures are merely "rubber stamps" or ceremonial personages with plenty of style but little substance. During times of crisis, parliamentary heads of state take on critical roles. They become arbiters of power, deciding who could lead governments, and at times even usurped the role of government to exercise complete authority, effectively ruling by decree.

Kumarasingham further theorizes three rights that define their scope of action during political crises: the right to rule (assume sovereign powers like an absolute monarch), to uphold (guard the principles and procedures of the constitution) and to oblige (do nothing and take on a detached path in conformity with the executive's whims).[97] Another crucial element that influences the manoeuvrability of the parliamentary heads of state is the "viceregal-premier axis" or the relationship between the head of state and the head of government, the latter usually titled as prime minister. In decolonizing contexts, the relationship between both of them was crucial in ensuring the success of the constitutions of would-be sovereign nations.[98] As Lee Kuan Yew stated when Yusof was sworn in as Yang di-Pertuan Negara, the 1958 Constitution was fully realized only when the Malayan-born appointee entered office, suggesting the fulfilment of the decolonizing spirit behind the Constitution. This transition was in a sense a covenant between the Yang di-Pertuan Negara and the prime minister because it seemingly expunged the coloniality that remained stuck in the structure of the Singaporean state. With the departure of the last colonial governor of Singapore, Yusof's ascendence helped manufacture legitimacy for the PAP regime, creating the impression of a "genuine" anti-colonial government in the age of global decolonization.

In recounting Singapore's historical experience with the Yang di-Pertuan Negara, this book provides two interventions which supplement the scholarly inquiry in *Viceregalism*. First, it demonstrates that much could be gained in understanding the political character of parliamentary heads of state by extending analysis beyond episodes of crisis. While Kumarasingham is accurate in stating that exigencies bring out the extent of powers invested in parliamentary heads of states, their political importance also predate their constitutional operation. The struggles that precipitated during the conception of these offices need to be taken just as seriously to better sketch a complete picture of their political inflexions. The overt political efforts to design the Yang di-Pertuan Negara both exposed and engendered strains in existing power relations.

This leads to the second intervention. What if political crises were treated as perennial? Power asymmetries are in consistent flux, and so too were the roles of parliamentary heads of state. Their positions within prevailing power relations require constant negotiations. Kumarasingham and the other authors hope to attend to the political roles of parliamentary heads of states and not confine them merely to ceremonial functions. But is the distinction between the political and the ceremonial a helpful one? The importance of the Yang di-Pertuan Negara lies in the polemics of its political and cultural dimensions. If a source of authority for these viceregal offices was symbolic power to give politics a "dignified" representation, it becomes even more critical to look at the everyday making of their significance to better contemplate their roles as political actors. Symbolic practices through national rituals help perpetuate the idea of social contracts and a certain ordering of society.[99] The term "viceregalism" must therefore be stretched to better consider the ceremonial as a political idiom because it invests symbolic substance in these offices, endowing them with authority as living totems.

Yang di-Pertuan Negara: Avatar of Empire, Class and Race

The theoretical buttress thus far sets the stage for a stirring story of the Yang di-Pertuan Negara. To tell this story, the chapters ahead follow three discursive frames: empire, class and race. These frames form the basis of meaning-making in the historical context and provide suitable entry points to access the historical struggles to represent the nation through the Yang di-Pertuan Negara. All three frames, however, are not mutually exclusive; in the historical context, they bled into and fused with one another. But this artificial separation of chapters has its advantages. It allows for the contemplation of the Yang di-Pertuan Negara on different terms, distilling the different registers of decolonization in Singapore and the textures of competing attempts to define the office.

To construct the spirited nature of power struggles in the historical context, each frame engages with three broad "counter-values" which Singaporean leaders advanced through their political projects and which the Yang di-Pertuan Negara, as the representation of the nation of intent, was supposed to personify—anti-colonialism, equality and multi-racial unity.[100] Singaporean leaders churned and transmitted these ideas to communicate the breakdown of the status quo and establish political capital for themselves as heroes of self-determination. It is also not an accident that these three counter-values to the colonial order conjure affinity with the values of the French Revolution, a historical event that has conventionally marked the widespread acceptance of the "nation" as the subject of human loyalties.[101] Further attesting to the revolutionary claims of nationalism, anti-colonial nationalist movements, including the ones in Singapore, were claimants to the Revolution's aspirations of liberty, equality and fraternity. By treating the Yang di-Pertuan Negara as a historical artefact that was made meaningful by the discursive frames of the time, the dynamic relations of power in a decolonizing Singapore take centre stage.

Each chapter constructs the unfurling of different struggles, casting the Yang di-Pertuan Negara in a constant state of ambivalence. This narrative structure borrows Sujit Sivasundaram's framework of "recycling and movement". Rather than fixating on continuity and change, "recycling and movement" connotes the idea that "change is constant, and every change is changed in turn, and continuity is there but in that continuity the very idea of what came in the past...is repackaged and redefined".[102] While Sivasundaram looks at an instance of colonial transition in Ceylon, the lens he offers enlightens the *decolonizing* transition taking place in Singapore. There was no overhaul of the colonial order, but what took place were conjoined efforts to dramatize change and reinvent the status quo in the service of power. The slipperiness between the values of the colonial order and counter-values of the nationalist alternative reinforces the idea that the dichotomies between these concepts were permeable enough to be absorbed into the political projects of different historical actors depending on what suited them best. These actors reinterpreted elements of continuity entrenched under British rule while selectively deploying signs of novelty. The Yang di-Pertuan Negara existed in the interstices of what was "colonial" or "anti-colonial", deployed to mean either way based on what was expedient.

Besides centring on the pliable nature of the Yang di-Pertuan Negara, structuring the book according to discursive frames has an additional effect of de-emphasizing the linear flow of time. A straightforward chronological order might produce the impression that self-government was a "logical" or "natural" stage of decolonization or human progress, leading ultimately to the formation of the nation-state. This might reproduce what Prasenjit Duara calls, "the false unity of self-same, national subject moving through time", a narrative model typical in most national histories.[103] To circumvent this, the narrative that tie the chapters traces and re-traces its temporal steps because it plays with what came before and what came after, or to employ Rudolf Mrázek's description, "less as a chronology, than as, let us say, shifting sands".[104] The temporal manoeuvres capture the Yang di-Pertuan Negara's historical existence as a palimpsest of multiple layers of memory; the office's meanings were inexact, contingent and dependent on the interaction of elements from past and present.

In terms of space, the narrative also weaves multiple scales that stretch from the macro to the micro, encompassing global geopolitics, imperial-colony tensions and the conscious decisions of individual personalities. These narrative strategies represent the chaotic realities influencing the historical actors, underlining how decolonization played out in an open-ended, provisional and uncertain manner. Chapter 2 is an exception. It serves as an entry point and uses a conventional linear narrative to foreground the wave of change enveloping the postwar world and to better situate the intellectual inquiry undertaken in subsequent chapters.

Following Chapter 2's contextual basis, Chapter 3 traces the efforts to subvert empire through the 1958 Constitution and the counter-efforts to preserve the British imperial system. Nationalist governments, including the one in Singapore, sought ways to uphold the status of their states as an equal, dignified political entity in the postwar world system. In everyday life, Singaporean leaders curtailed the excesses of imperial rituals which had entrenched consciousness of the supranational hierarchy of empire. They tweaked the ritualistic practices of the colonial order to project an impression of Singapore's existence as a liberated ex-colony. The British Crown, which was at the apex of the imperial hierarchy, became the subject of nationalist harassment. At the time when the Yang di-Pertuan Negara was established, two major newly independent former colonies, Pakistan and India, had emulated Ireland by dissolving the post of governor-general in their territories to remove their links with the British monarch. The case was more violent for former British dependencies in the Middle East as local kings and chieftains, previously propped up by colonial governments, were overthrown.[105]

But different historical situations produce different configurations. The nationalist government of the Federation of Malaya, avoiding the fervour of its other ex-colonial contemporaries, continued to indulge the Malay rulers—all nine of them—as the colonial masters once did.[106] As an aspiring member of the Federation, Singapore faced an interesting dilemma upon PAP's rise to power: stick to the party's socialist and anti-monarchical principles as displayed by many decolonizing states in Afro-Asia, or embrace the monarchical culture of her neighbour up north to "fit in". Furthermore, geopolitical concerns of the Cold War arrested the attempts of Singaporean leaders to demand complete emancipation from colonial rule. Through a critical scrutiny of the Yang di-Pertuan Negara's blueprint and the subsequent operation of the office, Chapter 3 grapples with these questions: how did the imperial hierarchy survive in a global context of decolonization and the Cold War, and conversely, how did the nationalist leaders attempt to reconcile the lingering presence of the imperial hierarchy?

Chapter 4 complements Chapter 3, baring the situation of ambiguity that was dawning on Singapore. By delving into the design and performance of the Yang di-Pertuan Negara, one can observe the extent to which Singaporean leaders continued to be trapped in practices of class distinctions that were ingrained in the colonial order. The social practices of everyday life which emphasized these distinctions continued to haunt the "new" self-governing Singapore. In trying to launch a social revolution through the promotion of their nationalist ideas, class distinctions maintained by the colonial state endured in other ways. At times, Singaporean leaders even affirmed them. With the class of White colonial administrators no longer directly governing Singapore's internal affairs, a rising class of non-White elites had risen to power, taking the places of their former imperial overlords. This situation was intimately tied to the social position of the Yang di-Pertuan Negara. In apparent harmony with the socialist ideals of the PAP, Yusof was promoted as a commoner and exalted as an "anti-colonialist". But in doing so, what elements of colonial class privileges—privileges enjoyed by dominant sections of the nationalist leadership—endured? How could an egalitarian symbol concurrently and contradictorily serve as a stubborn symbol of class distinctions?

Alongside the presence of imperial hierarchies and the practice of class distinctions, the spectre of race also shaped the rationalities of colonial rule. Chapter 5 elaborates on the racialized dimensions of class issues which hardened as a result of the many decades of colonial capitalism. The colonial order consolidated racial identities as observed in the colonial division of labour and politics in British Malaya. The hierarchy of class existed in tandem with a parallel hierarchy of race in which White Europeans were ranked higher than coloured peoples. The coming of self-government did not completely liberate the Yang di-Pertuan Negara from the racialist modality of colonial society. When the office was first conceptualized, British suspicions toward an Asian personage occupying Governor House were motivation enough for them to think of safeguards to preserve the racial hierarchy of the colonial order. In an attempt to overturn this hierarchy, Singaporean leaders sought to revolutionize the standards of the former office of colonial governor by installing a non-European, Malayan-born man to remediate the inequalities of White rule over non-White imperial subjects. This visible "overthrow" of White dominance presumably destroyed the image of racial hierarchy to produce symbolic meaning in the era of decolonization. During self-government, Yusof—notwithstanding his very obvious non-European heritage—was furthermore promoted as a multi-racial symbol and was conspicuously draped with the rhetoric of freedom from communalism. But in doing so, what aspects of race did Singaporean leaders continue to accept and perpetuate to consolidate their political projects?

This book responds to these questions by curating information from a range of primary sources. These sources form the discursive structure in the historical context, depicting the ideas and actions of multiple parties, including the British officials, politicians from both Singapore and the Federation as well as ordinary people. The first group of primary sources consists of declassified official records produced and compiled by the ministries of the British government, namely the Colonial Office and the Dominion Office (later reconstituted as the Commonwealth Relations Office), respectively organized under the CO 1030 and DO 35 file series. Correspondences and reports transmitted between the British government in London and the governor in Singapore (later on, with the United Kingdom commissioner) account for the bulk of contents in CO 1030. Meanwhile, the DO 35 series is made up of a range of documents circulated within Whitehall as well as exchanges between the British government and other Commonwealth countries. These files provide crucial details on the circumstances that shaped the creation of the Yang di-Pertuan Negara not only because they contain the thoughts of British officials, but also because they record the actions, interactions and concerns of Singaporean leaders. Moreover, these declassified documents reflect the ideological traces of the colonizing power which are disguised, more often than not, by banal bureaucratic concerns. It is precisely because of their ideological nature that the documents become invaluable historical material to expose the struggle for power involved in the making and establishment of the Yang di-Pertuan Negara.

Debates in the Singapore Legislative Assembly published in *The Hansard* comprise another corpus of primary information, capturing the political rhetoric prevalent in the context in question, specifically amongst the elected representatives of the island state. Besides official documents, party periodicals and newspapers have been invaluable in examining the ideological discourse of nationalism in the historical context because they were a dominant medium of communication accessible to the reading public then. These publications not only record the voices of the political parties and activities of workaday persons, but also help to recover the details of public appearances and speeches undertaken by the Yang di-Pertuan Negara. Autobiographical material and oral histories further supplement these sources.

As much as these historical sources ground the information presented in this book, the telling of history itself remains an inconclusive project. History, perhaps not unlike the Yang di-Pertuan Negara, is as much a form of cultural expression as a representation of the political. It is an open-ended medium to depict the power relations and stratifications of human society in the past. As readers might realize even before reaching the ending of this particular account of the Yang di-Pertuan Negara, the discursive legacies of colonial Singapore, just like in any other ex-colonial contexts, still haunt contemporary life on the island, albeit subject to creative reinvention.

As a historical account rooted in the present, this book deliberately strives to accommodate the heterogenous reality during Singapore's decolonization and does not pretend to offer *the* definitive account of the Yang di-Pertuan Negara, nor Singapore's experience with decolonization for that matter. Its modest aim is very much shaped by current challenges of the Singaporean nation-state, imploring readers to reflect on historical trappings and inequalities that persist today, not just in Singapore but in the global system. The thrust of this book is therefore simple, provoking and productive—*He Who is Made Lord* portrays the Yang di-Pertuan Negara as an artefact from the past with the potential to cast a different light on the present, inviting the imagining of a future that is unfettered by historical baggage, for both Singapore and the world.

Notes

1. *The Singapore Free Press (SFP)*, 2 December 1959, p. 1.
2. Government of Singapore, *Singapore (Constitution) Order in Council 1958* (Singapore: Government Printing Office, 1958), p. 55.
3. Government of Singapore, *Installation of the Yang di-Pertuan Negara of the State of Singapore* (Singapore: Government Printing Office, 1959), CO 1030/633, 30–34.
4. *SFP*, 3 December 1959, p. 1.

5. Chua Beng Huat, "Decoding the Political in Civic Spaces: An Interpretive Essay", in *Public Space: Design, Use and Management*, edited by Chua Beng Huat and Norman Edwards (Singapore: Singapore University Press, 1992), pp. 57–58. The building was former home to the municipal offices of the colonial government and was now the new home of the PAP government.

6. Kevin Tan, "A History of the Pandang", *Biblioasia* 18, no. 1 (2022), https://biblioasia.nlb.gov.sg/vol-18/issue-1/apr-to-jun-2022/history-padang (accessed 7 November 2022).

7. *Times*, 4 December 1959, DO 35/9888, 44.

8. *SFP*, 3 December 1959, p. 1.

9. *The Straits Times (ST)*, 12 November 1959, p. 11.

10. *SFP*, 2 December 1959, p. 1.

11. "Singapore Government Press Statement", 3 December 1959, CO 1030/480.

12. Ibid.

13. Ibid.

14. Ibid.

15. *Times*, 4 December 1959, DO 35/9888, 44.

16. *ST*, 4 December 1959, p. 4.

17. *ST*, 3 December 1959, p. 1.

18. *ST*, 8 November 1959, p. 1 and *ST*, 27 September 1959, p. 13.

19. David Cannadine, *Ornamentalism: How the British Saw Their Empire* (New York: Oxford University Press, 2001), pp. 121–35.

20. Karl Hack, "The Malayan Trajectory of Singapore's History", in *Singapore from Temasek to the 21st Century*, edited by Karl Hack, Jean-Louis Margolin and Karine Delaye (Singapore: National University of Singapore Press, 2010), pp. 243–91.

21. Krishnan Kumar, "Colony and Empire, Colonialism and Imperialism: A Meaningful Distinction?", *Comparative Studies in Society and History* 63, no. 2 (2021): 280–309.

22. Ibid. On empire as a world system, see John Darwin, *The Empire Project: The Rise and Fall of the British World System* (Cambridge: Cambridge University Press, 2009).

23. Partha Chatterjee, *The Nation and Its Fragments* (Princeton: Princeton University Press, 1993), pp. 26–34.

24. Jürgen Osterhammel, *Colonialism: A Theoretical Overview*, translated by Shelley Frisch (Princeton: Markus Wiener Publishers, 1997), p. 11.

25. For the full list of works consulted, see *Bibliography*. A few examples that will be cited include William R. Roff, *The Origins of Malay Nationalism* (Kuala Lumpur: University of Malaya Press, 1967); Anthony Milner, *The Invention of Politics in Colonial Malaya: Contesting Nationalism and the Expansion of the Public Sphere* (Cambridge: Cambridge University Press, 1994); Syed Muhd Khairudin Aljunied, *Radicals: Resistance and Protest in Colonial Malaya* (DeKalb: Northern Illinois University Press, 2015).

26. See *Bibliography*. For example, see C. F. Yong and R. B. McKenna, "The Kuomintang Movement in Malaya and Singapore, 1925–30", *Journal of Southeast Asian Studies* 15, no. 1 (March 1984): 91–107.

27. K. G. Tregonning, "Tan Cheng Lock: A Malayan Nationalist", *Journal of Southeast Asian Studies* 10, no. 1 (March 1979): 25–76.

28. C.F. Yong, *The Origins of Malayan Communism* (Singapore: South Seas Society, 1997), pp. 128–50. Also see *Bibliography*.

29. Sai Siew-Min, "Educating Multicultural Citizens: Colonial Nationalism, Imperial Citizenship and Education in Late Colonial Singapore", *Journal of Southeast Asian Studies* 44, no. 1 (2013): 49–73 and Sai Siew-Min, "Dressing Up Subjecthood: Straits Chinese, the Queue, and Contested Citizenship in Colonial Singapore", *The Journal of Imperial and Commonwealth History* 47, no. 3 (2019): 446–73.

30. Cheah Boon Kheng, *Red Star Over Malaya: Resistance and Social Conflict during and after the Japanese Occupation, 1941–1946* (Singapore: Singapore University Press, 1983), pp. 56–123 and Aljunied, *Radicals*, pp. 73–101.

31. Karl Hack points out that this understanding of empire was part of an "Oxbridge school" which goes back to the works of Jack Gallagher and Ronald Robinson and later furthered by John Darwin, see Karl Hack, "Unfinished Decolonisation and Globalisation", *The Journal of Imperial and Commonwealth History* 47, no. 5 (2019): 818–50.

32. Krishnan Srinivasan, "Nobody's Commonwealth? The Commonwealth in Britain's Post-imperial Adjustment", *Commonwealth & Comparative Politics* 44, no. 2 (July 2006): 259–65.

33. John D. Kelly and Martha Kaplan, *Represented Communities: Fiji and World Decolonization* (Chicago and London: University of Chicago Press, 2001), pp. 9–15.

34. Adom Getachew, *Worldmaking after Empire: The Rise and Fall of Self-determination* (Princeton and Oxford: Princeton University Press, 2019), pp. 71–106.

35. John Drysdale, *Singapore: Struggle for Success* (Singapore: Times Books International, 1984). Also see Yeo Kim Wah, *Political Development in Singapore* (Singapore: Singapore University Press, 1973).

36. C.M. Turnbull, *A History of Modern Singapore, 1819–2005*, new ed. (Singapore: NUS Press, 2020).

37. For example, see the first 11 contributions in Michael Barr and Carl Trocki, eds., *Paths Not Taken: Political Pluralism in Post-war Singapore* (Singapore: NUS Press, 2008) and Loh Kah Seng, Edgar Liao, Cheng Tju Lim and Guo-Quan Seng, *The University Socialist Club and the Contest for Malaya: Tangled Strands of Modernity* (Singapore: NUS Press, 2012).

38. For example, see Drysdale, *Struggle for Success*, pp. 85, 237; Edwin Lee, *Singapore: The Unexpected Nation* (Singapore: Institute of Southeast Asian Studies, 2008), p. 165; Mohd Azhar Terimo, "From Self-government to

Independence: UMNO and Malay Politics in Singapore, 1959–1965", in *Malays/Muslims in Singapore: Selected Readings in History 1819–1965*, edited by Khoo Kay Kim, Elinah Abdullah, and Wan Meng Hao (Subang Jaya: Pelanduk, 2006), p. 493; also see chapters by Timothy P. Barnard and Jan van der Putten as well as Lily Zubaidah Rahim in *Paths Not Taken*, pp. 102, 139, 149.

39. H. Kumarasingham, "Viceregalism", in *Viceregalism: The Crown as Head of State in Political Crises in the Postwar Commonwealth*, edited by H. Kumarasingham (Cham: Palgrave Macmillan, 2020), pp. 15–35.

40. Martin Shipway, *Decolonization and Its Impact: A Comparative Approach to the End of Colonial Empires* (Oxford: Blackwell, 2008), pp. 8–9 and John Darwin, *Britain and Decolonisation: The Retreat from Empire in the Postwar World* (Basingstoke and London: Macmillan Press, 1988), pp. 3–25.

41. T.N. Harper, *The End of Empire and the Making of Malaya* (Cambridge: Cambridge University Press, 1999).

42. Karl Hack, *Defence and Decolonisation in Southeast Asia* (Surrey: Curzon, 2001).

43. Karl Hack, "Theories and Approaches to British Decolonization in Southeast Asia", in *The Transformation of Southeast Asia: International Perspectives on Decolonization*, edited by Marc Frey, Ronald W. Pruessen and Tan Tai Yong (London and New York: Routledge, 2003), pp. 105–26.

44. Jan Jansen and Jürgen Osterhammel, *Decolonization: A Short History*, translated by Jeremiah Riemer (Princeton: Princeton University Press, 2017), p. 2.

45. Ibid., pp. 6–13.

46. Ibid., p. 2 and Hack, "Unfinished Decolonisation and Globalisation", pp. 839–40.

47. Hack, "Unfinished Decolonisation and Globalisation", pp. 841–43.

48. Amongst others, Martin Shipway has advocated for this approach, treating decolonization as a complex outcome of a dialectic between the colonizer and the colonized, see Shipway, *Decolonization*, p. 5. Meanwhile, Kelly and Kaplan are sceptical of the dialectical approach, opting for the view that decolonization was a complex dialogical process beyond the colonizer-colonized divide involving an infinite number of subject-subject relations, see Kelly and Kaplan, *Represented Communities*, pp. 6–9.

49. Friedrich Nietzsche, "On the Uses and Disadvantages of History for Life", in *Untimely Meditations*, edited by Daniel Breazeale, translated by R.J. Hollingdale (Cambridge: Cambridge University Press, 1997), p. 62.

50. The term "foundation myth" is not denoting untruthfulness but rather a "a simplistic, usually rosy version of events" used as a foundational basis for a social collective, see John Tosh, *The Pursuit of History: Aims, Methods and New Directions in the Study of History*, 7th ed. (London and New York: Routledge, 2022), p. 3.

51. Lee Ting Hui, *The Open United Front: The Communist Struggle in Singapore 1954–1966* (Singapore: South Seas Society, 1996) and Poh Soo Kai, Tan Kok Fang and Hong Lysa, *The 1963 Operation Coldstore in Singapore: Commemorating 50 Years* (Kuala Lumpur: SIRD, 2013). Also see *Bibliography*.

52. On "worldmaking" efforts by leaders of the Global South, see Getachew, *Worldmaking after Empire* and Christopher J. Lee, ed., *Making a World after Empire: The Bandung Moment and its Political Afterlives* (Athens: Ohio University Press, 2010).

53. Mohamed Noordin Sopiee, *From Malayan Union to Separation: Political Unification in the Malaysia Region 1945–1965* (Kuala Lumpur: University of Malaya Press, 2005) and Tan Tai Yong, *Creating "Greater Malaysia": Decolonisation and the Politics of Merger* (Singapore: Institute of Southeast Asian Studies, 2008).

54. Benedict Anderson, *Imagined Communities: Reflections on the Origins and Spread of Nationalism*, rev. ed. (London and New York: Verso, 2006).

55. Frantz Fanon, *The Wretched of the Earth* (New York: Grove Press, 1963), pp. 206–48.

56. Noor Fadilah Yusof, "Malayans First and Last: The Cultural Battle for Merger, from 1959 to 1963", (Unpublished academic exercise, Department of History, National University of Singapore, 2009).

57. Irene Ng, *The Singapore Lion: A Biography of S. Rajaratnam* (Singapore: Institute of Southeast Asian Studies, 2010).

58. See Lee, *Singapore*.

59. Melanie Chew, *A Biography of President Yusof bin Ishak* (Singapore: SNP, 1999).

60. Ibid., pp. 98–130.

61. They include Yusof's brother, Rahim Ishak, and former PAP cabinet minister, Othman Wok.

62. Norshahril Saat, *Yusof Ishak: Singapore's First President* (Singapore: Institute of Southeast Asian Studies, 2015).

63. Ibid., pp. 53–64.

64. Edmund Lim, *Yusof Ishak* (Singapore: Straits Times Press, 2017); Ooi Kee Beng, *Yusof Ishak: A Man of Many Firsts* (Singapore: Institute of Southeast Asian Studies, 2017) and Norshahril Saat, "Progressive Malay/Muslim Singaporeans—the Thoughts of Yusof Ishak", in *Majulah! 50 Years of Malay/ Muslim Community in Singapore*, edited by Zainul Abideen Rasheed and Norshahril Saat (Singapore: World Scientific, 2016), pp. 3–18.

65. Kevin Tan, *Puan Noor Aishah: Singapore's First Lady* (Singapore: Straits Times Press, 2017).

66. Kevin Tan and Lam Peng Er, *Managing Political Change in Singapore: The Elected Presidency* (London: Routledge, 1997) and Kevin Tan, *The Constitution of Singapore: A Contextual Analysis* (Oxford: Bloomsbury, 2015).

67. My claims are based on the historiographical review on "Modernism" in Umut Özkirimli, *Theories of Nationalism: A Critical Introduction* (Basingstoke: Palgrave Macmillan, 2010), pp. 72–142.
68. This phrase is Benedict Anderson's, see Anderson, *Imagined Communities*.
69. Ernest Gellner, *Nations and Nationalism*, 2nd ed. (Oxford: Wiley-Blackwell, 2006).
70. Chatterjee, *The Nation*, p. 5.
71. See Chakrabarty on historicism in Dipesh Chakrabarty, *Provincializing Europe: Postcolonial Thought and Historical Difference* (Princeton and Oxford: Princeton University Press, 2000), pp. 6–13.
72. Chatterjee, *The Nation*, pp. 6–13.
73. Anthony Reid, *Imperial Alchemy: Nationalism and Political Identity in Southeast Asia* (Cambridge: Cambridge University Press, 2016).
74. Kelly and Kaplan, *Represented Communities*, p. 22.
75. Craig Calhoun, *Nationalism* (Buckingham: Open University Press, 1997), pp. 3–6.
76. Alan Finlayson, "Ideology, Discourse and Nationalism", *Journal of Political Ideologies* 3, no. 1 (1998): 107–13.
77. Ibid., p. 105.
78. Michael Geisler, ed., *National Symbols, Fractured Identities: Contesting the National Narrative* (London: Middlebury College Press, 2005), pp. xiii–xlii.
79. Karen A. Cerulo, *Identity Designs: The Sights and Sounds of a Nation* (New Jersey: Rutgers University Press, 1995), p. 4.
80. Philip S. Gorski, "Nation-ization Struggles: A Bourdieusian Theory of Nationalism", in *Bourdieu and Historical Analysis*, edited by Philip S. Gorski (Durham and London: Duke University Press, 2013).
81. Ibid., p. 256.
82. Ibid., p. 257.
83. Gayatri Chakravorty Spivak, "Can the Subaltern Speak?", in *Colonial Discourse and Post-colonial Theory: A Reader*, edited by Patrick Williams and Laura Chrisman (New York: Columbia University Press, 1994), pp. 70–75.
84. For example, see contributions in M. Banerjee, Charlotte Backerra, and Cathleen Sarti, eds., *Transnational Histories of the 'Royal Nation'* (Cham: Palgrave Macmillan, 2017) and David Cannadine, "The Context, Performance and Meaning of Ritual: The British Monarchy and the 'Invention of Tradition', c. 1820–1977", in *The Invention of Tradition*, edited by Eric Hobsbawm and Terence Ranger (Cambridge: Cambridge University Press, 1983), pp. 101–64. Also see *Bibliography*.
85. Calhoun, *Nationalism*, pp. 42–58.
86. Eric Hobsbawm, "Mass Producing Traditions: Europe, 1870–1914", in *The Invention of Tradition*, edited by Eric Hobsbawm and Terence Ranger (Cambridge: Cambridge University Press, 1983), pp. 282–83.

87. Anthony Milner, *Kerajaan: Malay Political Culture on the Eve of Colonial Rule*, 2nd ed. (Petaling Jaya: SIRD, 2016), pp. 15–16.

88. Donna Amoroso, *Traditionalism and the Ascendancy of the Malay Ruling Class in Colonial Malaya* (Singapore: NUS Press, 2014), pp. 136–64.

89. Philip Murphy, *Monarchy and the End of Empire: The House of Windsor, the British government and the Postwar Commonwealth* (Oxford: Oxford University Press, 2019).

90. David Butler, "Introduction", in *Sovereigns and Surrogates: Constitutional Heads of States in the Commonwealth*, edited by David Butler and D.A. Low (London: Macmillan, 1991), pp. 1–8.

91. Ibid., p. 8.

92. Murphy, *Monarchy*, pp. 16–33. The "old Dominions" were Australia, Canada, New Zealand, the Irish Free State, South Africa and Newfoundland.

93. See ibid. for the cases of Australia and Canada.

94. Jess Ilse, "Milestones of a Monarch: Barbados becomes a Republic", *Royal Central*, 30 March 2022, https://royalcentral.co.uk/uk/milestones-of-a-monarch-barbados-becomes-a-republic-174721/ (accessed 24 April 2022).

95. Kumarasingham, "Viceregalism", pp. 2–3.

96. Ibid., p. v.

97. Ibid., pp. 15–35.

98. Ibid., p. 12.

99. Kelly and Kaplan, *Represented Communities*, pp. 140–41.

100. These counter-values to colonialism correspond to the PAP's founding objectives, see *ST*, 22 November 1954, p. 1. Chatterjee has argued that the nationalism is a "derivative discourse" trapped in the intellectual premises of colonialism. Likewise, the counter-values offered by nationalism in Singapore accepted the same intellectual premises of the colonial order. See Partha Chatterjee, *Nationalist Thought and the Colonial World* (London: Zed Books, 1986), pp. 1–30.

101. Calhoun, *Nationalism*, p. 9.

102. Sujit Sivasundaram, *Islanded: Britain, Sri Lanka, and the Bounds of an Indian Ocean Colony* (Chicago: University of Chicago Press, 2013), p. 12.

103. Rudolf Mrázek, *Engineers of Happy Land: Technology and Nationalism in a Colony* (Princeton: Princeton University Press, 2002), p. xv.

104. Prasenjit Duara, *Rescuing History from the Nation: Questioning Narratives of Modern China* (Chicago and London: The University of Chicago Press), p. 4.

105. Ibid., pp. 154–73.

106. Ibid., pp. 174–75.

2

REDESIGNING THE COLONIAL STATE

Singapore Separated

Beneath the temporal layers of Yusof's swearing-in ceremony was Singapore's inextricable historical position as part of the Malay World. In 1819, 140 years before the coming of the Malayan-born Yang di-Pertuan Negara, the British East India Company enthroned Hussein Shah as sovereign ruler of Singapore. The island was at this time under the domain of the Johor-Riau Sultanate. As the eldest son of Sultan Mahmud Shah III, Hussein was in line to succeed his father but lost this claim due to a succession dispute. His younger brother, Abdul Rahman, received the backing of the Dutch and the Bugis chiefs and was instead crowned as sovereign. In exchange for recognition as sultan and a reasonable pension, Hussein gave his assent to an adventurer from the Company, Sir Stamford Raffles, the so-called "founder of modern Singapore", to build a factory on the island.[1]

The political role of the British-recognized sultan, however, withered after sovereignty over Singapore was later transferred to the British Crown in 1824.[2] Hussein's descendants nevertheless continued to live within the premises of the Istana Kampung Glam, the palace compound belonging to the sultan located on the south-eastern end of the island. Under the sovereign rule of Britain, Singapore gradually transformed into a colonial metropolis. It was later governed as part of the Straits Settlements, a collection of British-controlled port cities which included Penang and Melaka. From 1874, the British began to intervene in the polities of the Malay Peninsula due to increasing pressure from commercial interests who wanted greater stability in the Malay states.[3] Through treaties and protectorate agreements, the Malay rulers gradually ceded authority over most of their affairs to colonial officials, resulting in the bureaucratization of these polities in line with "enlightened" European standards and the facilitation of a more efficient economic system to exploit labour and natural resources.

The colonial regime reordered the island of Singapore and the other peninsular polities under a loose (and at times contested) conglomeration of "British Malaya". In Singapore, the British abolished Malay kingship in favour of direct colonial rule, but they opted for a different strategy in the peninsular states, choosing instead to strengthen the positions of the traditional elites and legitimize the sovereign status of the Malay rulers. With the consolidation of the rulers' sovereignty in the colonial state, there was a pretence that the pre-colonial socio-political order of the *kerajaan* had been preserved; under the *kerajaan*, the ruler was the centre of his subjects' political consciousness.[4] Singapore was embedded within the *kerajaan* order prior to British rule and shared the wider political culture of the Malay World. Similar to Singapore, British paramountcy brought vast demographic and socio-economic changes to the peninsular states. The Malay ruling class found it sensible to collaborate with the imperial power amid these vast transformations, thereby securing their privileges in the new colonial order.

Even after the side-lining of its Malay ruler, Singapore was not completely severed from the political landscape of the peninsula. The governor of the Straits Settlements based in Singapore held the joint office of high commissioner of the Federated Malay States (FMS), the federative framework which fastened the states of Selangor, Pahang, Perak and Negri Sembilan together under British rule. Other peninsular states which later came under the fold of British Malaya were referred to as the Unfederated Malay States (UMS). The governor in Singapore, as the highest-ranking Crown representative in British Malaya, maintained oversight of these territories. Besides housing the seat of British power in the region, Singapore served as an important entrepôt and a node for capital. Booming economic activity further attracted a large immigrant population to the colonial city, facilitated in large part by exploitative practices like indentured and penal labour.[5] As a colony, Singapore continued to be deeply embedded in the Malay World and Britain's global empire. The future office of Yang di-Pertuan Negara was to carry the historical traces of this political heritage.

This British-dominated political system, however, came to a dramatic end during the Second World War when the Japanese, allied with Italy and Germany, conquered European outposts of empire in Southeast Asia.[6] The change in imperial overlordship altered the political configurations of the region. British Malaya as well as the entire Malay Archipelago came to be united under the rule of a single hegemonic power. In contrast to the previous British-dominated order, the Japanese authorities in Malaya were not bounded by treaties, and they chose not to legitimize the sovereignty of the Malay rulers, at least at first. But as the war situation deteriorated, the Japanese accorded greater privileges to the rulers, making use of their royal prestige to win the fidelity of the people.[7]

In spite of their nebulous relationship with the Malay rulers, the new imperial masters accorded greater opportunities for other local elites to lead. The Japanese assigned responsibilities of former British expatriate managers to bureaucrats from the Malay aristocratic class.[8] Meanwhile, anti-colonial leaders persecuted under British rule, like those from the *Kesatuan Melayu Muda* (Young Malays Union, or KMM), were tasked with mobilizing the population through the creation of militias and taking charge of propaganda efforts.[9] The Japanese also supported the creation of the Indian Independence League. This military division came under the command of a former leader of the Indian National Congress, Subhas Chandra Bose, who persuaded ex-sepoys and local Indians in Malaya to collaborate with the Japanese to liberate India from Britain.[10] But these political opportunities did not spare the local population from the terror and violence of the Japanese regime. The Chinese community received the brunt of wartime horrors due to their anti-Japanese campaign during the Sino-Japanese War. To sabotage Japanese war efforts, some of them later joined guerrilla operations under the banner of the Malayan People's

Anti-Japanese Army (MPAJA).[11] Japanese rule acquainted colonial society with military struggle and civic participation in political causes. In the years to come, these elements would come to play a critical role in influencing the pace and trajectory of decolonization in both the Malayan Peninsula and Singapore.

Final victory did not belong to the Japanese. Twin American atomic bombs dropped on the Japanese cities of Hiroshima and Nagasaki, forcing the last standing Axis power to capitulate to Allied forces. When the British returned to Malaya in 1945, the colonial status quo that was in place before the war had been severely disrupted. The British, as part of their response to the changing geopolitical conditions of the postwar world, announced plans to guide their imperial dependents towards eventual independence. These plans were however taken with much cynicism. Talk of independence for Malaya was merely aspirational and set in an indefinite future. The interracial bloodshed as a result of revenge killings in the interregnum after Japanese surrender reinforced justifications for continued British governance in Malaya to better manage relations between different racial groups. In this vein, the British implemented the Malayan Union plan in 1946 with the aim of "preparing" Malaya for independence. This political arrangement introduced a centralized government and a common citizenship for the resident population regardless of race should they choose to make Malaya the subject of their national loyalty.[12]

But Singapore became a casualty under the Malayan Union. The re-ordering of Malaya meant that the island would be constitutionally separated from the peninsula and then re-established as a British Crown Colony.[13] Singapore's severance from the peninsular states was one of many projects of partitioning in the British Empire and predated the violent 1947 partition of the Indian subcontinent by a year. The process of partition materialized the imperial intent to create distinctiveness between connected territories.[14] Besides Singapore, the institution of the Malay kingship also fell victim to the Malayan Union. Since the British governed this new political unit as a colony under direct rule, the Malay rulers had to relinquish sovereignty over their respective states to the British Crown. The Johor aristocrat Dato' Onn Bin Jaafar later led UMNO to oppose the Malayan Union in a clarion call to restore the rulers' sovereignty and Malay political dominance over Malaya.[15] The British, overwhelmed by UMNO's campaign of civil disobedience, eventually relented in favour of a federative arrangement. During negotiations with the rulers during the course of 1947, the British agreed to restore the sovereignty of the former and tightened the criteria for citizenship for the immigrant population. The federal proposals, however, did not reverse Singapore's constitutional separation from the peninsula in spite of the long-standing historical and cultural ties between both territories.

The federal proposals were not satisfactory for some in the anti-colonial nationalist movement. In 1947, a host of disparate parties formed the All-Malayan Council for Joint Action (AMCJA) and launched a *hartal* (strike) to oppose the proposals. Working with the *Pusat Tenaga Rakyat* (Centre of People's Power, or PUTERA), a Malay left-wing alliance, the coalition demanded for "a united Malaya, including Singapore".[16] The movement's effort to unify Singapore with the peninsula was cut short in June 1948 when the British declared a state of emergency to quell a spate of violent attacks against European plantation managers. As part of counter-insurgency measures, the British took a hard stance against "subversive" activities by launching military action against the MCP and outlawing many left-wing political organizations.[17] By this time, Cold War tensions had also engulfed the world. Europe was bifurcated along Soviet and American spheres, while revolutionary struggles led by communist forces were unfolding in China and Southeast Asia.

The MCP had taken full advantage of the postwar "liberal" politics in Malaya. Its cadres engineered strikes and labour unrests to agitate for better socio-economic conditions for the working class in pursuance of their goal of establishing an independent communist republic. This was a direct threat to British interests because keeping Malaya open to British capital was vital to rebuild Britain's battered postwar economy. Framing the MCP strategy as part of global communist onslaught to destabilize the capitalist system, the Emergency was therefore largely fought to "make Southeast Asia safe for British business".[18] The war imposed a wide range of consequences in Malaya. Through its strategy of "exclusion", the colonial state pushed historical actors who had alternative, class-based ideas of establishing an independent non-communal Malaya into the fringes of society, clearing the path for the dominance of concessionary politics between elites representing Malaya's dominant racial communities. This led to the establishment of the "racial state", which meant that the discourse of race became a primary medium to negotiate resources and rights. The elite-based concessionary politics was exemplified by the rise of the Alliance, a political coalition comprised of UMNO, the Malayan Chinese Association (MCA) and the Malayan Indian Congress (MIC), which rose to power in the Federation under these repressive circumstances.[19]

Representative Politics in Singapore

Singapore was not exempted from emergency regulations. In response to communist infiltration of political parties and trade unions as part of the MCP's "open united front" strategy, the British imposed laws to detain individuals and ban any organization deemed as a threat to public safety.[20] These measures continued to remain in place even as the city-state embarked on a separate constitutional path from the peninsula.[21] From 1948, the British began to introduce a limited measure of electoral politics in Singapore. Most of the Legislative Council's members, however, were still unelected and appointed to their seats by the British governor. Moreover, only British subjects could vote. Since the vast majority of Singapore's immigrant population were still legally recognized as foreigners, most were not able to participate in the polls.[22]

This situation changed in 1955. Following the enactment of the Rendel Constitution and reforms to British citizenship laws, many long-term residents in Singapore could finally cast their vote. The island's legislature was reconstituted into a Legislative Assembly with a majority of elected seats, thus allowing the people of Singapore to elect a state government.[23] The general elections later that year led to the appointment of David Marshall as Singapore's first chief minister. His party, the Labour Front, formed a coalition government with the Singapore Alliance, which was itself comprised of the Singaporean branches of UMNO and MCA together with the *Kesatuan Melayu Singapura* (Singapore Malay Union, or KMS).[24] Singapore's first elected government aimed to carry out the people's mandate and bring the city-state much closer to self-determination through merger with the Federation.

Marshall's tenure as chief minister, however, was largely turbulent. Popular politics manifested in regular occurrences of strikes and unrests, forcing Marshall to balance negotiating with protestors and taking tough measures to restore order.[25] His remit was further curtailed by the British governor, who wielded extensive reserve powers and supervised key areas of governance like security and finance. Colonial officials thus kept a close watch over the elected government in Singapore.[26] Still, the British tolerated Marshall. A collapse of his government would not only delegitimize the British experiment to introduce self-government in Singapore, but also result in the rise of the PAP, a more radical left-wing party already infiltrated by communists.

Things came to head during a constitutional crisis in July 1955 when Governor Robert Black refused to approve Marshall's request for the appointment of four assistant ministers. The conflict then became fixed on the scope of the governor's discretionary powers. Marshall argued that the governor should adopt the most "liberal" interpretation of the Rendel Constitution and merely dispense the functions of the constitutional monarch in Britain. In other words, Marshall believed that the governor must oblige to executive advice from the elected Singaporean ministers. The Colonial Office, however, supported Black's right to use his discretionary powers to veto policies, resulting in Marshall threatening to resign from government. The crisis was resolved only after direct mediation by Alan Lennox-Boyd, the British colonial secretary, resulting in the Colonial Office's acquiescence to Marshall's demands.[27] The contentious figure of the colonial governor as Singapore's Crown representative would play an important role in shaping the demands of the Singaporean delegation during constitutional talks in 1956.

The unfolding of the 1955 constitutional crisis in Singapore resonated with the anti-colonial mood engulfing the Afro-Asian world. National leaders from Africa and Asia convened at the 1955 Bandung Conference barely two weeks after the Marshall government was sworn in. Condemning the colonialism of European and American powers, they affirmed new principles of the global order, in particular the equality of all races and respect for national sovereignty. A *Times* article speculated that Marshall's brash attitude came from the restlessness towards Singapore's constitutional position as Afro-Asian leaders began to assert themselves in remaking the international order. The Conference was also a blatant reminder of the island's "inferior" position in Afro-Asia since Singapore was not seen as coeval with the other sovereign nations represented in Bandung.[28]

Although the structure of representative politics in Singapore had barely taken shape, Marshall was aggressive in pushing for the city-state's decolonization. He pressed for the Malayanization of the civil service to reduce the reliance on expatriate manpower in the management of the state.[29] The Assembly later passed his resolution to demand from the British full self-government. The all-party effort granted the chief minister overwhelming support, proving that self-determination was a uniting cause. This was remarkable because other opposition parties were ruthless in their criticisms of Marshall's leadership, while his own party suffered from heavy infighting.[30] The anti-colonial momentum in Singapore was furthermore in line with ongoing debates taking place in the UN Human Rights Council, which began equating colonialism to slavery and linking individual rights to the achievement of self-determination for colonized states.[31]

But what did "full self-government" actually mean? Britain and the other colonial powers had committed themselves to granting self-government to their imperial dependents as part of their postwar plans for the global order. This followed the spirit of the Atlantic Charter, the founding document of the UN, which enshrined the principle of self-determination for all peoples. Nationalists in colonial territories were nevertheless sceptical. Even as far back in 1945, anti-colonial critics were outspoken about the term "self-government". Vijaya Lakshmi Pandit, the sister of the Indian premier Jawaharlal Nehru, called it an "ancient weasel word" for Western powers to defer granting independence for their colonial territories.[32] It was a vague term that could mean mere concessions to representative politics rather than complete sovereign independence.

While the specifics of what constituted "self-government" were nothing less than hazy, for Singaporean leaders, the term encapsulated the idea of a fully elected local government which would aim for full independence through merger with the Federation. Since the 1955 elections, political parties in Singapore had campaigned for the inclusion of Singapore in a united Malaya, taking up the mantle from the AMCJA-PUTERA coalition. They construed self-government as a means to reverse the partitioning of Singapore and the peninsula, although the parties differed on their approaches to achieve this complex project of political reunification.[33] In line with the aim of achieving merger, the idea of being "Malayan" was therefore the main receptacle of a local nationality for residents of Singapore.

Marshall tried to court the Federation chief minister, Tunku Abdul Rahman, to form a joint effort at achieving an independent united Malaya. The latter, however, was hesitant to offer any overt support.[34] The UMNO-led Alliance government was already negotiating for a constitution for an independent Federation of Malaya. Drawing Singapore into the equation might aggravate existing constitutional knots and delay independence for the Federation. The island's massive Chinese population also posed a nasty problem in the eyes of the Tunku.[35] From the perspective of his UMNO support base, the Malays had already compromised with the Chinese community in the peninsula by giving them citizenship rights. Adding a million Singaporean Chinese into the Federation's demographic mix could exacerbate inter-racial tensions. The Tunku was furthermore public with his distrust of the Singaporean government's ability to handle communist elements in the city-state.[36] Merger, at least at this juncture, had to be deferred.

Constitutional Demands from Singapore

In April 1956, a 13-man delegation from Singapore arrived in London in a hopeful attempt to negotiate self-government for the city-state. Later named the "Marshall delegation", it comprised of members from the ruling coalition and the opposition, including PAP assemblymen Lee Kuan Yew and Lim Chin Siong.[37] On the other side of the negotiating table, Colonial Secretary Lennox-Boyd led British officials from both Singapore and London. The Singaporean representatives had a clear position: defence and external affairs were to remain under British jurisdiction, while the city-state was to attain the status of an "independent territory" within the Commonwealth and get its own local-born governor-general as Crown representative.[38] The replacement of the governor with the governor-general would signal Singapore's status as equivalent to other Commonwealth countries with their own governor-generals, like New Zealand and Australia.

For the British, however, independence was out of the question. They had to maintain their strategic interests in the region through their military bases in Singapore. Allowing the island to exist as a sovereign state was simply not viable due to its size and vulnerability to a communist takeover. In short, a sovereign Singapore, whether communist or otherwise, may encumber access to these bases and hinder British defence commitments to other allies in the region. Even though the colonial power was willing to accord a greater degree of local autonomy over Singapore's internal affairs, the island's independence could only be considered if it was part of a united, stable, British-friendly Malaya. But these concerns did not stop Marshall from trying to humbug the British to grant *"merdeka"* (independence) for Singapore rather than self-government.[39] Negotiations soon became a game of semantics.

Despite the gulf in negotiating positions, both delegations nevertheless agreed to the establishment of a "Defence and Security Council" to coordinate overall security. But differences arose as to its staffing; the British wanted a majority in the Council, while Singaporean delegates believed that elected local ministers ought to form the majority. Marshall later compromised through a somewhat creative solution. He proposed parity in the number of British and Singaporean members with a representative from the Federation serving as chair with a tiebreaker vote. Federation presence in the Council would not only trim potential excesses of colonial power but also encourage a united Malaya by giving Federation leaders a greater say in Singapore's affairs. Such an arrangement, however, was erroneous—it meant that non-British representatives could overrule British officials in the affairs of a British colony. Even though Marshall argued that strategic interests of Britain and the Federation were largely aligned, the British delegation rabidly hounded down his proposition and insisted that the British government retain "ultimate authority" over defence and internal security in Singapore.[40] The deadlock on the security issue notwithstanding, the British endorsed the Singaporean delegates' unanimous expression of the island's eventual unification with Malaya.[41] There was also consensus on all other points of discussion, including the issues of a local Singaporean citizenship and a fully elected legislature.

The security issue overshadowed another matter: a future Crown representative who would serve the titular functions of head of state. The British wanted to design this viceregal office along the lines of a British high commissioner to reflect the city-state's "advanced status" in the Commonwealth.[42] The high commissioner was envisioned as the representative of both the Crown and the British government. This office would be parallel to the high commissioner in Malaya following the 1948 Federation of Malaya Agreement.[43] Taking on this proposal, however, would make the office of high commissioner hardly any different from the current British governorship. The former would continue to wield the extensive powers which included the authority to suspend the Constitution, act on matters relating to defence and external relations as well as decide on key appointments to the security organs of the state.[44] It was no surprise that the Marshall delegation was hostile towards such a proposal. Singaporean leaders were adamant that the future Crown representative should be strictly apolitical:

> We are of the view that Her Majesty's representative should be a symbol of the State, outside all political conflicts and one to whom, whoever he may be, the people of Singapore should look up to and give their loyalty.[45]

The Marshall delegation wanted a non-British, local-born "Malayan governor-general" for Singapore, while the high commissioner, as the representative of the British government, would administer the island's defence and external affairs.[46] By separating the representative of the Crown from the representative of the British government, this proposal called for an effective split in the office of governor.

The British delegates, however, could not accept the "Malayan governor-general" proposal. According to them, a governor-general for Singapore would raise unspecified "difficulties".[47] A governor-general and a high commissioner serving in one territory was nevertheless not an extraordinary occurrence in Commonwealth countries. This was true back in 1956 as it is today.[48] A governor-general acts as the representative of the British Crown and serves the titular function of a constitutional monarch, while a high commissioner is a diplomat representing the British government. The defining problem was that Singapore was still a colonial dependent of Britain. The separation of the Crown representative's functions from the office of British government representative was an exclusive privilege reserved for sovereign nations in the Commonwealth realms.

With the British and Singapore delegates at an impasse, the governor-general proposal along with the entire platform of the 1956 Singapore Constitutional Conference, were eventually declared dead. Marshall explained to the press that the talks collapsed because Lennox-Boyd had offered him, in what would become a famous quote, "Christmas pudding with arsenic sauce".[49] Taking ownership of his failure, Marshall subsequently resigned, allowing Lim Yew Hock, the minister for labour and welfare, to take over as chief minister. After settling into his new office, Lim travelled to London in July 1956 to informally confer with the colonial secretary about Singapore's constitutional status. The chief minister felt that attaining independence through a united Malaya was a difficult prospect for Singapore.

Given the circumstances, Lim believed that the city-state needed to tread its own constitutional path towards greater self-determination. He speculated that the Tunku "would only last for two years or so" and in all likelihood be replaced by his deputy, Abdul Razak, who was seen as more popular among the youth.[50] But until there was another window of opportunity to discuss merger with a post-Tunku Federation government, Lim was eager to obtain a settlement on Singapore's constitutional status to appease nationalist sentiments in the city-state. Diverging from his predecessor, he was content with Singapore remaining a colonial dependent of Britain and did not attempt to sneak independence into proposed constitutional arrangements. But Lim stuck with the proposals of the Marshall delegation on two key issues: the need for a Malayan-born Crown representative and a British non-majority in the Defence and Security Council.[51] The failed Malayan governor-general proposal would provide a mould for the future office of Yang di-Pertuan Negara.

While the British were primarily worried about the Defence and Security Council's ability to function effectively and guarantee the safety of their bases in Singapore, Lim placed a greater emphasis on the

Malayan governor-general as an important *precondition* to assure British strategic interests. The chief minister told Lennox-Boyd that he was completely fine with the British government choosing the Malayan-born appointee.[52] Furthermore, according to Lim, the governor-general would just be a "purely ornamental figure" and that "everything will be easy" once there was an impression that Malayans have taken over Government House, the official residence of the British governor in Singapore.[53] He even claimed that the PAP's Lee Kuan Yew, who was supposedly more radical than he was, equated independence with having a local man in Government House.

Reporting on Lim's subsequent talks with British officials, John Chadwick from the Colonial Office believed that the chief minister's thoughts on the security issue was cogent. Lim seemed quite satisfied with the idea of the British maintaining absolute jurisdiction over defence and external affairs and accepted Lennox-Boyd's proposition of having three Singaporean, two British and one Federation representative on the Defence and Security Council. But there was a catch to this proposal: apart from the two British representatives, the British high commissioner would preside over the Council as chair and would cast a tiebreaker vote in the event of a deadlock.[54] This suggestion departed from Marshall's earlier position on having a representative from the Federation to chair the Council. Moreover, the chair would have the final say on when to convene the Council and decide on meeting agendas. With the British high commissioner as chair, Whitehall would therefore be in a dominant position to influence proceedings and resolutions. The British high commissioner, according to Lennox-Boyd's proposition, would also have the power to suspend the Constitution and rule by decree should any of the council's resolutions run contrary to British interests. The ingenuity of this arrangement lies in the optics—while there would be a non-British majority in the Council, ultimate discretion over Singapore's security still lay firmly in British hands.

Although Lim was amicable towards the proposals outlined for the Defence and Security Council, Chadwick reported that the chief minister remained "quite unshakeable" when it came to the proposal for a Malayan governor-general:

He (Lim) did not want an independent Singapore. He argued that a Malayan in Government House would be a symbol of emancipation that would entirely satisfy the masses and a constitution on such an arrangement might well be able to run along for ten to fifteen years without difficulty ... He pointed out that so long as Singapore remained in some state short of independence, even though there were no merger with the Federation for many years to come our bases would be safe in that Singapore was still a British territory and maintained that the only political agreement which would make this possible would be our acceptance of a Malayan Governor-General so that the population would feel that they were in fact running their own affairs and had all they needed.[55]

Seen as a stabilizing element to satisfy the anti-colonial mood in the city-state, the Malayan governor-general was to Lim an even more fundamental issue than the Singaporean government's complete control over internal security.

The chief minister later told Chadwick that any solution that was short of a Malayan governor-general would give communists the necessary fodder to hijack nationalist sentiments and continue instigating disorder in the city-state. Lim's political finesse was at its best. With the appropriate invocation of the prevailing Cold War anxieties, he stoked British fears of an anarchic Singapore under communist insurgency. Whitehall officials continued to worry that the compound effect of a Malayan governor-general and a British minority in the Council would dangerously give a false signal of British withdrawal at a time when Cold War geopolitics was threatening to destabilize the region. But Lim refused to budge. When asked what he would do should British ministers deny the governor-general proposal, Lim impressed on Whitehall officials that "he could not see any solution to the problem at present".[56]

In the meantime, the Tunku pulled further away from discussions on Singapore's constitutional issues. Like Marshall before him, Lim failed to persuade the Federation chief minister to mount a joint effort with Singapore to wrestle independence from Britain. In August 1956, the Tunku even joked with British officials that after the Federation's *merdeka*, he would personally put down a "rubber curtain" at the Johor-Singapore causeway.[57] But to the surprise of British officials, Lim still managed to charm the Tunku, convincing the latter to send a ministerial representative from the Federation to Singapore's Defence and Security Council.[58] Having secured the Federation government's agreement to participate in the Council, there was one less obstacle to a constitutional settlement for Singapore.

As the Colonial Office continued to deliberate on Lim's proposals, the chief minister sought to win British confidence and improve his negotiating position by supressing "communist-driven" civil agitation. Lim was clearly more hard-handed on the issue of public order in contrast to his predecessor. After banning several key unions which were under suspicion of being communist-front organizations, tensions between Lim and the left-wing movement climaxed during the Chinese Middle School riots in October 1956. The clashes resulted in the detention of its ringleaders, among them the PAP's Lim Chin Siong.[59] The chief minister, having consolidated his position, led another all-party delegation to London in March 1957 to re-negotiate full self-government for Singapore.[60] This opportunity was Lim's moment. Since informal talks in July and August 1956, the Colonial Office had deliberated Lim's proposals with the Commonwealth Relations Office and the Ministry of Defence with plenty of back and forth. The British government, pleased with Lim's anti-communist drive, finally decided to back Lim's propositions on the Malayan governor-general and the earlier agreement on the Defence and Security Council's composition.[61] Whitehall officials began to see the value of reaching a political settlement with Lim as they harboured fears that extremist anti-colonial quarters would weaponize a second collapse of constitutional talks to instigate violence in the city-state.[62]

Larger forces were also at play in shaping the constitutional settlement for Singapore. There was an urgent need for the British to recover their moral prestige after a humiliating defeat during the Suez Crisis, which unravelled just days after the Chinese Middle School riots. The colonial powers of France and Britain failed to not only overthrow Egyptian President Gamal Abdul Nasser but also reverse his nationalization of the Suez Canal. Besides the resignation of Anthony Eden as British prime minister, the catastrophic fumble further intensified global pressure to accelerate the decolonizing process.[63] Commonwealth allies, particularly the Australian and New Zealand governments, were also increasingly sensitive to the global mood for decolonization. While they stressed that the British should have the final say on internal security in Singapore, the Antipodean powers admired Lim for his handling of the October riots and saw a deal with Singaporean leaders as necessary to ensure that the island remain conducive as a base for Commonwealth forces.[64] It was in the aftermath of Suez and a freefall in British prestige that the March 1957 constitutional talks unfolded.

New Constitution, New Controversies

During this second round of constitutional talks, Whitehall acquiesced to a new constitution which would recognize Singapore as a self-governing state with a fully elected legislature and its own prime minister. The new constitutional agreements were largely in conformity with Lim's position that the Singaporean government would have autonomy in all matters except for defence and external affairs, both of which would fall under the responsibility of the British government. To administer both these domains, a "United Kingdom commissioner" would represent the British government on the island state. He was to be responsible to the colonial secretary.[65] The previously proposed Defence and Security Council was reconceptualized as an Internal Security Council (ISC), an all-powerful body with the ability to pass binding resolutions to manage Singapore's internal security. The British commissioner would chair the Council, and with him included, there would be a parity of three members each to represent the Singaporean and British governments. The Federation government would also get a seat in the ISC. As an additional restraint on a potentially recalcitrant Singaporean government, the British commissioner was to have reserve powers, including the ability to suspend the constitution and assume direct control over the government of Singapore.[66]

Besides the security framework, the constitutional agreements included other important concessions. One of them was the provision for a separate Singapore citizenship, liberally catered for the island's immigrant population.[67] Another significant point was a clause in the constitution's preamble that recognized the indigenous status of the Singaporean Malays.[68] This clause committed the government to the community's interests, paralleling similar provisions in the Federal Constitution of Malaya.[69] There was, however, one issue that invited disagreement: a "subversive clause" would be implemented to bar political detainees from electoral contest while in detention. The Singaporean delegation asserted that such a clause was "contrary to the practice of democratic states", but the British refused to give in.[70] Forced to accept the British position, the Singapore delegates acknowledged this decision with "regret".[71] Finally, both delegations resolved to revise the proposed constitution four years after its implementation.[72]

On the issue of the Crown representative, the British agreed to name the office "Yang di-Pertuan Negara"—a translation of "head of state" in the Malay language—as proposed by the Singapore delegation. The Constitutional Report, however, does not mention the identity of title's original proponent.[73] During the initial six months of the constitution's implementation, an interim Yang di-Pertuan Negara who need not be Malayan-born would concurrently serve as the British commissioner.[74] He would make way for a Malayan-born successor after his term of office expires. Based on the points of agreement, the British government agreed to *consult* the Singaporean government on the appointment of the Malayan Yang di-Pertuan Negara before advising the Queen to appoint the nominee.

The office would be modelled and styled along the lines of other governor-generals in the Commonwealth. As Crown representative, the Yang di-Pertuan Negara would have the discretion to appoint as prime minister the lawmaker who has the support of a majority in the Assembly following a general election. Furthermore, under the advice of the prime minister, the Yang di-Pertuan Negara would have the authority to dissolve the Assembly and hold fresh elections. If the Yang di-Pertuan Negara found the sitting prime minister unable to command the Assembly's confidence, he could dismiss the incumbent and appoint a replacement.[75] All bills passed by the Assembly must also have the Yang di-Pertuan Negara's assent to become law.[76] Except the aforementioned discretionary powers, his other constitutional duties would be bound to ministerial advice.[77] The only specific qualification for the office was that the appointee must be of "Malayan-born personage" except during the six-month interim.[78]

Reaching compromise on all major issues, the 1956 constitutional talks were largely regarded as a success for both the British and Singaporean delegations. Singapore's all-party delegation returned home, lauded as heroes in some quarters, while reviled as colonial collaborators in others. Even with the promise of a Malayan-born Crown representative in the form of the Yang di-Pertuan Negara, the Assembly was far more concerned with other issues in the constitutional package, particularly the existence of the "subversive clause".[79] The most hostile response, however, came from the ex-chief minister. Marshall mordantly attacked the constitutional agreement, calling it a "murder-ka document", playing on the Malay word "*merdeka*", since it killed the people's aspirations for self-determination.[80] He pointed out that the delegation was short-changed. With its ability to pass resolutions that were binding for the Singaporean government, the ISC would condemn the role of elected lawmakers on security issues to irrelevance. The ISC was therefore practically accountable to no one.

During the 1956 talks, the British had proposed to the Marshall delegation that any joint council on security was only consultative, not all-powerful like the ISC.[81] Marshall lamented:

> this constitution is … in fact and in essence, a colonial constitution and the improvements are not to be brought into force until an indefinite period when it so pleases His Excellency the colonial official … the Chief Minister knows full well that what he has got back is a thing that is deformed and a thing of shame.[82]

The ex-chief minister then urged the Assembly to be courageous enough to fight for Singapore's full independence instead of being beholden to the Tunku's whims.[83] Lee Kuan Yew rubbished this suggestion. The PAP assemblyman asserted that only someone who was "anti-Malayan" and a "sell-out" could propose independence without merger.[84] To challenge this principle, Marshall dared Lee to resign from his seat and compete in a by-election so that the people could decide who was the real "sell-out". After vacating his seat, Marshall, however, decided not to contest in the subsequent by-election and announced his retirement from politics.[85]

Although Marshall effectively shuffled himself out of the Assembly, he was not wrong in pointing out that the new constitutional arrangements made little practical difference to the separation of British and Singaporean jurisdictions. In a bid to allay reservations from his cabinet colleagues, Colonial Secretary Lennox-Boyd confessed that the 1958 Constitution affirmed the status quo. In practice, under the 1955 Rendel Constitution, the existing Council of Ministers, which was made up of a majority of Singaporean ministers, jointly exercised control over internal security.[86] Beneath the issue of the ISC was more subterfuge. While portraying themselves as vocal heroes resisting the "subversive clause", historian Albert Lau has pointed out that both Lim and Lee had privately expressed support for the clause to British officials and had in fact actively pursued the ban.[87] Such a measure would damper the careers of their left-wing political opponents who were currently in detention. The constitutional handicap was a potent strategy to ensure that the detainees could not come into power and seize control of the government. Rather than unanimously uniting the divergent political forces in Singapore, the Constitution became a tool to strive for power whether it came to Chief Minister Lim, the PAP's Lee or the British government.

Singaporean leaders were increasingly nervous about legitimizing their successes partly because the Federation of Malaya had attained its independence on 31 August 1957. Three weeks after this date, the Tunku—now the newly minted prime minister of the sovereign Federation of Malaya—made an official visit to Singapore. He ruled out the possibility of island's merger with the Federation, and to add insult to injury, announced a plan to introduce a "pass system" to stop unrestricted entry of Singaporean residents into the Federation.[88] The Tunku, however, articulated a degree of receptiveness to the vague idea that sometime in the future, the Federation could accept Singapore but only with the inclusion of North Borneo and Sarawak.[89] Until this complicated arrangement was ironed out, there was to be no merger for Singapore.

The winds of *merdeka* blowing from the peninsula were therefore both liberating and suffocating for the Singaporean leaders as the city-state appeared to be stuck in the status of perpetual colony. As time ticked for the nationalist careers of Singaporean leaders, the Colonial Office got busy with the drafting of the proposed legal document. Its officials believed that Anthony Rushford, a legal assistant to the ministry, was the best man for the job since he was privy to both constitutional talks for Singapore, but he was already engaged with the drafting of Nigeria's Constitution. The Colonial Office was furthermore concurrently occupied with formulating a constitution for Malta.[90] After repeated demands from Lim and Governor Black, a working deadline of January 1958 was set, with Henry Steel, another legal advisor, assigned to draft the constitution. Steel himself was fresh from his involvement in seeking a constitutional settlement for the Cyprus Emergency.[91] The Colonial Office expedited the draft, largely basing provisions for Singapore on the Constitutions of Malaya and those of other self-governing colonies. For instance, the Colonial Office modelled the clauses concerning the tenure of judges after the constitution of Nigeria.[92] These civil servants and legal advisors connected the city-state with the rest of the decolonizing empire. Singapore's new constitution therefore bore the hues of other decolonizing experiences elsewhere. It was only the latest addition to the Westminster-style constitutional network, a legacy of a fading British imperium.

Amid the impending passage of the new constitution, Lim became paranoid about his own political survival. He privately hinted to Black that he should receive "special assistance" to guarantee a future Singaporean government that was friendly to British interests. The chief minister even persuaded the governor to keep his party's links to the Chinese secret societies a secret.[93] When the draft of the Constitution was released in February 1958 after much delay, it gave Lim another opportunity to plot his stay in power. In the subsequent weeks, the Colonial Office sent copies to Singapore and to the other British ministries to solicit feedback. Much of the re-drafting involved the legal instruments for the ISC.[94] Opposition lawmakers then pressured Lim to release information on the draft constitution since there were rumours that the British were sneaking in secret provisions.[95] Lim explained to the Assembly on 22 April 1958 that there was no draft, but confessed that he had discussed some of its points with the Colonial Office.[96] A month earlier, however, in a letter dated 14 March 1958, Sir William Goode, Black's successor as governor, informed the Colonial Office that he had already given full copies of the draft to Lim. Goode pointed out that the chief minister had refused to disclose the draft to anyone, even to his own ministers.[97] Either Goode was delusional, or Lim had intended to monopolize Singapore's voice in the shaping of the Constitution.

For someone who had claimed ignorance about the draft Constitution, Lim had plenty to say on its stipulations. In his report to the Colonial Office, Governor Goode relayed Lim's feedback on the draft; the chief minister had no less than 29 different comments on 29 specific clauses.[98] One noteworthy point was his suggestion to re-name the Council of Ministers as "the Cabinet" to accord it more prestige. This was in line with an earlier agreement during constitutional talks to renew the office of chief minister as "prime minister" to achieve the same dignifying effect in line with other self-governing colonies.[99] On the Yang di-Pertuan Negara, Lim maintained that the titular Crown representative should retain discretionary powers over the dissolution of the Legislative Assembly as a check against the executive.[100]

In May 1958, Lim headed another all-party delegation to London to confirm details of the Constitution.[101] In an all too familiar strategy of false concession, the British agreed to remove the controversial "subversive clause" from the Constitution but would still ban detainees from participating in elections via separate legislation. It seemed that Whitehall needed to avoid opening another can of worms by enshrining a controversial "undemocratic" clause into the constitution of one of its colonies, particularly when the world's patience with colonial repression was wearing thin. Even though Lee played an active part in finalizing the Constitution as the PAP's representative, he tactfully exhibited a non-committal position, perhaps not to betray his closet enthusiasm in keeping his detained comrades unelectable.[102]

While the issue of the "subversives clause" became potent material for a political controversy, there was confusion behind the scenes among British civil servants over the Yang di-Pertuan Negara. The Colonial Office initially planned to channel all lines of communication between the British government and Singaporean government via the Yang di-Pertuan Negara since he was the Queen's representative. The British commissioner would then be engaged only in matters of defence and external affairs.[103] This protocol was later revised—all communication with the British government must go through the British commissioner.

By the same token, Singaporean ministers would have no direct access to the Queen except through the British commissioner and the colonial secretary.[104] The Colonial Office later issued an official guidance for Whitehall's circulation to eliminate any further confusion. It asserted that despite the change in title from "Colony of Singapore" to "The State of Singapore", the island "will remain a dependency of the United Kingdom and under the responsibility of the secretary of state for the colonies".[105] These were deliberate moves to show that the British commissioner in Singapore was no mere diplomat. The Commonwealth Relations Office stressed that he would be much closer to the typical colonial governor rather than the high commissioners stationed in the independent member states of the Commonwealth.[106]

Besides these manoeuvres, the draft constitution and the final legislation specified that current laws implemented in the name of the governor would henceforth be replaced with the name of the Yang di-Pertuan Negara since he was now the Crown representative.[107] The Constitution entitled the Yang di-Pertuan Negara to all information available to the Cabinet and also a civil list, which stipulated his allowance to meet official duties. These two points were modelled after the Federation's head of state, the Yang di-Pertuan Agong.[108] The State of Singapore Act—the bill that would officiate the new constitution—later became law on 1 August 1958 after its passage through the Houses of Parliament in Westminster.[109] The Act legitimized the "1958 Singapore Order-in-Council" ("the Constitution") and would come into full force once a new Singaporean government takes office after a general election.

Rise of the PAP

Uncertainty nevertheless plagued prospects for the Constitution's success. Sharing British anxieties of having to deal with a potential PAP-led radical government, the Federation began displaying a greater interest in its future role in Singapore's affairs. Dr Ismail, the Malayan Home Affairs Minister, announced that the Federation should not participate in the ISC, rattling officials in Whitehall.[110] In October 1958, the Tunku himself cautioned that he would withdraw the Federation's representative from the ISC should the future Singaporean government take actions contrary to his advice.[111] After writing to the Tunku to clarify his position, officials from the Colonial Office were relieved when the Federation prime minister gave a written confirmation that his government would fully cooperate with the British in the ISC regardless of the political party governing Singapore. The Tunku admitted that the political grandstanding was to ensure that any future Singaporean government would think twice before offending the interests of the Federation.[112] Besides being privy to the ISC together with the ministerial representative from the Federation, it is important to remember that the party that was to form the next Singaporean government would also get to nominate the future Malayan-born Yang di-Pertuan Negara following the transition period of six months.

The political party that was best organized and presented a united front was the PAP. Even before the Constitution's successful passage through Westminster, the party was well-poised to form the next Singaporean government. It had demonstrated its popular appeal by attaining a resounding victory during the City Council elections held in December 1957, resulting in Ong Eng Guan's rise as mayor.[113] But the PAP's superb organization and party discipline belied a dangerous schism brewing within the party. This rift was between a more "moderate", English-educated faction who dominated the party leadership and an extremist faction affiliated with the "Middle Group" trade unions, the latter of which was under the control of communist elements. Chief Minister Lim had intended to entice Lee's group to join him in forming a broad "National United Front" with the aim of achieving merger, but the strength of the PAP's extremist elements forestalled any serious effort for a coalition.[114]

As the general elections drew nearer, the PAP was awarded a political gift. Two major scandals rocked the incumbent government. The first was a damaging corruption case against Lim's right-hand man, Chew Swee Kee, who had served as minister for education. The case also implicated the wife of Abdul Hamid Jumat, the deputy chief minister and leader of the Singaporean branch of UMNO. This was followed by botched investigations into the wrongdoings of a government-friendly councilman, P.C. Marcus.[115] As the integrity of his leadership eroded, Lim had to explain away unsubstantiated claims that he was pandering to the British because he coveted the office of Yang di-Pertuan Negara. He insisted that he was too devoted to party politics to become a non-partisan Crown representative.[116] In putting out these fires, the chief minister attempted to re-brand his leadership in November 1958 by establishing a new party, the Singapore People's Alliance (SPA), superseding the crumbling Labour Front.[117] But Lim's government could not stem the tide of trouble in the final months of his term: unemployment was worsening, crime rate was rocketing, the social welfare budget was outspent, housing was in shortage and a rapidly rising population threatened the quality of life.[118]

It was in this context of poor governance that the PAP mounted its bid for power. In a display of outstanding morale, it was the only party to contest all 51 seats after the dissolution of the Assembly on 31 March 1959.[119] The PAP portrayed itself as a cohesive party, free from the infighting and defections prevalent in other political parties. The party ridiculed its opponents by labelling them "rojak party" and "mah-jong players" to describe their shifting loyalties.[120] Despite the communist elements within the party, the PAP had established itself in 1954 as an anti-colonial political force, consistently pledging itself to achieve a "free, independent, democratic, non-communist Malaya".[121] Based on its brand of socialism, one of the PAP's foremost ideological principles was equality. As forcefully expressed in its 1959 election manifesto, the party stood for "equality of opportunity for education, for employment, for a decent life".[122]

Its election manifesto was practical as it was hopeful. The party outlined a five-year plan for Singapore which included an industrialization policy under a Malayan common market, investment in technical skills, an affordable healthcare system, improvements to social welfare and the prolific building of public housing.[123] Underlining these proposals, however, was the posturing "towards a Malayan nation", affirming the party's commitment to a united independent Malaya through union with the Federation.[124] The PAP was offering a refreshing vision for a new Singapore—a stable society rising from the inequalities of the colonial order, holding the promise of better living standards for all.

To counter the PAP's campaign, the SPA mainly relied on Lim's prestige as the incumbent chief minister and pledged itself to a successful delivery of merger. The party invoked its close relationship with the Alliance government in Kuala Lumpur to sell the idea that a vote for the SPA would mean a better chance for a united Malaya.[125] Federation ministers also "implicitly" endorsed Lim by awarding the chief minister the Federation's highest honour, the *Seri Maharaja Mangku Negara* (S.M.N.), which carries the title of *Tun*.[126] In February 1959, a British official reported to Governor Goode that there were rumours on the grapevine that Lim's "lack of energy" in getting his affairs in order was because he had made a deal with Lee Kuan Yew; should the PAP form the next government, Lee promised to appoint Lim as Yang di-Pertuan Negara.[127] These claims, however, remained hearsay. The chief minister and other political opponents continued to be militant during the election campaign, barraging the PAP with allegations that it would bring Singapore under communist influence.[128]

Polling Day on 30 May nevertheless witnessed the triumph of the PAP. Winning a landslide 43 out of 51 Legislative Assembly seats, it was able to comfortably form the next government. Meanwhile, the SPA shrivelled into an opposition party with only four seats. Lim's political ally and coalition partner, the UMNO-led Singapore Alliance, won the electoral contests in three Malay-majority constituencies. The last remaining seat went to A.P. Rajah, an independent candidate.[129] The people of Singapore had given the PAP a compelling mandate to lead the city-state.

The transition of power was smooth despite initial hurdles. After a day of celebrations, Lee announced the PAP's intention to honour its election promise to not occupy government until the release of its detained party leaders, all of whom, owing to the ban on detainees contesting the elections, were unelected and thus ineligible as prime minister.[130] Lee was then confirmed as the party's choice for the office.[131] On 3 June 1959, Goode was sworn in as Singapore's inaugural Yang di-Pertuan Negara and the ex-officio British commissioner. With the colonial secretary's approval, Goode freed eight PAP detainees in one of his final decrees as governor so as to avoid a constitutional crisis and to foster goodwill with the incoming PAP government.[132]

Symbolic changes were already visible even before the PAP got on with the business of governing. The swearing-in ceremony for the Cabinet on 5 June took place in City Hall which was counter to the long-established practice of having officials sworn in at Government House. The PAP also announced that the seat of government would move from Empress Place to City Hall to further emphasize a transition from the colonial order.[133] The PAP Cabinet turned up for the ceremony in their signature white shirts and slacks instead of suits, with Lee proudly telling the press that his government was not in favour of cocktail parties, a practice of elite circles in colonial society.[134] As congratulatory messages poured in, Deputy Primer Minister Tun Razak, speaking on behalf of Kuala Lumpur, promised that the Federation government "[would] be fair" when participating in the ISC.[135] With Alliance-PAP relations in a benign state, Singapore seemed closer to independence from colonial rule. Perhaps it is best to hear straight from the PAP about what was in store for Singapore under its new nationalist regime:

> A new era is dawning upon us ... The clean keen scent of spring begins to fill the air. And with the coming of spring, all freedom loving peoples feel an upsurge of joy and thrill of exhilaration as they march forward towards a new life and as they direct their creative energies to their new tasks—the building of a new clean and just society, where man does not exploit man, where the free development of each is the condition for the free development of all.[136]

The Yang di-Pertuan Negara was to carry this sense of hope and rupture peddled by the PAP government. Beneath the overt invocations of change, however, the office reinstituted Singapore's enduring place in the cross-territorial imperial system. The next chapter goes deeper into this quandary. It contemplates the Yang di-Pertuan Negara as a symbol of Singapore's "rebirth" and unfurls the power struggles that came to shape the meanings of the office.

Notes

1. Turnbull's account of the founding of modern Singapore has been largely regarded as the most dominant account, see Turnbull, *A History of Modern Singapore*, pp. 29–81. Her account, however, has been disputed for supressing the agency of the Malay aristocracy. For an alternative account, see Carl Trocki's work cited below. A summary of this historiographical controversy can also be found in Michael D. Barr, "Singapore Comes to Terms with its Malay Past: The Politics of Crafting a National History", *Asian Studies Review* (2021): 1–19.
2. After excluding Hussein from Singapore's political affairs, the British stopped recognizing his descendants as sultan following the death of Hussein and his son, Ali. See Carl Trocki, *Prince of Pirates: The Temenggongs and the Development of Johor and Singapore 1784–1885* (Singapore: NUS Press, 2007), pp. 75–160, 191.
3. On the different narratives on colonial expansion in the Malay Peninsula, see Gareth Knapman, "The Liberal Security Experiment in Southeast Asia", in *Liberalism and the British Empire in Southeast Asia*, edited by Gareth Knapman, Anthony Milner and Mary Quilty (London and New York: Routledge, 2019), pp. 192–214.
4. Milner, *Kerajaan*, pp. 15–16.
5. Turnbull, *A History of Modern Singapore*, pp. 86–89.
6. On the region's governance during the Second World War, see Nicholas Tarling, *A Sudden Rampage: The Japanese Occupation of Southeast Asia, 1941–1945* (London: Hurst and Company, 2001). On the fate of the Malay rulers during the Second World War, see Akashi Yoji, "Japanese Military Administration in Malaya: Its Formation and Evolution in Reference to the Sultans, the Islamic Religion and the Moslem-Malays, 1941–1945", *Asian Studies* 7, no. 1 (1969): 61–89.
7. Ibid.
8. Amoroso, *Traditionalism*, pp. 108–14.
9. Aljunied, *Radicals*, pp. 73–100 and Cheah, *Red Star*, pp. 102–14.
10. Paul H. Kratoska, *The Japanese Occupation of Malaya and Singapore, 1941–45*, 2nd ed. (Singapore: NUS Press, 2018), pp. 108–14 and Tarling, *A Sudden Rampage*, p. 201.
11. Cheah, *Red Star*, pp. 57–101.
12. On British wartime planning for the Malayan Union, see Albert Lau, *The Malayan Union Controversy* (Singapore: Oxford University Press, 1991).
13. Sopiee, *Malayan Union*, pp. 15–31.
14. On the concept of partition, Sujit Sivasundaram has provided a useful breakdown, see Sivasundaram, *Islanded*, pp. 14–17.
15. Amoroso, *Traditionalism*, pp. 136–65.
16. Sopiee, *Malayan Union*, pp. 38–57, 95–100.
17. Harper, *The End of Empire*, pp. 94–148 and Cheah, *Red Star*, pp. 241–65.

18. Harper, *The End of Empire*, p. 200.
19. Amrita Malhi, "Race, Space, and the Malayan Emergency: Expelling Malay Muslim Communism and Reconstituting Malaya's Racial State, 1945–1954", *Itinerario*, 24 November 2021: 1–4.
20. Lee, *United Front*, pp. 40–78.
21. Drysdale, *Struggle for Success*, pp. 19–30.
22. Yeo, *Political Development*, pp. 251–77. Voting was allowed for British subjects with a minimum one-year residency.
23. Ibid., pp. 259–62.
24. Singapore branch of UMNO will not be abbreviated as "SUMNO" as conventionally upheld in the scholarly literature. This is to reflect the terminological realities of the historical context and to emphasize the branch's links with its parent organization based in Kuala Lumpur. When referring specifically to the party's Singapore branch, it will be indicated as necessary.
25. Ibid., pp. 45–50.
26. James Low, "Kept in a Position: The Labour Front-Alliance Government of Chief Minister David Marshall", *Journal of Southeast Asian Studies* 35, no. 1 (2004): 45–57.
27. Ibid., pp. 50–54.
28. *Times*, 17 August 1955, DO 35/6289, 167.
29. Yeo, *Political Development*, p. 85.
30. Drysdale, *Struggle for Success*, p. 87. Also see *SLAD*, Vol. 1, Sitting No. 8, Col. 463–506 (25 July 1955).
31. For a critical appraisal of the Atlantic Charter and the debates leading up the UN Resolution 1514, see Getachew, *Worldmaking after Empire*, pp. 71–92.
32. Cited in Ian Sanjay Patel, *We are Here Because You were There: Immigration and the End of Empire* (London and New York: Verso, 2021), p. 136.
33. Sopiee, *Malayan Union*, pp. 105–8.
34. Low, "Kept in a Position", p. 56 and Lee, *Singapore*, pp. 116–21.
35. Sopiee, *Malayan Union*, pp. 108–9.
36. Extract from Malaya monthly report no. 33, 15 January to 15 February 1956, DO 35/9865, 18.
37. See the full report of the 1956 Conference in Colonial Office, *Singapore Constitutional Conference* (London: Her Majesty's Stationery Office, 1956), CO 1030/161 [hereinafter *Singapore Conference 1956*]. For a thorough analysis on the 1956 constitutional talks, see Albert Lau, "The Colonial Office and the Singapore Merdeka Mission, 23 April to 15 May 1956", *Journal of the South Seas Society* 49 (1994): 104–22.
38. Colonial Office, *Singapore Conference 1956*, p. 10.
39. Lau, "Decolonization", pp. 46–47.
40. Colonial Office, *Singapore Conference 1956*, pp. 21–22.
41. Ibid., pp. 24–25.

42. Ibid., pp. 14, 20.
43. Ibid., pp. 20–21.
44. Ibid.
45. Ibid., p. 27.
46. Ibid., pp. 27–28.
47. Ibid., p. 33.
48. Murphy, *Monarchy*, pp. 16–33.
49. Lim Yew Hock, *Reflections* (Kuala Lumpur: Pustaka Antara, 1986), p. 65 and *ST*, 16 May 1956, p. 1.
50. Minute by A. Lennox-Boyd, 25 July 1959, DO 35/9872.
51. Lau, "Decolonization", pp. 49–50.
52. Quoted in ibid., 49. This is based on Minute by A. Lennox-Boyd, 25 July 1959, DO 35/9872.
53. Minute by A. Lennox-Boyd, 25 July 1959, DO 35/9872.
54. Letter from J. Chadwick to R. Black, 3 August 1957, DO 35/9872.
55. Ibid.
56. Letter from J. Chadwick to R. Black, 8 August 1957, DO 35/9872.
57. Letter from D. Watherston to J.B. Johnston, 15 August 1956, CO 1030/83, 341.
58. Letter from R. Black to E. Melville, 12 September 1956, CO 1030/83, 346.
59. Lee, *Singapore*, pp. 131–39. Lim Yew Hock was pressured by his allies to arrest Lee Kuan Yew, but he resisted their pleas. See Lim, *Reflections*, pp. 77–84.
60. On the deliberations and circumstances concerning the re-opening of constitutional talks, see Albert Lau, "Decolonization and the Cold War in Singapore, 1955–9", in *Southeast Asia and the Cold War*, edited by Albert Lau (Oxon and New York: Routledge, 2012), pp. 47–60.
61. Lau, "Decolonization", pp. 55–61.
62. Memorandum from A. Lennox-Boyd to the British Cabinet, 30 November 1956, CO 1030/122.
63. S.R. Joey Long, "Bringing the International and Transnational Back in: Singapore, Decolonisation, and the Cold War", in *Singapore in Global History*, edited by Derek Heng and Syed Muhd Khairudin Aljunied (Amsterdam: Amsterdam University Press, 2011), pp. 218–23 and Peter Lyon, "The Commonwealth and the Suez Crisis", in *Suez 1956: The Crisis and its Consequences*, edited by Wm. Roger Louis and Roger Owen (New York: Oxford University Press, 1991), pp. 257–74.
64. Telegram from UK High Commissioner in Canberra to the Commonwealth Relations Office, 20 December 1956, DO 35/9873, 634 and Cablegram from New Zealand government to the New Zealand High Commissioner in London, 13 December 1956, DO 35/9873, 629.
65. See Colonial Office, *Report of the Singapore Constitutional Conference* (London: Her Majesty's Stationery Office, 1957) in CO 1030/468 [hereafter *Singapore Conference 1957*].

66. Ibid., pp. 14–15.
67. Ibid., pp. 15–16.
68. Ibid., p. 5.
69. See Articles 152 and 153 in Government of Malaya, *Federation of Malaya: Constitutional Proposals* (Kuala Lumpur: Government Press, 1957), pp. 73–76.
70. Colonial Office, *Singapore Conference 1957*, p. 10.
71. Ibid.
72. Ibid., p. 15.
73. Ibid., p. 6.
74. Ibid., p. 5.
75. Ibid., p. 6.
76. Ibid.
77. Ibid., p. 6.
78. Ibid.
79. *SLAD*, Vol. 3, Sitting No. 7–9, Col. 1639–1868 (26–30 April 1957).
80. *SLAD*, Vol. 3, Sitting No. 7, Col. 1686 (26 April 1957).
81. Colonial Office, *Singapore Conference 1956*, pp. 31–32.
82. *SLAD*, Vol. 3, Sitting No. 7, Col. 1688 (26 April 1957).
83. Ibid., Col. 1678–1680.
84. *SLAD*, Vol. 3, Sitting No. 8, Col. 1767 (27 April 1957).
85. Kevin Tan, *Marshall of Singapore: A Biography* (Singapore: Institute of Southeast Asian Studies, 2008), pp. 394–98.
86. Lau, "Decolonization", p. 59.
87. Letter from R. Black to E. Melville, 3 December 1957, CO 1030/468, 209–10. Also see Lau, "Decolonization", pp. 60–61.
88. *Hindustan Standard*, 24 September 1957, DO 35/9865, 24.
89. Extract from dispatch from the UK High Commissioner in Kuala Lumpur, 18 October 1957, DO 35/9868, 26.
90. Letter from K. Roberts-Wray to R. Black, 1 October 1957, CO 1030/468, 229–31.
91. Ibid.
92. Letter from H. Steel to A.J.N. Patterson, 27 January 1958, CO 1030/468, 193–94.
93. Letter from R. Black to E. Melville, 3 December 1957, CO 1030/468, 209–10.
94. The deliberations can mostly be found in CO 1030/471, CO 1030/472 and CO 1030/473.
95. *ST*, 23 April 1958, p. 6.
96. *SLAD*, Vol. 6, Sitting No. 2, Col. 17–19 (22 April 1958).
97. Letter from W. Goode to W.I.J. Wallace, 14 March 1958, CO 1030/469, 214. The CO concurred that copies were sent to Singapore for Lim's vetting, see Secret Memorandum by W.I.J. Wallace (19 February 1958), CO 1030/468, 52–53.

98. "Comments on the Draft Royal Instructions and Part I to VII of the Draft Constitution Order-in-Council", 14 March 1958, CO 1030/469, 215.

99. See the different "types" of prime ministers in the Commonwealth in Murphy, *Monarchy*, pp. 54–60.

100. "Comments on the Draft Royal Instructions and Draft Constitution Order-in-Council", CO 1030/469, 222–23.

101. *ST*, 11 May 1958, p. 1.

102. Ibid.

103. See deliberations in CO 1030/472. The Yang di-Pertuan Negara's function as the official line of communication with Her Majesty's Government was initially enshrined in the draft Constitution but removed in the final legislation, see "Draft Order-in-Council", CO 1030/468, 94 and Government of Singapore, *Singapore (Constitution) 1958*, pp. 10–13.

104. Note by the Colonial Office Establishment and Organisation Department, 26 June 1959, CO 1030/877, 13.

105. Ibid.

106. Letter from Larmour to W.I.J. Wallace, 5 May 1958 in CO 1030/473, 20–21 and "Comments on Draft Constitution" by W.I.J. Wallace in CO 1030/469, 181.

107. Comments on the draft are in CO 1030/468. The suggested changes were enshrined in the Fourth Schedule of the final Constitution, see Government of Singapore, *Singapore (Constitution) 1958*, p. 57.

108. Memorandum from J. Hennings, CO 1030/469, 11–17.

109. See well wishes from the British Houses of Parliament to Singapore in CO 1030/475.

110. Letter from A.W. Snelling to G. Tory, 20 June 1958, CO 1030/476, 165–66.

111. *BH*, 28 October 1958, p. 1.

112. Letter from Tunku Abdul Rahman to G. Tory, 8 November 1958, CO 1030/476, 52–53.

113. Drysdale, *Struggle for Success*, pp. 186–94.

114. Extract from "Malaya Monthly Emergency and Political Report, 15 June to 15 July 1957", DO 35/9872.

115. Ong Chit Chung, "The 1959 Singapore General Election", *Journal of Southeast Asian Studies* 6, no. 1 (1975): 64–70.

116. *BH*, 25 March 1958, p. 1 and *The Straits Budget (SB)*, 30 April 1958, p. 9.

117. *ST*, 11 November 1958, p. 1.

118. See the evidence of the abovementioned problems in respective order: Department of Social Studies, University of Malaya, *Report on a Survey of Applications to the Singapore Labour Department Employment Exchange* (Singapore: University of Malaya, 1959), p. 15; *ST*, 7 May 1959, p. 4; *ST*, 2 January 1959, p. 4; *SS*, 12 January 1959, p. 4; *ST*, 8 May 1959, p. 12; *ST*, 1 March 1959, p. 1.

119. Ong, "1959 Singapore General Election", p. 81.
120. PAP, *Petir* 2, 1 (January 1959), p. 1.
121. *ST*, 17 May 1955, p. 1.
122. PAP, *The Tasks Ahead I: PAP's Five-Year Plan 1959–1964* (Singapore: Petir, 1959), pp. 4–5.
123. See ibid. and PAP, *The Tasks Ahead II: PAP's Five-Year Plan 1959–1964* (Singapore: Petir, 1959).
124. PAP, *The Tasks Ahead I*, p. 8.
125. Ong, "1959 Singapore General Election", pp. 74–77.
126. *ST*, 31 August 1958, p. 1. Also see Perpustakaan Negara Malaysia, *Senarai Gelaran Melayu* (Kuala Lumpur: Perpustakaan Negara, 1980).
127. Letter from W.I.J. Wallace to W. Goode, 25 February 1959, FCO 141/15022, 13.
128. Ong, "1959 Singapore General Election", pp. 70–74.
129. For the election results, see ibid., p. 86 and *ST*, 31 May 1959, p. 4.
130. Amongst them were Lim Chin Siong and Devan Nair. For the deliberations on the release of the detainees, see CO 1030/630.
131. *ST*, 2 June 1959, p. 1.
132. Telegram from W. Goode to Colonial Office, 1 June 1959, CO 1030/650, 125–26.
133. *SS*, 6 June 1959, p. 1 and *ST*, 6 June 1959, p. 1.
134. *SS*, 6 June 1959, p. 1.
135. *ST*, 3 June 1959, p. 1. For messages from other world leaders, see *SS*, 9 June 1959, p. 5.
136. PAP, *Petir*, 2, 5 (May 1959), p. 1.

3

IMPERIAL, OR MALAY(AN) SYMBOL?

Singapore in the British World System

Six months after the PAP's electoral victory, Yusof was inaugurated as Yang di-Pertuan Negara. This moment was celebrated as the complete realization of the 1958 Constitution. The opening section of this book has recounted the subterranean tensions prickling the symbolic gestures of the Yusof's swearing-in ceremony. Even though both Lee and Yusof heralded a sense of emancipation from colonial rule, the procedures reinforced Singapore's position as a component of the British imperial system.[1] Indeed, the appointment of the Malayan-born Yang di-Pertuan Negara was legitimized through familiar rituals which upheld the sovereign authority of Britain over Singapore. Yusof acceded to Royal Instructions from the Queen and also recited the pledge of allegiance to the British Crown. Meanwhile, imperial symbols like *God Save the Queen* were still given ceremonial deference.[2]

In the global age of decolonization, Singapore had transformed into a layered political entity which met both the needs of colonial control and the growing demands of self-determination. The implementation of the 1958 Constitution conjured a graphic change in Singapore by replacing the British governor with the Yang di-Pertuan Negara. Designers of the latter envisioned its appointee as a captivating ornamental figure, a personage who could signify the city-state's transition to self-government. But the imperial clothes of the governor's successor were not so easily shed. Paradoxes and perplexities interrupted attempts to make the Yang di-Pertuan Negara meaningful. These questions animate the story ahead: how did the office of Yang di-Pertuan Negara embody both a breakdown and an entrenchment of Singapore's colonial status? How was sovereignty performed to muddle the city-state's continued standing as a British colony?

To expose the contestations behind Singapore's colonial status, it may be helpful to retrace the steps of Singaporean leaders, taking a closer look at the granular details of the two constitutional talks in 1956 and 1957. During these negotiations, the British were firm in their stance to keep Singapore as a vassal state that was firmly within the ambit of the United Kingdom. The Singaporean delegations, uncomfortable with the prospects of perpetual colonial rule, sought to abate complete British hegemony over the city-state. With this aim in mind, the 1956 Marshall delegation proposed "dominion status" for Singapore. The idea first came to Marshall at the behest of Jawaharlal Nehru, the prime minister of India.[3] Dominionhood was a type of governing structure which characterized the dependency relations of the colony and the metropole. It had developed during the interwar years and was later consolidated through the 1931 Statute of Westminster, which bestowed sovereign equality to the White settler colonies—South Africa, Canada, Ireland, New Zealand and Australia—collectively referred to as the "old dominions". Dominionhood for Singapore could therefore subvert the island's subordinate status in relation to Britain.

Dominions were components of a larger "British world system". In this international ordering of states, Britain exercised varying degrees of control over other foreign territories, for instance through forming coercive relationships with seemingly sovereign polities, establishing semi-independent protectorates and exercising direct colonial rule.[4] Viewing empire as the creation of this British-dominated world system, the "Oxbridge school" of imperialism see decolonization as a waning of this system. Historians like John Darwin and W. David McIntyre have appreciated transformations in the relationship between Britain and its dependencies after the Second World War, identifying the movement towards equality of status for the latter.[5] At the heart of dominionhood was a historical effort by British imperialists to reconcile imperial unity with local demands for self-determination. These tensions between centralizing and secessionist forces were already in motion since the formation of empire itself. By the turn of the twentieth century, Britain had introduced limited measures of representative government in the settler colonies while reining in local demands for more autonomy. This "privilege", however, was reserved for the White settler colonies only. Local elites in colonies like India and the British West Indies demanded for covealness but faced constant disappointment.[6]

During the First World War, the participation of the White settler colonies in the British war effort gave these territories even more leverage to agitate for greater independence from the United Kingdom. As dominions, their demands for self-determination could be accommodated without severing important links defined by mutual defence, capital flows and a shared loyalty to the British Crown. The White settler colonies would thus shift "from autonomy to equality" upon their transition into dominions.[7] Over time, the "British Empire" became fungible with the idea of a "British Commonwealth of Nations". The latter became a flexuous term to absorb the idea of dominion parity with Britain. It sustained the self-serving liberalism of the imperial project, conceptualizing the empire-Commonwealth as an association of diverse tribes and nations under the enlightened guidance of Britain. Some of the Commonwealth's architects nevertheless affirmed this cross-territorial fraternity as a testament to White dominance in the global order.[8] By reinventing their ties with the dominions, the British rejuvenated their paramountcy in this world system.

The dominion formula was pliant precisely because of its ambiguities. There were hardly any legal stipulations which governed relations between Britain and its former settler colonies. Politicians, both from the metropole and dominions, enjoyed sufficient latitude to straddle their political stances between imperial unity and local nationalism depending on their interests at particular moments in time.[9] After the Second World War, the bestowal of dominion status and equal membership to India, Pakistan and Ceylon signified a new phase for the Commonwealth. The

South Asian ex-colonial states took on the dominion model of sovereignty for the sake of expedience, prestige and strategy.[10] With the removal of the colour bar imposed during the interwar years, the Commonwealth began to display an ostensible inclusiveness. Multiracialism and equality were now founding principles of this revitalized fraternity of states.[11] In the form of this revitalized Commonwealth, the British imperial system had become more amenable to the principle of self-determination as enshrined in the Atlantic Charter, the foundational basis of the postwar international system. This seismic shift universalized the regime of "Westphalian sovereignty", entailing a legal commitment to upholding equality and non-intervention in the relationship between states.

Inequalities in global wealth and power, however, continued to burden the global order.[12] Far from being the harbinger of British imperial decline, the postwar Commonwealth carried the mantle of the old imperial system and demonstrated a degree of robustness in withstanding the pressures of global change. British officials saw the Commonwealth as a "progressive" stage of British global influence and a "logical" step for the civilizing impulse of imperialism.[13] Marshall intended to latch onto this liberal British outlook. With the aim of attaining sovereign equality for Singapore, he proposed that the city-state could attain sovereign status as a dominion first and later cede control over its defence and external affairs to Britain.[14] A dominion of Singapore would also get its own governor-general as its Crown representative. The intended effect was simple: Singapore would become a sovereign state, equal in status to Britain and other Commonwealth members.[15]

Scholarship has not really appreciated the ingenuity of Marshall's dominion proposal. Considering Singapore's precarious situation in the second half of the 1950s, dominionhood was a promising basis for nation-building. A common heritage of Westminster institutions and ideas, or what John Darwin calls a "shared Britishness", had a unifying potential in diverse societies where a common national culture was absent.[16] This formula, at least in theory, was practical as much as it was romantic. Its prospective application could bring together the multi-ethnic and immigrant-based social fabric in Singapore. A dominion of Singapore under the umbrella of the Commonwealth would renew shared links—both symbolic and in substance—with the United Kingdom and other ex-colonial British territories.

Another important element of the dominion proposal was the city-state's future relationship with the Crown. In the postwar Commonwealth, the British took great pains to adjust the relationship of the British monarch with member countries so that republican ex-colonies would feel less apprehensive towards membership. Ireland had set a precedent by quitting the organization in 1949 after becoming a republic, while Burma refused membership following independence in 1948 based on the same premise.[17] To prevent India from breaking away from the Commonwealth with the passing of its new republican constitution in 1949, the British monarch was eventually given a dampened magisterial title—"Head of the Commonwealth"—to symbolize an act of "common will" between members, rather than being validated as a shared symbol of allegiance as was the case before the Second World War.[18] Loyalty to the Crown was no longer a prerequisite for Commonwealth membership.

These symbolic gestures notwithstanding, the Commonwealth remained in many respects a "surrogate for colonial rule" and the cornerstone of British global influence in the postwar era, particularly in the official mind of Whitehall.[19] For Marshall, dominion status was a strategic compromise to British interests in order to achieve Singapore's recognition as an independent state. This is similar to how membership of the UN legitimizes the sovereign equality enjoyed by a country by being a member of the global community of nation-states.[20] The British would also be able to continue playing a part in the island's defence in line with their strategic interests. As a state liberated from colonial rule, Singapore could retain its place in the existing Commonwealth defence arrangements through treaties with Britain, Australia, Malaya and New Zealand.[21] Continued association with Britain and the Crown was therefore a means to validate Singapore's stature as an ex-colony in a post-imperial world.

Colonialism, Communism and the Commonwealth

The 1956 talks, however, collapsed because the British remained adamant on having an unequivocal guarantee of its security interests in Singapore.

They were averse towards granting dominionhood or the status of independent Commonwealth member to the city-state because it might compromise their existing rights to defence installations on the island, frustrating British military obligations to other Commonwealth partners and the Southeast Asia Treaty Organization (SEATO). An independent Singapore in the postwar global order—whether as a dominion or a communist republic—might very well choose to exercise its sovereign right and expel foreign British forces from the island.

The British felt no need to gamble their current position of dominance because there was no guarantee that a local government would consent to British military presence on the island in perpetuity. Singapore must therefore remain as a colonial dependent, at least for the time being. Furthermore, by the 1950s, dominionhood was largely defunct as a system of self-government. As the British stumbled to search for suitable jargon for self-governing status short of full independence, ex-colonial states began to invest their sovereign sense of being in the terminology of "Commonwealth country", a term which better reflected the equality they enjoyed in relation to the former imperial centre.[22] The British nevertheless offered to vouchsafe a "special status" for Singapore, another dubious terminology in British imperial parlance which in practical terms meant very little.[23] Concessions like the creation of a separate Singaporean citizenship fell short of the coveted recognition as an equal, dignified Commonwealth member.

As opposed to a sovereign former colony, having a titular governor-general acting as the Crown representative in a dependent territory did not become the norm in the postwar Commonwealth. There were exceptions like in the cases of Nigeria and the Federation of Rhodesia and Nyasaland. These territories, however, were semi-independent assemblages of different dependents with disparate constitutional statuses. In the Federation of Rhodesia and Nyasaland, the governor-general was the titular Crown representative. The component state of Southern Rhodesia already had an autonomous status and was under the watch of the Commonwealth Relations Office, the ministry which mainly dealt with diplomatic affairs concerning the former dominions and the independent ex-colonies. Meanwhile, the other component states of Northern Rhodesia and Nyasaland were protectorates managed by the Colonial Office, the ministry directly responsible for the governance of dependent territories. This meant that both states were established via treaties with local rulers, not unlike the situation in the respective sultanates of the Federation of Malaya.[24] In contrast, Singapore was constitutionally islanded as a colony with a direct subordinate relationship to the imperial metropole.

During the 1956 talks, Marshall argued for Singapore's transfer from the Colonial Office to the Commonwealth Relations Office. This move would presumably elevate Singapore's status towards equality with the other independent countries of the Commonwealth.[25] His successor as chief minister later denigrated this particular proposal. To Lim Yew Hock, the transfer made little difference since the Colonial Office and the Commonwealth Relations Office were both ministries of the British government.[26] Every one of Marshall's attempts to clinch dominionhood for Singapore as part of the 1956 delegation made little headway.

The 1956 Marshall delegation faced one rejection after another, particularly when it came to any initiative that could give any semblance of recognition as a sovereign nation-state to Singapore. During the preparatory stages of the 1956 constitutional talks, Marshall even provided statistical evidence to Colonial Secretary Alan Lennox-Boyd to prove that Singapore was on par with many independent countries in terms of wealth, population and geographical size.[27] The idea that the city-state had to be continuously reliant on the protection of the United Kingdom was therefore a misdiagnosis. On British responsibilities of defence, Marshall cited the cases of independent Ceylon and the former dominions. They had defence treaties with the United Kingdom in both matters, and yet they were recognized as sovereign countries.[28] With British approval and technical assistance, Marshall further believed that Singapore would merely need a few years to build its own military force.[29] But his arguments were not treated seriously. The British felt that their military bases on the island were too important to leave to the whims of Singaporean politicians who might have no qualms about violating defence treaties. While credit could be given to Marshall for his imaginative overtures to seek equal Commonwealth membership for Singapore, the venture was tantamount to flogging a dead horse.

The British still had to find ways to pacify the demands of the 1956 Singaporean delegation. First, the colonial power maintained that it was impossible for Singapore to gain equal membership of the Commonwealth because of precedence. In spite of the accelerated decay of the British world system in the age of decolonization, the thought of a colonial state with a status equal to Britain and the other sovereign ex-colonies seemed erroneous since such an arrangement breached the ongoing practice of decolonization in the British Empire. Other colonial states, like Malta and the Gold Coast, were denied a similar recognition even after attaining self-governing status.[30] Having rejected these demands for sovereign equality during the 1956 talks, the British delegation attempted to provide medicament to calm the nationalist fever of Singaporean leaders:

> It must be made clear beyond doubt that in expressing reservations on this subject Her Majesty's Government in no way seek to impugn good faith of the present Government of Singapore, in which they have every confidence, or to comment on any alternative Government there might be at say a time in the near future.[31]

These words indicate that the British judged Singapore as simply unfit for complete independence. But typical of the paternalism of colonial governance, the British assured Singaporean leaders that the city-state might be ready sometime in the indefinite future. This rhetoric of dependency and the continued deferment of self-determination prolonged colonial power in Singapore.

The British cited Singapore's vulnerability to communism as the second justification. Singapore's wealth was dependent on its port and an open economy, and thus the island, at least according to the British, would face total collapse should it convert into a centrally driven, closed economy typical of communist states. Complementing their capital interests, British anxieties hinged on the fate of their bases in Singapore because their military presence ensured that in the event of widespread unrest or an armed insurrection by communist forces, British soldiers could be deployed to restore order. Marshall's counterargument was that Singapore's vulnerability to communism was not exceptional. The Federation of Malaya, for instance, was still fighting a guerrilla war with the MCP and yet there were already initiatives in motion to offer the Federation complete independence. The threat of communism in Singapore should therefore not be taken as prejudicial to its demand for self-determination.[32]

Furthermore, the spectre of race loomed over the island's fate. The face of communism in Singapore and Malaya was a Chinese one.[33] While not explicitly mentioned during the constitutional talks, the temptation for a Chinese-majority Singapore to embrace communism was a daunting possibility for the British since Commonwealth forces were still embroiled at this time in the war against the MCP, a predominantly ethnic Chinese militant group believed to be the proxy of Mao Zedong's China.[34] This somewhat racist view persisted in Whitehall circles.[35] Moreover, in the eyes of the Alliance-led regime in the Federation, the future government of Chinese-majority Singapore would also be Chinese-dominated and therefore more susceptible to communist influence.[36] This became part of the reason why the Alliance government resisted incorporating Singapore into the Federation.

The British further dismissed Marshall's argument that the risk of a communist takeover would defuse with the city-state's independence, even though they were aware of the ideological potency which came with the miscegenation of anti-colonialism and communism.[37] An independent Singapore could be tantalized by communism's promises of a freer and equal society—if not now, then perhaps in the future. The only guarantee for the safety of British bases was colonial rule.

Though the British were predominantly worried about their bases on the island, Lim's insistence on retaining Marshall's proposal of a Malayan governor-general pushed the British to confront the implications of having a non-British person as the Crown representative in Singapore. One puzzle that had initially befuddled British officials was the proposed split in the existing functions of the colonial governorship. By keeping the offices of Crown representative and the British government representative separate, a local-born person appointed to the former would be ranked higher than the latter in the hierarchy of a colony. The Colonial Office maintained that "it is not right that at this stage of constitutional development the representative of the UK government should be placed in a subordinate position".[38] An independent-minded Malayan Crown representative might refuse executive advice or even veto the policies initiated by the representative of the British government. Regulations and acts would only have legal effect after the Crown representative signed them into law, and hence his cooperation was vital to ensure a healthy operation of British authority over Singapore's defence and external affairs.

In addition to this potential hindrance, Whitehall officials were alarmed that the British government representative might lose access to confidential Cabinet papers and security reports—a privilege previously reserved for the Crown representative—thereby impeding his ability to carry out his duties.[39] Lim's British advisors from the Colonial Office even added that the proposed Malayan governor-general might handicap future efforts towards merger to further dissuade the chief minister from pursuing the idea. If political union with the Federation was to happen, Singapore had to establish a new relationship with the Federation's sovereign head of state. This would result in two possibilities: first, the office of governor-general would be abolished and become a wasteful constitutional exercise, or second, "vested interests" reliant on the prestige and privileges of the office could obstruct merger.[40] Lim's proposal for the Malayan-born Crown representative thus met with the same British apprehension as it had run into during the 1956 talks.

After further discussions, this hard-line attitude began to soften as the British realized that Lim would never yield on the issue. They registered that Lim "attached so much importance to symbol of Government House" and that negotiations "should not get very far towards the meeting of minds" unless there was some concession to the idea of a Malayan titular figure occupying Government House.[41] Governor Black even patronizingly called the issue of a Malayan governor-general Lim's "obsession".[42] Moreover, the eventual concession on the part of the British government was a crucial attempt to bolster the prestige of political "moderates" in the eyes of the electorate, particularly with respect to the new chief minister.[43] In a memorandum to the British Cabinet prior to the 1957 talks, the colonial secretary informed his cabinet colleagues:

> ... I recognise that the appointment of a local personage as Head of State would be unprecedented at the present stage of constitutional development, and that for Commonwealth reasons he would have to have some other title besides 'Governor-General'. But this is the first of our 'smaller territories'—those whom we can foresee no ultimate independence on their own—to have made this suggestion, and it may well be that, if we devise an arrangement on these lines that satisfies local

national pride without making the territory independent of the United Kingdom, we shall have taken a pragmatic step towards the solution of a difficult constitutional problem, and shall have demonstrated once more the adaptability of our Commonwealth arrangements.[44]

A local-born representative of the Crown in the context of a colony was therefore an important symbolic venture to extend the life of British sovereignty over Singapore. But the British remained nervous about a future Malayan Crown representative encumbering their authority. Accordingly, they began to think of creative safeguards to make the idea work to their benefit.

Concessions (Terms and Conditions Apply)

The first sticking point was the title of "governor-general". Governor-generals are viceregal officers who act as surrogates of the British Crown. They serve in Commonwealth countries where the British monarch continue to reign as head of state following the territory's formal independence from Britain. British officials were bothered that a local-born governor-general in Singapore might equate the island's status to the sovereign Commonwealth countries with their own governor-generals. The British commissioner-general in Southeast Asia, Robert Scott, cautioned that a governor-general for Singapore was too "pretentious" for a British colony.[45] His views were in line with the wisdom circulating within the Colonial Office which maintained that other Commonwealth countries would become "jealous" since the governor-general represented their independence from Britain.[46]

But British speculations about the reaction of other Commonwealth countries towards the Malayan governor-general in Singapore were not completely accurate. Both the high commissioners of Australia and New Zealand in London relayed that their respective governments were less preoccupied with the symbolic value of the governor-general and more concerned with practical difficulties in administering defence in Singapore. They were worried that the split between the offices of Crown representative and British government representative might compromise existing military arrangements. The New Zealand high commissioner insisted that the governor-general issue should not be a "breaking point", whereas the Australian high commissioner was more withdrawn, stressing that the British government was in the best position to decide on the matter.[47] British officials, erring on the side of caution, still believed this future viceregal office should be renamed so as to dispel any confusion about Singapore's status as a colony.

The British eventually acquiesced to the symbolic office to appease national pride, but on the condition that the office should not take on the title of "governor-general". The move to rename the Crown representative in Singapore soon became a source of chronic confusion. During the 1957 talks, the British gave a nod to the Singaporean delegation's proposal to style the office as "Yang di-Pertuan Negara". The ingenuity behind the office's name will be dissected later, but what needs to be emphasized is that this concession—the opportunity to rename the office of Crown representative—in the context of a British colony was unprecedented. Singapore's colonial masters kept their guard up. Any slippages might overstate this exceptional opportunity as a sign of the city-state's independence. Should these liberal interpretations arise, it would not only result in diplomatic hassle for the British government, but also send a false signal to communist forces in the region that the British were withdrawing from Southeast Asia.

Yet, when "Yang di-Pertuan Negara" was revealed as the new name for the Crown representative in Singapore, local politicians highlighted that foreign visitors were "confused" as to why the city-state would be governed by the Colonial Office under the proposed constitution and still have a Yang di-Pertuan Negara as a "head of state", which alluded to the false impression that Singapore had its own sovereign ruler.[48] This confounding issue could be explained by developments taking place north of Singapore. The Federation of Malaya at this time was waiting for its imminent independence from Britain and had designated the title of its future head of state as "Yang di-Pertuan Agong". Ironically, the title of "Yang di-Pertuan Negara", as a rechristened name for the Malayan governor-general, was even more of an overreach. If the entire purpose of the rebranding exercise was to prevent confusion, this new ostentatious title achieved the complete opposite and further generated a semantic mess.

This was an unpleasant situation for officials in the Commonwealth Relations Office. They appealed to their colleagues in the Colonial Office to clarify that Singapore's head of state in constitutional terms was still the Queen—the Yang di-Pertuan Negara was only Her Majesty's representative. The main concern of the Commonwealth Relations Office was that the Yang di-Pertuan Negara was not of equal standing with other heads of state in sovereign Commonwealth countries and ought not to be mistaken as such, even though the office had a unique "indigenized" name.[49] Officials were already uncomfortable with the use of "high commissioner" for the representative of the British government, pointing out that it was a misnomer; other high commissioners were appointed to independent Commonwealth countries as diplomats with ambassadorial duties, not as colonial administrators with gubernatorial authority as was the case in Singapore. The high commissioner of Malaya—the colonial official who administered the Federation when it was a British dependent—was an aberration, and thus this office should not be emulated in the city-state's future Constitution.[50] The dissenting voices pushed the Colonial Office to eventually style the office of British government representative as "United Kingdom commissioner" during the 1957 talks.

Fearing excesses in the office of Yang di-Pertuan Negara, the British constrained the eventual appointee with bureaucratic procedures. For instance, the Yang di-Pertuan Negara could only go on leave with the gracious approval of the colonial secretary to stress Singapore's enduring colonial status.[51] In conjunction with this debilitating enforcement of hierarchy, the Yang di-Pertuan Negara did not have direct access to the Queen, even though it was his duty to accept petitions on Her Majesty's behalf. Instead, he had to forward these petitions to the colonial secretary, who would then submit it to the Queen.[52] This anxiety within Whitehall came close to paranoia. When drafting the public announcement of Yusof's appointment to the office in November 1959, Goode, who was at this time holding the joint office of the interim Yang di-Pertuan Negara and British commissioner, proposed that the message should start with the phrase "Her Majesty has been pleased to approve the appointment". The Colonial Office was careful to revise the message by prefacing the statement with the phrase "it is announced by the Secretary of State for the Colonies, Mr Ian McLeod, that" to eschew any interpretation that might suggest a change in Singapore's colonial status.[53] The British were resolute in emphasizing Singapore's lesser position in the hierarchy of nations.

In tandem with issues of rank and hierarchy, the British needed compliance from the Yang di-Pertuan Negara because the office was a component of the state's security organ. Unlike more innocuous symbols like a flag or a crest, he would have concrete powers since any form of legislation needed his endorsement to become law. As Marshall pointed out when debating the outcome of the 1957 talks, the Yang di-Pertuan Negara must assent to all ISC resolutions. This could tarnish the prestige of the office because any blame for any repressive ISC measures could shift to the Yang di-Pertuan Negara.[54] The entanglement of the office with the mechanism of colonial control was far removed from Marshall's vision of the Malayan governor-general. During the 1956 talks, Singaporean delegates imagined the Malayan governor-general as a symbol of independence within the Commonwealth, with much less of the securitized inflexions since internal security—based on Marshall's failed proposals—would completely be in the hands of an elected Singaporean government. The ISC, however, was an unelected council consisting of only a minority of Singaporean representatives.

Despite the fact that the Yang di-Pertuan Negara was the Crown representative, the British commissioner, as representative of the British government, still had wide-ranging powers. He was the channel of all official correspondence from Singapore to London and enjoyed the privilege of access to Cabinet papers and confidential security documents. Most importantly, the authority to suspend the Constitution and impose emergency rule over Singapore lay in his hands. In making contingency plans during an event of emergency rule, the colonial authorities were fully aware of potential complications because the Yang di-Pertuan Negara would still remain in office as a form of respect for a Crown representative.

Yet, under the circumstances of emergency rule, the Yang di-Pertuan Negara would be reduced to a petty functionary of the colonial power because he must assent to the decrees of the British commissioner in all matters.[55] When officials first drafted the Constitution, there were misgivings within the Colonial Office about a non-compliant Yang di-Pertuan Negara who could hinder British emergency rule. John Hennings, a senior official in the Colonial Office, nevertheless assured his colleagues:

> If the holder of that office refuses to cooperate, he can be removed—he holds the office during Her Majesty's pleasure—and if no local replacement can be found, the offices of United Kingdom Commissioner and Yang di-Pertuan Negara can be held by the same person.[56]

It was possible for the British commissioner to seize control over Singapore with relative ease, pacify an already emasculated Yang di-Pertuan Negara and then override all the supposed gains from the Constitution. Britain's ability to exert its will over Singapore did not change in substance but was only tweaked in form. In spite of the celebratory atmosphere ushered in by these supposed constitutional gains, Singapore remained a colony, with the British receiving a new lease of life as paramount power.

Even the confirmation of an appointee as Yang di-Pertuan Negara was within British discretion. The Queen would only appoint a candidate under executive advice from a British cabinet minister, namely the secretary of state for the colonies, who in turn would nominate someone in consultation with the Singaporean government. In the case of a "proper" governor-general, the British monarch would be legally obliged to act on direct advice from the government in the Commonwealth country, with no meddling from Whitehall intermediaries. Again, it was Marshall who publicly exposed the veto power of the British government over the appointment of the Yang di-Pertuan Negara.[57] As enshrined in the Constitution, the appointee may only stay in office "at Her Majesty's pleasure", and thus the British government could dismiss him at any time through executive advice to the Queen.[58]

This situation was not historically atypical. During the interwar years, the appointment of governor-generals occasionally came under Whitehall's oversight. While the British monarch conventionally obliged to the advice of dominion governments when appointing governor-generals, there were episodes when the British government politically influenced the acceptance or rejection of candidates.[59] But these episodes largely fizzled away after the Second World War with the post of governor-general becoming more institutionalized. With the gradual phasing out of dominionhood, the British government refrained from interfering with governor-general appointments to avoid infringing upon the sovereignty of their former dependents—sovereign equality is after all a foundational principle of the new postwar Commonwealth.

Through persuasive parlance and legal acrobatics, the colonial power managed to renew its sovereignty over Singapore in spite of the concessions it made during the 1956 and 1957 constitutional talks. As Chatterjee argues, "the notion that colonial rule was not really about colonial rule but something else was a persistent theme in the rhetoric of colonial rule itself".[60] Singapore was denied independence over its affairs because a radical, "communist-influenced" government could compromise British strategic concerns in the Far East.[61] The justifications employed by the British all point to Singapore being "not ready", glazed with the same paternalistic fervour of "the White Man's burden", as wilfully summoned during the advent of colonial rule.[62] This invocation of Singapore's vulnerability became a potent rhetorical device to substantiate the city-state's unreadiness to govern itself, thereby tailoring the situation to suit British interests. The diminishing pool of colonies in the British world system needed to be organized based on a different discursive frame in the postwar world, and thus the atmosphere of the Cold War provided a significant bearing for the recalibration of colonial rule.

Inextricable from the geopolitical factor was the structure of the postwar Commonwealth. While the Marshall delegation saw the organization as a means to independence and affirm their allegiance to British interests, it was ironically also because of the Commonwealth that Singapore was situated in a new international hierarchy. The Commonwealth structure placed the island state on a universal plane shared with other ex-colonial nations and became a way to determine Singapore's readiness for independence in relation to other territories. Philip Murphy has pointed out that the Commonwealth, at least during the initial postwar years, still displayed trappings of the imperial hierarchy. Like restrictive practices of a gentleman's club, prospective members had to fulfil certain requirements to qualify for membership. This hierarchy also manifested in the symbolic practices in Commonwealth ceremonies. During the

1953 coronation of Elizabeth II, the sitting location of representatives from the Commonwealth—whether they were seated inside or outside Westminster Abbey—depended on their respective status on the ladder of self-determination.[63]

Decolonization since the end of the Second World War had led to the existence of an unequal global order not just between the colonizer on one side and the colonized and formerly colonized on the other. An increasingly layered international hierarchy had begun to take shape with colonies placed below the newly independent countries. For the British, Singapore could not qualify for a full Commonwealth membership because it was not a sovereign independent state, and it could not be one because of its susceptibility to communism. For Singaporean leaders, the city-state remained susceptible to communism because it was not a sovereign independent state, and it could not be one if it was denied full Commonwealth membership. It was an impossible situation.

Facing this impasse, Singaporean leaders had little room to manoeuvre. Instead of furthering attempts to dismantle the rhetoric enforcing Singapore's vulnerability to communism—a force which also threatened to compromise their own political fortunes—the 1957 Singapore delegation accepted the premise that Singapore was in exceptional peril of a communist takeover and that the British should retain powers over Singapore's security apparatus. Still, the British entertained the Marshall delegation's earlier suggestion to have a representative from the Federation in the ISC, since the pro-British Tunku would play his part as an additional restraint on the Singaporean government.[64] In his autobiography, Lim Yew Hock describes the 1957 talks as "festive" and "smooth sailing" after he succeeded in persuading the Tunku to keep a watchful eye over Singapore through an ISC representative from the Federation.[65] While publicly expressing reservations over the "subversive clause", the 1957 delegation embraced the other points of agreement, suggesting the triumph of political expedience on all sides.[66]

After the catastrophe at Suez, the British were looking for a symbolic victory to regain its crumbling international prestige and were eager to grant symbolic concessions to the city-state while maintaining their absolute authority over the island. Colonialism, as it was at its advent and now towards its very end, was lasting due to the collaboration of the elites from the colonized society. It seemed that the 1957 Singapore delegation had developed an acquired taste for what Marshall had called "Christmas pudding in arsenic sauce" rather than admitting that there was nothing good for dessert. By appeasing British strategic concerns, the Singaporean delegation saw opportunity to accumulate political capital. The success of attaining the new self-governing Constitution would mean a chance to legitimize themselves as genuine anti-colonial nationalists—a victory which Lim, as leader of the 1957 Singaporean delegation, was only too delighted to gloat about.[67]

Singaporean leaders needed to communicate a sense of change to the electorate despite their failure to revise the status quo. While there was a greater level of autonomy for locally elected leaders in most of the city-state's affairs, these were burdensome responsibilities that the British were already willing to abandon at the very start of the 1956 talks, and as highlighted earlier, Lennox-Boyd admitted that executive power in Singapore was in practice already exercised by local ministers under the Rendel Constitution.[68] A failure on the constitutional front to achieve sovereign independence did not stop nationalists from displaying anti-colonial fervour through symbolic persuasion; new, tangible idioms were needed to further mitigate the continued presence of colonial control while providing political mileage for Singaporean leaders.

Singaporean attempts to represent a rupture of the colonial order, however, must be done without inviting British suspicions of falling into the temptation of communism. Decolonization needed to be performed, and nationalists found a ripe target: the Crown. In a setting where political competition amounted to slandering competitors as "imperialist stooges", Singaporean leaders needed to urgently display the breakdown of the colonial status quo to further prove themselves as effective nationalists. If Singapore was denied the status of an independent sovereign entity untethered to British rule, perhaps the city-state could at the very least muster a performance to conjure an image of being an independent sovereign entity.

The Singaporean delegations during both constitutional talks embraced continued links with the British Crown for different reasons, but Chief Minister Lim thought it was best to further camouflage Singapore's colonial status more actively. In his comments on the constitutional draft, he insisted that references to the Queen should only be used minimally.[69] With a vocal opponent like Marshall expressing relentless contempt for the 1958 Constitution, such requests to mitigate association with the Crown indicated that Singaporean leaders were fully cautious—and to some extent insecure—about the burden of coloniality that the Constitution carried. Even before the passage of the Constitution, Lim had his worries about unnecessary association with the Crown. In July 1956, Lennox-Boyd asked Lim about a possible visit of the Duke of Edinburgh to Singapore. The chief minister merely replied, "could he not come unannounced?", although he clarified that if it was the Queen who intended to visit, Singaporean leaders would "spread themselves in a big way" because Her Majesty was still the sovereign of Singapore.[70]

In February 1959, while still in opposition, the PAP called for a boycott of the Duke's visit to the island. According to the party, the royal family was a "symbol of overlordship of the British Raj".[71] In response, a *Straits Times* editorial lectured the party by pointing out that Ong Eng Guan's position as mayor in the PAP-led City Council was established via Royal Charter. The writer further penned a blistering reprisal by asking whether the PAP's attitude towards the Crown would jeopardize their potential relationship with the Yang di-Pertuan Negara, who was after all the Queen's future representative.[72] The PAP continued to express further defiance towards the British monarch. The press reported that the Queen's portrait in City Hall was removed during the swearing-in of the PAP government.[73] This was the dialectic at the centre of the anti-colonial project in Singapore: affinity with the British Crown was a representation of imperial subordination, but the "pragmatism" needed for a greater degree of self-government dictated that Singapore should remain a colony. How then did nationalist leaders in Singapore decolonize the Yang di-Pertuan Negara, a figure who served as the island's constitutional link to the British Crown?

Romantics of Malay(an) Political Culture

The stylistic segment of the office could therefore be seen as a site of nationalist attempt to subvert, or perhaps disguise, its colonial underpinnings. Singaporean leaders wanted to infuse a meaningful sense of change into the office, affirming a shift from the Rendel Constitution. The title of Yang di-Pertuan Negara was translated in the 1957 constitutional report as "head of state".[74] The name, however, is not a neutral term divorced from historical imprints. On the contrary, it was testament to the reworking of Singapore's historical emplacement within the Malay World for the service of overlapping political projects. A "Yang di-Pertuan" of Singapore was not an unfamiliar occurrence in the recent history of the island. The title, which directly translates to "he who is made lord", had its origins in Malay political culture and was understood in pre-colonial texts from the region as a title used by royalty.[75]

During the assertion of Bugis influence in the Johor-Riau Sultanate from 1722, a new position with the hereditary title of "Yang di-Pertuan Muda" or "junior king" (also translated as "Yamtuan Muda") was created for the Bugis leader who had helped Sultan Sulaiman defend his throne against Raja Kecil from Siak.[76] Upon being confirmed by the British in 1819 as the rightful heir to the Johor-Riau throne, Sultan Hussein explained to his younger brother, the reigning sultan of Johor-Riau, that he was not a usurper but was compelled to accede to British demands. Hussein nevertheless addressed himself as the "Yang di-Pertuan Singapura" or "lord of Singapore". Meanwhile, Raja Ali Haji, the renowned court historian of Johor-Riau, called Hussein "Yang di-Pertuan Selat" or "lord of the straits".[77] Singapore, however, ceased having its own sovereign "Yang di-Pertuan" after the complete surrender of the island's sovereignty to the British Crown. But one could argue that the British monarch was in fact both the de facto and de jure "Yang di-Pertuan" of Singapore when the island came under colonial rule.

In spite of its genealogy, the title of Yang di-Pertuan Negara was a product of innovation. The fixture "*negara*" transformed the title into something new. In the Malay language, "*negara*" has come to connote the modern nation-state. The title of Yang di-Pertuan, long dead in the history of Singapore's royal court, was thereafter resurrected as an "invented tradition". According to Eric Hobsbawm:

> "[i]nvented traditions" is taken to mean a set of practices, normally governed by overtly or tacitly accepted rules and of a ritual or symbolic

nature, which seek to inculcate certain values and norms of behaviour by repetition, which automatically implies continuity with the past.[78]

Such practices were not merely a blind reconstruction of ancient materials but were selectively adapted for new purposes under novel circumstances.[79] Invented traditions manifest in a variety of forms encompassing ceremonies, songs or even costumes to convey a sense of stability amid relentless change. Hobsbawm goes on to identify three main functions of invented traditions, namely, to demonstrate social cohesion, to legitimize institutions or relations of authority and finally, to foster "value systems and conventions of behaviour".[80] In the modern era, they inculcate values and display the character of the nation, fostering a sense of stability within the structure of the nation-state.[81] The adaptation of "Yang di-Pertuan" now served a new purpose in a different historical juncture. The title, as well as the rituals and ceremonies in which the future appointee would participate, aimed to generate a new norm in social relations.

The invocation of the island's pre-colonial heritage in self-governing Singapore was an overt endeavour to dramatize change while communicating stability—as contradictory as this may sound. The titular office of the land was an institution of the colonial state, but it still tapped into the symbolic authority of a political heritage which had been buried in the island's past. The title of Yang di-Pertuan Negara was part of a wider creative effort of Singaporean leaders to adapt elements of the past in the service of decolonization. On the one hand, by invoking a past that was once "lost", they indicated a sense of relief from colonial rule to the people of Singapore in a new era of self-determination, conjuring the island's historical emplacement in the larger Malay World. On the other hand, as representative of the British Crown, the Yang di-Pertuan Negara would signal a sense of stability rather than a complete revolutionary overhaul, dispelling British worries of radical "communist" leanings amongst Singaporean leaders and cementing a sense of continuity within the prevailing structure of the British imperial system. In other words, change was embraced but cautiously adjusted depending on the circumstance and audience.

In their efforts to balance the representation of change, the distinction between what was characteristically "Malay" (an elusive, primordial ethno-cultural identity believed to be existent since the days of ancient past) and what was "Malayan" (a descriptive terminology of political features associated with the British-constructed Federation of Malaya) became conflated at times. The idea of inventiveness discussed below depends on the interplay of both ideas and on the slippages inherent in both terms—the modern and seemingly archaic, the contemporary and what appeared to be ancient. The term "Malay(an)" employed hereinafter to refer to invented elements of political culture will therefore be more suitable.

The Malay(an) character of the Yang di-Pertuan Negara stirred the monarchical connotations which came with the title's genealogy. According to Rahim Ishak, Yusof's younger brother and former PAP minister, the Tunku was the title's architect.[82] The Federation prime minister was a staunch defender of the institution of Malay monarchy and was after all a prince from the state of Kedah. Meanwhile, newspaper reports note similarities between the title and royal precedents in the Federation, drawing comparisons to the Yang di-Pertuan Besar, who is head of state in Negri Sembilan, and the federal head of state, the Yang di-Pertuan Agong.[83] Both positions were interestingly *elected* positions. Negri Sembilan is a confederation of smaller provinces. The chiefs of these provinces choose from amongst their ranks a Yang di-Pertuan Besar to serve as the state's ruler. The Tunku, inspired by this arrangement, transposed this model at the federal level when negotiating constitutional arrangements for an independent Malaya. The nine peninsular rulers would select one of their brother rulers to become Yang di-Pertuan Agong for a term of five years.

The point is that the Yang di-Pertuan Negara was modelled after royalty. Anonymous observers privy to the constitutional talks publicly hailed that the similarities between the Yang di-Pertuan Negara and the Yang di-Pertuan Agong as "evident synthesis" which pointed to eventual reunification of Singapore and the Federation.[84] Elsewhere in the region, Brunei's sultan was also called "Yang di-Pertuan Brunei" before the territory's independence from Britain in 1984.[85] The covealness of these examples emphasize the insinuations of royalty which were affixed to the title of Yang di-Pertuan Negara. In one critical editorial written in response to the formulation of the title, the office is described as "synthetic" and a "pseudo-monarchy", condemning Lim Yew Hock's government for its abandonment of left-wing principles. The commentator speculates that merger could result in a royal personality from the Federation occupying the post of Yang di-Pertuan Negara, thereby turning the office into a seat of a new monarchical dynasty.[86] When the details of the Constitution were finalized in May 1958, another article from the *Sunday Standard* could not resist calling the Yang di-Pertuan Negara as the colony's "king".[87] Even after the constitutional contours of the office were finalized, the title persisted in generating royal signification.

The royal signification of the title notwithstanding, Singaporean leaders had other options. They could have adopted the model offered by Penang and Melaka, Singapore's sister cities of the former Straits Settlements. Unlike the other constitutive states of the Federation, both Penang and Melaka have no sovereign monarch as head of state. In July 1956, Lim informed British officials that he was waiting for the proposals of the Reid Commission which would outline constitutional arrangements for the soon-to-be independent Federation of Malaya. More particularly, he was paying close attention to the Commission's plans for the ceremonial head of state in Penang and Melaka, hoping to base Singapore's future "governor-general" along the lines of the proposals.[88]

The Commission, however, later outlined that the offices ought to carry the title of "governor" ("*gabnor*" in Malay) in accordance with the defunct British precedent. After all, it was the colonial governor based in Singapore who had administered both states as British colonies.[89] Other colonial territories, like Malta or Ghana for instance, also retained the governor as titular office when they first transitioned to self-government. In these cases, the governor, who was under the direction of the Colonial Office, wielded substantial executive and emergency powers as well as responsibility over the affairs which fell under British jurisdiction.[90] When opposing the co-option of the governor-general title for a dependent territory, the permanent secretary in the Commonwealth Relations Office, Sir Gilbert Laithwaite, opined that even an advanced "State" like Singapore ought to keep the governor as the Crown representative.[91] The offices of governor in Penang and Melaka were only renamed "Yang di-Pertua Negeri" in 1976 to follow the examples provided by Sabah and Sarawak when they, together with Singapore, joined the Federation in 1963.[92] Compared to the prefix of "Yang di-Pertuan", "Yang di-Pertua" is not exclusively reserved for royalty. It was used then as it is today to denote the office of a chairperson or leader who presides over an establishment, organization or political party.[93]

Seeing that the models chosen for Penang and Melaka failed to communicate a sense of change, it was likely that Lim, perhaps in consultation with the Tunku, decided to tailor the designation of "Yang di-Pertuan Agong" to suit the office of Crown representative in Singapore. By adapting the title used for the Federation head of state, the entire re-naming exercise became an undisguised initiative to eliminate the colonial association of the governorship. The constitutional reforms in Singapore would therefore be more closely associated with those taking place in the Federation. In discussing the feasibility of the proposal for a governor-general for the city-state, Whitehall officials were initially baffled as to why the title of "governor" was seen as derogatory to Singaporean leaders.[94] L.B. Walsh Atkins from the Commonwealth Relations Office even suggested the "splendid and handsome" title of "viceroy" as an alternative in a romantic appeal to the imperial heritage of the British Raj.[95] Walsh Atkins nevertheless made an important caveat: the title of viceroy should only be used in the Malay translation to suit the specific context of Singapore because such a grand title had the potential to be put to better use elsewhere in the British Empire and the Commonwealth.

British fears of using the title of governor-general became motivation for Whitehall officials to sprout other potential names for the Crown representative in Singapore. Their brilliant ideas included "Queen's deputy" and "Queen's commissioner", both of which would emphasize Singapore's subordinate status as a dependent colonial territory.[96] Whitehall officials went on to complain that Shakespeare's tongue lacked the ability to express Singapore's "new state of being" in spite of their faith in English, the official language of the Commonwealth, as the best medium for the title.[97] Officials in London clearly revelled in the legacy of empire. For the British, accepting the title of Yang di-Pertuan Negara as recommended by Singaporean leaders was an outcome of the familiar dialectic of mollifying demands of self-determination to prolong British domination. Their final decision to acquiesce to a new Malay name for Singapore's viceregal office was a politically convenient measure which only came as a begrudging final resort. Modifying New Zealand Prime

Minister David Lange's descriptor for the governor-general, the Yang di-Pertuan Negara was effectively the Queen in Malay(an) drag.[98]

There is one final component in the innovative title of "Yang di-Pertuan Negara" that needs to be taken apart. Why was the term "*negara*" significant? One can only speculate that it was meant to reflect Singapore's distinct status amid its own constitutional journey. "*Negara*" and "*negeri*" have been used since classical times in the larger region. According to Clifford Geertz, both terms are based on the same Sanskrit loanword, connoting the "city", "capital" or "state", as opposed to the word "*desa*", meaning "countryside" or "village".[99] In the context of British Malaya before the Second World War, the slippage between "*negara*" and "*negeri*" were frequent occurrences. Although "*negeri*" was the common term used to refer to both the Malay states and all states in general—whether they were completely sovereign or not—by the early twentieth century, it began to replace the term "*kerajaan*" (the condition of living under a *raja*) in conceptualizing the notion of the state as a modern political structure.[100]

Following the Second World War, however, the nation-state became increasingly represented as the only viable form of modern community in the world system. "*Negara*" soon became commonplace in the nomenclature to refer to an expansive sense of pan-Malayan nationhood beyond the parochial bounds of each peninsular state or the *negeri*, for instance in context of "Warta Negara" or "Parti Negara". While "*negara*" has come to mean a fully sovereign nation-state or country, the use of "*negeri*" has gradually been reserved to connote a constitutive state or province within a larger political conglomeration. It was understood that the Federation of Malaya fully transitioned into a *negara* when it attained independence from Britain in 1957, denoting its transition to an independent nation-state, while a state like Kedah or Johor for example remained a constituent *negeri*. The Federation's national anthem, *Negaraku*, could also be translated as "my country".[101] Furthermore, during the constitutional negotiations in 1956 and 1957, the Negara Republik Indonesia (NRI) was already a sovereign country, offering another contemporaneous use of "*negara*".[102]

Singapore, under the terms of its new Constitution, was strictly not a *negara* in the sense that it was not a sovereign nation-state. The island was instead a modern (colonial) state with a centralized administration. The term "*negara*" was therefore a rather extravagant stylistic device to signify the new "State of Singapore" which was birthed from the 1958 Constitution, jumbling the fact that the island was neither an independent sovereign state nor a constituent state of the Federation. If the Tunku was truly the main progenitor of "Yang di-Pertuan Negara", one could appreciate the use of "*negara*" as a terminological deference that emphasized Singapore's otherness, that it was distinct and not a *negeri* of the Federation. This was consistent with the well-established understanding that the Tunku was disinclined to accept Singapore into the Federation before discussions on the "Malaysia Plan" in 1961.[103]

Whether or not the Tunku deliberately coined the title to create further distance between Singapore and Malaya, political representatives of the city-state still embraced the new name of their Crown representative to represent the political change embodied in the new Constitution. The liminal status of being a British colony that aspired to be part of the Federation trapped Singapore in ambiguity. This became a serviceable condition for the political projects of Singaporean leaders. In July 1958, Marshall put forth a gambit in order to free Singapore from this ambiguity. The ex-chief minister, now leader of the newly formed Workers' Party, dared the Tunku to sign a binding agreement which would incorporate the city-state into the Federation. In return the Federation prime minister would not only get to nominate the Yang di-Pertuan Negara but also all of Singapore's lawmakers.[104] While this wager would free Singapore from British rule and demonstrate Singapore's absolute loyalty to the Federation, it was treated as mere political gimmick.

But the full praxis of this equivocal situation could be seen after the implementation of the Constitution. The PAP government regularly called for loyalty to the "Singapore State" rather than more contentious terms like a "Singaporean nation", which may misrepresent the city-state as not Malayan. Connoting a sense of community and of imagined belonging, the term "nation" was therefore reserved in the context of a "Malayan nation" to reflect a commitment to a united Malaya.[105] Although British official discourse perpetuated the idea of a fully sovereign Singapore as beyond the accepted bounds of possibility, it was the PAP government that went on to preserve this understanding by relegating others who called for Singapore's separate independence from Malaya as lackeys of communism.[106] By accepting the invented title of Yang di-Pertuan Negara, Singaporean leaders could package the office of Crown representative as a sovereign head of state in line with the independent Federation. This form of symbolic resistance against the reality of the Queen's lasting reign dressed up Singapore's colonial status. The Singaporean nationalist leadership, whether under Lim Yew Hock or Lee Kuan Yew, did not blindly mimic the models in the Federation. They craftily applied the medium of a stylistic change and the ambiguities that came with it to satisfy their political needs.

A Sultan for Singapore

The Yang di-Pertuan Negara fell into further controversy in September 1958 when the Singaporean branch of UMNO openly called for the revival of the Sultanate of Singapore. The party boldly proposed that Singaporean Malays should elect one of the descendants of Hussein Shah or someone from the lineage of the Temenggong Abdul Rahman—whose descendants rule the modern State of Johor—to be crowned as sultan of the island.[107] According to UMNO, a sovereign Malay ruler would guarantee the rights of the Malays in the Chinese-majority city-state. By establishing this prospective sovereign, all political authority exercised in Singapore would emanate from a local royal figure rather than from the British monarch, thereby severing the colonial link to Britain. Singapore would therefore be constitutionally sovereign. For UMNO, the idea was also about correcting a historical injustice by restoring the sovereignty of Hussein Shah's lineage, whose right to rule the island was "forcefully" taken away by the British in 1824.[108]

Internal party support for the proposal, however, was not unanimous. UMNO's youth wing and one of the party's prominent leaders, Syed Ali Redha Alsagoff, became vocal opponents.[109] One member, Sahid Sahooman, recounted that the Singaporean branch of UMNO was split between traditionalist and socialist factions. According to him, Singapore "need[ed] its own Yang di-Pertuan" in order to restore Malay sovereignty over the island.[110] Defenders of the proposal wrote to *Berita Harian* to clarify that the party's plan should not be misconstrued as an effort to return to a time of absolute rulers. It was a legitimate means of restoring

Singapore's political independence since a sultan would serve as the embodiment of the sovereign status of a parliamentary democracy in accordance with the Westminster system.[111]

During the party's annual assembly in October 1958, delegates passed a resolution to restore the sultanate and adopt the proposal as part of its election platform. The delegates voted with a 33–23 majority with only two abstentions. Party members and observers jeered at the speakers opposing the motion.[112] The Tunku, who was himself present to grace the assembly, endorsed the resolution. The Federation prime minister nevertheless maintained a shrewd position, qualifying that the establishment of a sultanate was in itself an inadequate basis for merger.[113] As true as it was in earlier proposals for the city-state's independence, the most fanciful ideas to establish Singapore's sovereignty were as imaginative as they were problematic.

The reaction of other party leaders to UMNO's sultanate proposal was, at best, mixed. Lim Yew Hock, still the chief minister at this time, indicated an openness to the proposal. But he also pointed out that it was a matter for the future Singaporean government and harped on the fact that the most urgent goal was still merger. Upon Singapore's entry into the Federation, Lim explained that the central government in Kuala Lumpur could unilaterally decide on the nature of Singapore's head of state. He sympathetically assured proponents of the Sultanate of Singapore that for the time being, the city-state had little choice but to be content with the Yang di-Pertuan Negara.[114] Lim's predecessor, however, vehemently opposed the plans. Marshall stated categorically that he was against any effort to set up "a special class for descendants of former aristocracy", while E.K. Tan, leader of the Liberal Socialists, was evasive, highlighting that the "Malays themselves [were] not synonymous with the issue".[115]

In a somewhat surprising response, the anti-colonial and radical left-wing PAP seemed ambivalent towards the idea. Lee was tactful enough not to step on the toes of the Tunku because the Federation prime minister had publicly endorsed the sultanate proposal. When asked about the possibility of crowning Singapore's very own sultan, Lee replied:

> The all-party delegation, which includes the Singapore UMNO representative, has agreed to the constitutional progress regarding the Yang di-Pertuan Negara. No one expects to leave in a hurry for another

constitutional conference in London to undo this and to postpone the
general elections.[116]

The responses of other political parties did not kill enthusiasm for the
sultanate proposal. Sahid remembered how some UMNO members took
a drastic measure by calling for continued British colonialism because
the fate of the Malays would at least be protected by their colonial
masters.[117] The racial anxieties expressed by the Singaporean branch
of UMNO will be discussed more extensively in a later chapter, but as
for the fate of the sultanate proposal, it never materialized due to the
party's isolation on the issue.

More importantly, the reactions of other Singaporean leaders and their
use of the Yang di-Pertuan Negara as an olive branch to UMNO suggest
that the office was to some degree seen as a temporary placeholder, a
substitute for the idea of a sovereign sultan or raja reigning in Singapore.
With the exception of Marshall, the other political leaders did not
completely rule out the idea. They cited instead the impracticalities of
re-negotiating another constitutional agreement and the issue of non-
consensus. The proposal, rather than being demolished completely, was
instead deferred to an indefinite future. Even though the sultanate proposal
could not boast a spectacular take-off, this episode tied the symbolic
meaning of the Yang di-Pertuan Negara much closer to the romantic
notions of having a local sovereign ruler in Singapore, gesturing at the
city-state's rehabilitation into a Malay(an) political culture.

If the proposal to re-constitute the office of Yang di-Pertuan Negara
into a sovereign monarchy did not take off, perhaps the next best outcome
was to appoint someone of royal personage to the office. This solution
was precisely what a few politicians contemplated during the course of
1959 as discussions on the future Malayan-born Yang di-Pertuan Negara
took on a life of its own. On 10 February, the KMS, which had recently
ended cooperation with the Singaporean branch of UMNO, submitted a
petition to the Queen to appoint a descendant of Hussein Shah as Yang
di-Pertuan Negara.[118] This proposal was self-serving. Governor Goode
recognized that the KMS party chief, Tengku Muda Mohamed, had
every motive to push for the petition. As the most senior member of
the Hussein Shah's lineage, Goode presumed that Tengku Muda would
take on the office of Yang di-Pertuan Negara should the British approve

KMS's initiative. The governor further told the Colonial Office that the proposal held little weight because KMS was only a minor party.[119]

But the idea to reconstitute the Yang di-Pertuan Negara as a sovereign monarchical post endured. As late as March 1959, and closer to the general elections in May, an outpost of the Singaporean branch of UMNO modified the party's earlier sultanate proposal, calling for a member from one of the royal families in the Federation to be appointed as Yang di-Pertuan Negara.[120] Later during the election campaign, KMS adopted UMNO's original proposal, pledging the party to the sultanate's establishment.[121] A writer to the *Berita Harian* expressed hopes in April 1959 that the Yang di-Pertuan Negara would have a "Hari Raya Message", a similar practice of the Yang di-Pertuan Agong.[122] This call to imitate a tradition modelled after the sovereign ruler of the Federation indicated the stubborn attachment of the Yang di-Pertuan Negara to royal pretentions.

After Governor Goode transfigured into the interim Yang di-Pertuan Negara in June 1959, there was a further twist. The Singaporean branch of the Pan-Malayan Islamic Party (PMIP) submitted a letter to Queen Elizabeth II, appealing to Her Majesty to use "royal and monarchical tactics" and seek the recommendation of the Yang di-Pertuan Agong when appointing Singapore's Yang di-Pertuan Negara.[123] According to the petition, should Her Majesty confer with the Yang di-Pertuan Agong, it would foster goodwill between citizens of Singapore and the Federation. The Colonial Office, wanting to avoid any further complications, did not hesitate to put down the request because the arrangements of the new Constitution were already in place.[124] PMIP's strategy was probably also intended to veil the direct link between the Yang di-Pertuan Negara and the British Crown. By "borrowing" the sovereignty of the Yang di-Pertuan Agong, the appointment of the Yang di-Pertuan Negara would in some measure ordain Singapore's status as a constituent part of the already sovereign Federation and spotlight the island's perceived detachment from Britain.

Decolonizing the Governor

The embroidery of Malay(an) motifs into the design and blueprint of Yang di-Pertuan Negara became material in the embodied performance of the Yang di-Pertuan Negara. The British monarch was usually touted as the source of the "fountain of authority" in the empire; all acts of governance in British territorial possessions—charters and treaties, enactments and ordinances—were legitimized in the name of the monarch.[125] It is thus unsurprising that in the Commonwealth, there was a distaste for continued association with the Crown amongst ex-colonies. Singapore, like other British dependents throughout the empire, was endowed with a certain political culture to display British overlordship. Celebrations of imperial coronations and holidays, the singing of *God Save the Queen*, martial displays, the naming of places after royal persons and pioneers of empire—all these practices tied Singapore to the larger imperial hierarchy and persuaded its subjects of the empire's reach.[126] As Jan Morris aptly puts it, "spectacle was always an instrument of British imperialism".[127] These features were also forms of invented traditions entrenched by British rule throughout the empire. They inculcated a sense of stability and concreteness of the imperial system while tying dependents together under the hierarchical subjugation of the Crown.

The particularities of British Malaya conditioned Singapore's political culture as part of empire. During the inception of imperial intervention in the Malay Peninsula, the British began to rearrange the pre-colonial order of the *kerajaan* to suit the demands of colonial administration. They integrated the peninsular polities into a larger imperial system without dissolving social stratifications between the royal, aristocratic and subject classes. This strategy became a cost-effective approach to manufacture legitimacy for British rule throughout the empire, particularly when it came to societies with complicated social hierarchies of their own.[128] Historian Donna Amoroso has demonstrated that the continued reification of the sovereign status of the Malay rulers protected the privileges of the indigenous ruling and aristocratic classes.[129]

As the British consolidated their system of governance to ascend as paramount power in the peninsula, both the British and indigenous elites defended the principle that colonial officials only governed on behalf of the rulers. The latter was gradually remodelled into modern titular monarchs largely bereft of executive functions. In conjunction with this, the British appropriated Malay political idioms and ceremonial practices to exalt the rulers as the continued source of authority in the polity. A discourse of "traditionalism" espousing the preservation of the rulers and the social structure of Malay society consequently came to be the official rationale for continued British intervention as opposed to the rhetoric of revolution and progressive change. These practices sustained the impression of an unchanging *kerajaan* order, concealing the vast reordering of the Malay states as a result of the bureaucratization of administration, the formation of the colonial capitalist system and unprecedented immigration from elsewhere in Asia.[130]

Many of the invented traditions of British Malaya were retained even after the Federation of Malaya attained its independence. For instance, the British introduced the *durbar* or the ceremonial gathering of kings which borrowed from the imperial political culture of the British Raj. Known as the Majlis Raja-Raja (Conference of Rulers), it was originally a forum for the rulers from the FMS.[131] This royal assembly was later constitutionalized and extended to include the rest of the peninsular rulers following the establishment of the Federation. It continues to the present day as an official platform for the Malay rulers to deliberate on matters under their discretion. By reinvesting and institutionalizing the concept of sovereignty in the royal personages of the rulers, these practices preserved Malay political dominance over the modern state to the benefit of the UMNO-led government. The British-sponsored political culture of pomp and pageantry later served as the template for national traditions in both the Federation and Singapore.

Singapore had no less of the glittering trappings even though the Malay(an) elements were not as pronounced. With the indigenous ruler deposed as an intermediary, the island state was heavily steeped in the imperial rituals and symbolic practices which conveyed the sovereign rule of the British Crown. To accentuate Singapore's affinity with the Federation in the context of decolonization, Singaporean leaders adapted Malay(an) adornments to renovate existing rituals of the colonial order. These leaders, however, applied a discursive premise that was directly opposite to the traditionalism during the advent of British rule in the peninsular states: the discourse of change and transition was invoked rather than preservation and protection. Malay(an) elements were repurposed to engineer the appearance of a nationalist revolution even though the British remained paramount power in Singapore. Through the selective use of symbols from an imagined, serviceable past, Singaporean leaders hacked the rhythms and rituals of the colonial order which previously communicated the continuity of British imperial rule. This allowed the new nationalist rulers of Singapore to accumulate political legitimacy in the revolutionary age of decolonization.

As part of their efforts to accumulate political legitimacy, Singaporean leaders poured Malay(an) varnish over the White governor to decolonize the figure. His colonial personage was a particular problem for these leaders because the governorship represented the island's non-sovereign, subjugated position in the imperial hierarchy. Like in other colonies, the British governor in colonial Singapore presided over the public ceremonial, whether it was to legitimize practices, officiate buildings and institutions or reward the conduct of colonial subjects.[132] He was, over the span of a hundred years, Singapore's Crown representative. David Cannadine has argued that

> [g]overnors were not only powerful politically; as the direct, personal representative of the sovereign, they were at the apex of the colonial social hierarchy, they legitimised and completed it, and they linked it directly and personally to the monarch and the mother country.[133]

The Yang di-Pertuan Negara was in constitutional terms Singapore's link to the British monarch upon the demise of the office of governor. He was therefore the new "apex of the colonial social hierarchy" and was in the position to speak for the Queen like "how a priest (spoke) for God", as his predecessor once did.[134] As the Queen's surrogate in Singapore, the Yang di-Pertuan Negara bonded the island to the larger hierarchy of the British Empire.

Goode renewed the glue of this imperial bond when he transitioned from governor to become the inaugural Yang di-Pertuan Negara since many of his previous duties were largely maintained. For instance, he presented imperial honours to local residents on the occasion of the Queen's birthday in June 1959.[135] Goode later presided over the Queen's Birthday parade at the Padang, which was completed with the ceremonial glitziness of a 21-gun salute, a flypast by the Royal Air Force (RAF) and a formidable crowd of 20,000 individuals. The English press called the parade "the most impressive one held locally in years".[136] There was nevertheless an important specification: Goode was described as a "stately figure", seen wearing a lounge suit instead of carrying a pompous persona of a colonial governor. His ceremonial attire had shed the "cock-hat with white plumes"—a particular piece of peacockery which Lee evoked to describe colonial governors during the installation of Goode's successor in December 1959. Although Singapore had a new anti-colonial government in the guise of the PAP, the island's position under the new Constitution remained largely ambiguous amid the extant performance of imperial rituals.

Goode's six-month term as Yang di-Pertuan Negara was symbolically contentious as imperial rituals continued to be performed. During the opening of the first Assembly session under the new Constitution, the Yang di-Pertuan Negara's Address replaced the ritual of the Governor's Address which was in practice during the days of the Rendel Constitution. Similar to the Queen's speech in the United Kingdom, the titular head of the state would outline the policies of the government at the start of the legislative session. In terms of symbolic gesturing, the PAP government scored well in substantiating Singapore's re-birth as a self-governing State. While the address was recited by the same British man who had delivered the last Governor's Address a year before, the Yang di-Pertuan Negara made his speech in Malay, the national language and lingua franca of the region, to the pleasant surprise of the press and observers.[137] Such an act sought to demonstrate a perceived break from the status quo of the old Assembly, whereby the governor's speech was made in English. The ritual itself was analogous to the contents of the speech—in terms of form, the speech projected a nationalist victory, but its contents conveyed a renewed sense of stability. Previously wary of the PAP's perceived radicalism as a socialist party, traders and businessmen breathed easily after the government expressed support for existing economic practices, sparing their thick wallets from exorbitant taxes.[138]

Such an official occasion was also not complete without ceremonial display. During the Guard of Honour parade to welcome the Yang di-Pertuan Negara to the Assembly, the Armed Forces Band played the tune of *Pack up Your Troubles*, a British military song from the First World War, during Goode's inspection of the guard. *The Bridge of the River Kwai*—an orchestral counter for the *Colonel Bogey March* and popularized by the Academy Award-winning 1957 film *The Bridge of the*

River Kwai—was the initial choice but was replaced at the last minute by the Singaporean government as it was deemed "inappropriate".[139] The film portrays British prisoners-of-war in Thailand during Second World War. At the brink of death, the prisoners whistle the tune while marching to and from the internment camp as they undertake hard labour under the watchful eyes of Japanese soldiers.[140] Playing the popular tune as a British man kept to its tempo was a mockery. In order to avoid stoking sensitivities, the tune was changed to pay deference to the former colonial governor—a reminder of Singapore's continued status as part of empire.

The rituals of the colonial order still needed further reconditioning. In September 1959, after the Queen's Birthday parade described earlier, the PAP government decided that Singapore would stop celebrating the occasion altogether. To replace it, a National Day dated 3 June was officiated to commemorate the implementation of the new Constitution.[141] This move, similar to the other symbolic adjustments, purported Singapore's newfound emancipation, mimicking a similar practice in other ex-colonial countries to commemorate their independence as sovereign nation-states. As much as the British Crown granted constitutional validation for the Yang di-Pertuan Negara's authority, the imperial connection in these ceremonies was tapered to mitigate the reality of Britain's sovereignty over Singapore.

Upon the installation of Yusof as Yang di-Pertuan Negara in December 1959, the public performance of transition took on a more aggressive character. Many of the ceremonies previously graced by the ex-governor were henceforth graced by his Malayan-born successor. It was Yusof who presided over the grand performances during the first National Day celebrations in June 1960 to exhibit Singapore's "liberation" from the vestiges of the colonial order.[142] Taking a page out of the handbook for colonial governors, Yusof visited the people as a means to project the reach of the prevailing political order, just as the governors, proconsuls and monarchs once did to communicate the extent of imperial rule.[143] Furthermore, as part of the process of transition of the Malay rulers into modern titular monarchs, the British had encouraged similar tours to validate the lasting reign of rulers and the preservation of the *kerajaan*.[144] In self-governing Singapore, however, Yusof's visibility was used to simulate a sovereign status for the island state. Spectacles of the old empire were now renewed as nationalist spectacles with imperial spectres.

To simulate a sovereign status for the island state, Singaporean leaders used the Yang di-Pertuan Negara as a legitimizing symbol for their political projects. As more colonial states morphed into ex-colonial states, the "nation-states system", as concretized by the UN institution, gradually turned hegemonic, serving as the dominant mode of representation for communities to negotiate their existence in the new postwar global order.[145] Singapore, like many other colonized territories, had developed into a political entity with a representative mode of governance but remained trapped within a cross-territorial imperial hierarchy. The challenge for nationalist leaders was to recast the colonial system of representation in line with the emerging nation-states system. Looking to other sovereign nation-states, the PAP government had the same motivating force as the KMS and UMNO when they tried to re-establish the Sultanate of Singapore in the sense that they all wanted to choreograph a display of Singapore's very own "sovereign" head of state. Systems of representation under the colonial order, such as the institution of colonial governor, must be reworked in order to find synchrony with Singapore's aspirational status of being.

Singaporean leaders also had to weave narratives to represent this nationalist dream, and it is through national rituals that they could substantiate the reality of these claims. Anthropologists John Kelly and Martha Kaplan suggest that

> National rituals are the place where these narratives of social contract are made real. These narratives get made, ritually, when individuals or groups propose versions of relationships, group order, and history, past, present, and future, which they claim are not simply their own view or in their own interest, but instead are given, cosmologically, by gods, by tradition, or by principles of some sort.[146]

While the British constitutionally circumscribed Singapore's claim to sovereign equality, the political projects of Singaporean leaders were premised on the urgent need to manufacture the presence of a "new" socio-political order in the city-state, one which appeared to have trimmed the domination of Britain. As imperial dependents all over the world were rapidly gaining independence ahead of Singapore, the principle of self-determination became the prevailing political currency to stake Singapore's emerging position. It was also through a Federation of Malaya ticket that Singapore could be represented in the nation-states system. The message that gyrated during these rituals was overt: the colonial regime was on the way out, and in its place was an elected government that would bring Singapore closer towards inevitable fusion with the already independent Federation. This new "social contract" needed to be performed.

Performing Sovereignty

The Yang di-Pertuan Negara represented a crucial element in cementing the perceived realities of a breakdown of the colonial order. One captivating episode took place a month after Yusof's ascendency as Yang di-Pertuan Negara. In January 1960, he toured Singapore's Southern Islands to call on the islanders, many of whom were Malay fishermen. Some of them welcomed his visit by flying the Singapore flag on their rafts (*perahu*), while others assembled on the beaches. When Yusof descended onto the jetty, the village chiefs (*penghulu*) lined up to receive him. Children then sang *Majulah Singapura* to greet the Yang di-Pertuan Negara. The villagers displayed ostentatious buntings to arouse a festive mood, while a few of them played drums to foster a celebratory atmosphere. In his *Baju Melayu*, Yusof graced many acts of legitimization throughout the collection of small islands, including planting a tree in Pulau Seking and a stick in Pulau Bukhom Kechil to mark the site of a new mosque.[147] Speaking on a dais draped with State emblems, Yusof told the islanders, "all members of the Government are your representatives and I hope you will give them your full support in what they do".[148] Later, in another speech during the same leg of the tour, he declared, "I hope all of you here will co-operate with the new Government. Let's work together in whatever the Government wants us to do for the good of the country".[149]

Along with his calls for loyalty to the government, the Yang di-Pertuan Negara's visit came with bounties. Yusof announced that the islanders would get access to modern plumbing and electricity, vowing to take further steps to improve their lives.[150] Furthermore, he promised a \$20,000 water tank to villagers on Pulau Sudong to reduce the island's dependency on the mainland for its freshwater supply. Yusof also pledged further help to extend the perimeters of their fishing zones.[151] The audience greeted his speeches with chants of "*merdeka*". Even without extensive analytical scraping, hues of partisanship for the PAP government are already apparent. During his tours, ministers and Malay assemblymen from the PAP flanked the Yang di-Pertuan Negara.[152] The presence of the PAP politicians was significant considering that the Southern Islands was an opposition constituency. During the 1959 elections, the islanders gave the UMNO candidate, Ahmad Jabri, a landslide victory.[153]

There was a certain sense of magnificence to the entire affair, almost reminiscent of the flair when a royal potentate visits his or her subjects. The perimeters between the State and Yusof, the government and Yang di-Pertuan Negara, seemed increasingly difficult to differentiate. The islanders, some of them represented by their *penghulu*, even congregated in person to collectively pledge an oath of allegiance to Yusof.[154] In his presence, loyalty was declared to his person, similar to subjects pledging loyalty to a sovereign, or perhaps a more appropriate term, to a sultan. This practice demonstrated how the Yang di-Pertuan Negara had become, in Karen Cerulo's terms, a "modern totem"; through his physical being, the Yang di-Pertuan Negara manifested the State. Just like how nation-states sacralize their national symbols with the idea of their sovereignty, symbols of imperial rule were now replaced with Singapore's very own symbols—the State flag, *Majulah Singapura* and the Yang di-Pertuan Negara—to generate a sense of nationhood.

It was through events like the Southern Islands tour that the Yang di-Pertuan Negara performed and paraded sovereignty, obscuring Singapore's continued existence as a subordinate territory of Britain. The abstract structure of the State blended with the personage of the Yang di-Pertuan Negara, exalting him with a sense of authority, esteem and even a perceived ability to bequeath rewards onto the people, even if the largesse was dispensed on behalf of the elected government. As was the practice of colonial powers when they first sought to establish their authority over a subjugated polity, infrastructure projects acted as idioms to legitimize the governing power of the nationalist regime.[155] These practices in turn paralleled the practice of sovereign rulers who bestowed gifts and titles to win over their subjects' loyalty.[156] Through this symbolic occasion, the Yang di-Pertuan Negara captured the imagination of the islanders, building a sense of affinity between them and the State. The Yang di-Pertuan Negara was, at least through the public ceremonial, the perceived "fountain of authority" in the reincarnated Singapore State during the era of self-government. Ironically, he remained Singapore's constitutional link to the larger British imperial system.

Yusof also participated in the Malay(an) state rituals held in the Federation. This was *before* Singapore's entry into Malaysia and Yusof's involvement in the Majlis Raja-Raja. During ceremonial state occasions, Yusof represented the city-state in the grand spectacles alongside the other rulers. For instance, during the coronation of the new Yang di-Pertuan Agong in January 1961, Yusof sat with the royal figures on an elevated platform, in front of dignitaries, datuks and panglimas to witness the event. The entire ritual was majestic and marked with unmistakable grandeur. The presumptive Yang di-Pertuan Agong perched on top of his seven-tiered dais and was later crowned and blessed by the *mufti*, or the chief Islamic scholar. Other paraphernalia like the *keris* (daggers), *tombak* (spears), *berambu* (swords) as well as other regalia were conspicuously present to symbolically consecrate the position of the new king of the Federation in a clear testament to the notion of invented tradition.[157]

Yusof attended a similar elaborate ceremony for the funeral of the previous Yang di-Pertuan Agong who had died in office the year before.[158] Later, in January 1962, he took part in the opening ceremony of the new Dewan Bahasa building alongside the nine rulers.[159] His partaking in these rituals alongside other members of royalty added another layer of meaning to the office of Yang di-Pertuan Negara. They not only elevated him to a status similar to the other sovereigns but also transformed him into the connective ligament between Singapore and the socio-political hierarchy of the Federation.

The practice of adapting elements of Malay(an) political culture to symbolically subdue Singapore's continued status as a British dependent was extensive. Government House in Singapore was officially renamed "Istana Negara Singapura" or the "Palace of the State of Singapore" before Yusof took up his residence there, as if to further solidify the affiliation of the Yang di-Pertuan Negara with royalty. This move was at least significant at a symbolic level to destabilize Singapore's colonial status because Government Houses were built across the empire as physical testaments to British imperium over a territory.[160] Shedding the colonial baggage that came with the name was therefore consistent with the mood ushered in by the new Constitution, although it was still the same grandiose building.

This "fresh" rendition of the colonial era gubernatorial complex was also symbolically charged in a different way. It stood as Singapore's centre of state power in spite of the continued existence of the Istana Kampong Glam, which at this time was still home to the descendants of Hussein Shah. The re-branding exercise possibly communicated the Istana Negara Singapura's claim as the successor to the Malay(an) political heritage of the island or an invigorated version of the derelict Istana Kampong Glam to suit the needs of a modern, decolonizing Singapore. In addition to that, the "new" Istana also carried echoes of other "Istanas" in the peninsula, namely, the Istana Negara in Kuala Lumpur, the Yang di-Pertuan Agong's official residence, as well as the nine other palaces housing each of the respective rulers from the Federation. Now residing in his very own Istana, the Yang di-Pertuan Negara's image appeared ever more congruous with that of a reigning sovereign.

A cardinal-type persona further accompanied Yusof's elevation to the office of Yang di-Pertuan Negara. In June 1959, just days after taking office as the interim Yang di-Pertuan Negara, Goode received a memorandum from the Singaporean branch of UMNO, appealing for the release of eight rioters who were serving life sentences for their roles in the 1950 Maria Hertogh riots.[161] The party contended that since PAP detainees were released at the start of the new Constitution, there was no reason why these rioters should still be incarcerated. They were charged for inciting violence in response to a decision by the civil court to nullify the marriage of Maria Hertogh, a Dutch girl who wedded under Islamic rites.[162] They were therefore seen in some circles as victims of colonial injustices and as heroes who stood up against British authority to defend the sanctity of Muslim law.

UMNO's appeal for clemency for these rioters was rejected. This rejection, however, was conveyed via a letter from the advocate-general on behalf of Minister of Labour and Law K.M. Byrne, rather than from

Goode himself. UMNO interpreted this exercise as the PAP government's attempt at usurping the powers of the Yang di-Pertuan Negara. As the State's legal counsel, the advocate-general clarified that a minister replying on behalf of the Queen was the accepted convention in the United Kingdom. Byrne later stated that it was Goode who had personally asked for Cabinet advice.[163] Terribly displeased with the outcome, UMNO called for a Commission of Inquiry (COI) into the issue but was blocked by the PAP-dominated Assembly. A flustered Lee Kuan Yew even threatened Hamid Jumat, the former deputy chief minister and now an opposition UMNO assemblyman, by amending the terms of the proposed COI so as to also expose wrongdoings of ex-ministers from the last government.[164] While the issue came to a political halt because of the PAP dominance in the legislature, it was not satisfyingly resolved in moral terms—there was no catharsis for justice.

The situation changed with Yusof's appointment as the Yang di-Pertuan Negara. What was not possible was now possible. On the occasion of his swearing-in, Yusof gave a full pardon to Osman Ghani and four others implicated in the Maria Hertogh riots. The government statement on the matter was as follows:

> The Yang di-Pertuan Negara has expressed a desire to mark the occasion of his first installation as the first Malayan-born Yang di-Pertuan Negara of Singapore by exercising the prerogative of mercy on prisoners now serving sentences, who by their conduct and character in prison, have shown themselves worthy of such special regard. The Yang di-Pertuan Negara has, therefore, been graciously pleased, on the advice of his Ministers, to exercise the prerogative of mercy and to direct that the sentences of the following prisoners be remitted and that they be released with effect from Dec 4, 1959.[165]

Compared to six months earlier, it was with relative ease for the new Yang di-Pertuan Negara to express his "desire" to pardon the prisoners. The prerogative of mercy, as established earlier, was based on Cabinet decision, but the quoted statement above seems to aggrandize the role of the Yang di-Pertuan Negara in the decision-making process, attributing the decision mainly to him. Rather than being relayed through a letter from the advocate-general, this announcement also enjoyed more publicity.

While pardoning the prisoners could be a strategic move to remove political capital from UMNO, it conveyed the idea that Yusof was a benign figure who had authority reminiscent of the sovereign monarchs of old, that he had the power to grant freedom to the incarcerated, a feat that his predecessor had failed to perform. The royal prerogative of mercy was historically understood as privilege of kings as part of their divine rights of rule, but in modern times, it has been reformed as an "adjunct to democracy".[166] Even so, contexts shape the meanings of such a power. For instance, in the Anglo-European world, the royal prerogative of mercy has been historically marred with racist inflexions to keep the idea of moral supremacy attached to Whiteness afloat, thereby absolving White convicts from punitive measures.[167] From June to December 1959, what had changed tangibly, at least in the eyes of the public, was the appointee, not the powers of the office nor the deliberations of the Cabinet. This contributed to the manufacturing of a sovereign persona for Yusof, demonstrating that upon entry into the office of Yang di-Pertuan Negara, he had ushered a new era of benevolence and the defeat of colonial repression.

These ambivalent moments show that Yang di-Pertuan Negara operated in the semantic interstices of being both an imperial and Malay(an) symbol. The office generated a familiar dialectic at the core of British imperialism: the need to maintain an imperial world system while also satisfying demands of local self-determination. By granting the demand for a "Malayan governor-general", the British demonstrated the resilience of the imperial impulse. Their resolve to remain the colonial rulers of the island endured in spite of their blunder during the Suez Crisis and the ushering of a new global order in which justifications for colonialism had become increasingly difficult to sustain.

The British were proactive in trying to seize the decolonizing initiative. Whitehall officials fashioned the viceregal office on their terms, imposing safeguards to ensure that the future Crown representative could not frustrate British strategic interests. They simply could not allow the peddling of the idea that they were withdrawing from the city-state. Singaporean leaders, in the meantime, accepted dependency relations with Britain while taking liberties with the concession of a Malayan-born

Crown representative. Indeed, their political projects thrived on this ambiguity. The remodelling of the office of Crown representative, which took the form of governor in its previous incarnation, was one way in which the colonial system of political representation was appropriated to pass Singapore off as a sovereign polity with its own head of state, disguising the island's continued status as a colony. Since "governor-general" proved too sticky for the British, the office was recast in the form of a Malay(an) figurehead. Its new amorphous form allowed for the downplaying of imperial sovereignty over Singapore without radically altering the colonial status quo. The Yang di-Pertuan Negara was therefore, at least at its conception, an ingenious construction which entailed a win for all.

The political careers of Singaporean leaders counted on them being effective anti-colonial nationalists who could deliver self-determination for the island state. In fashioning the office of Crown representative to make colonial rule more palatable, they chose the invented title of "Yang di-Pertuan Negara", subsequently stirring a maelstrom of competing meanings with regard to the purpose and powers of the office. The title produced symbolic significance tied to the political culture of the Malay world. It bore a resemblance to the royal titles used in the Federation which were perceived to be enduring legacies from an ancient past. The Tunku's reluctance towards merger did not preclude Singaporean leaders from channelling these royal connotations to signal a sense of rupture from the colonial order and to tie Singapore much closer to the political culture of the Federation. Confusion about the office became entangled with the abortive project to restore the Sultanate of Singapore, bringing the Yang di-Pertuan Negara much closer to the captivating idea of establishing the island's very own sovereign.

After coming into power, the PAP government showed its innovative capacity by revamping imperial rituals for nationalist purposes. Symbolic practices of the colonial order were not erased but renewed under new terms following Yusof's appointment in December 1959. Through the efforts of Singaporean leaders across all political parties and Yusof's participation in "novel" national rituals, the Yang di-Pertuan Negara became sanctified as a quasi-sovereign ruler. The next chapter continues this story by following further creative efforts to dramatize a sense of transition in Singapore. In projecting sovereignty in the age of decolonization, the Yang di-Pertuan Negara became a malleable symbol to signify the breakdown of social hierarchies in the lived realities of the Singaporean people.

Notes

1. Speeches by Yusof Ishak and Lee Kuan Yew, CO 1030/480, 41–44.
2. The royal instructions for Yusof are contained in CO 1030/891. The pledge of allegiance is enshrined in the First Schedule of the Constitution: Government of Singapore, *Singapore (Constitution) 1958*, p. 55.
3. Low, "Kept in Position", p. 56.
4. Darwin, *The Empire Project*, pp. 1–12.
5. Ibid. See also Hack, "Unfinished Decolonisation and Globalisation" and W. David McIntyre, *The Commonwealth of Nations: Origins and Impact, 1869–1971* (Minneapolis: University of Minnesota Press, 1977), pp. 7–16.
6. Richard Drayton, "Commonwealth History from Below?: Caribbean National, Federal and Pan-African Renegotiations of the Empire Project, c. 1880–1950", in *Commonwealth History in the Twenty-first Century*, edited by Saul Dubow and Richard Drayton (Cham: Palgrave Macmillan, 2020), pp. 41–60 and John Darwin, "A Third British Empire? The Dominion Idea in Imperial Politics", in *The Oxford History of the British Empire: Volume IV: The Twentieth Century*, edited by Judith Brown and Wm. Roger Louis (Oxford: Oxford University Press, 1999), pp. 77–83.
7. Darwin, "A Third British Empire?", pp. 69–70.
8. McIntyre, *The Commonwealth of Nations*, pp. 4–7.
9. Darwin, "A Third British Empire", pp. 69–70.
10. H. Kumarasingham, "The 'Tropical Dominions': The Appeal of Dominion Status in the Decolonisation of India, Pakistan and Ceylon", *Transactions of the Royal Historical Society* 23 (2013): 223–45.
11. McIntyre, *Colonies to Commonwealth*, pp. 9–11 and McIntyre, *The Commonwealth of Nations*, pp. 442–56.
12. See Adom Getachew's deliberations on the principle of sovereign equality in Getachew, *Worldmaking after Empire*, pp. 15–30.
13. Srinivasan, "Nobody's Commonwealth?", pp. 257–69.
14. Low, "Kept in Position", p. 56.
15. Colonial Office, *Singapore Conference 1956*, pp. 10–19 and Low, "Kept in Position", p. 56. Also see Murphy, *Monarchy*, pp. 16–30.
16. Darwin, "A Third British Empire?", pp. 85–86.
17. Murphy, *Monarchy*, pp. 42–43.
18. Ibid., pp. 43–48.

19. Srinivasan, "Nobody's Commonwealth?", pp. 257–69.
20. Calhoun, *Nationalism*, pp. 118–19.
21. Colonial Office, *Singapore Conference 1956*, pp. 12–13.
22. W.D. McIntyre, "The Strange Death of Dominion Status", *The Journal of Imperial and Commonwealth History* 27, no. 2 (1999): 202–6.
23. Colonial Office, *Singapore Conference 1956*, p. 50.
24. Barnaby Crowcroft, "The Problem of Protectorates in the Age of Decolonisation: Britain and West Africa, 1955–60", in *Protection and Empire: A Global History*, edited by Lauren Brenton, Adam Clulow and Bain Attwood (Cambridge: Cambridge University Press, 2017), pp. 247–50.
25. Colonial Office, *Singapore Conference 1956*, pp. 14, 20. The British still refused the transfer in 1957, see Colonial Office, *Singapore Conference 1957*, pp. 16–17.
26. Minute by A. Lennox-Boyd, 25 July 1957, DO 35/9872, 567.
27. Colonial Office, *Singapore Conference 1956*, pp. 11–12.
28. Ibid., p. 13.
29. Ibid., p. 12. The National Service Ordinance was implemented since 1954 but was met with resistance, see Tim Huxley, *Defending the Lion City: The Armed Forces of Singapore* (St Leonards: Tim Huxley, 2000), p. 5.
30. Murphy, *Monarchy*, pp. 56–58.
31. Colonial Office, *Singapore Conference 1956*, p. 23.
32. Ibid., p. 22.
33. The communist movement in Singapore was active within Chinese-based organizations, most prominently the Chinese students' movement. Besides the works cited earlier in the introduction, also see Justus van der Kroef, *Communism in Malaysia and Singapore: A Contemporary Survey* (The Hague: Martinus Nijhoff, 1967), pp. 33–88. Suspicions of Chinese links to communism were harboured since 1922, see Turnbull, *A History of Modern Singapore*, pp. 226–33.
34. The Emergency only ended in 1960, but the communist threat, or at least perception of the threat, still lingered, see Cheah Boon Kheng, *Malaysia: The Making of a Nation* (Singapore: Institute of Southeast Asian Studies, 2002), pp. 80–81.
35. Lau, "Decolonization", p. 56.
36. Savingram from D. MacGillivray to Secretary of State for the Colonies (30 March 1956), CO 1030/122, 24.
37. Colonial Office, *Singapore Conference 1956*, p. 22.
38. Note for discussions prepared by the Colonial Office, July 1956, CO 1030/83, 297A.
39. Ibid.
40. Minute by Secretary of State recorded by J.B. Johnston, 24 July 1957, CO 1030/83, 301.
41. Telegram from Secretary of State for the Colonies to R. Black, 28 July 1956, CO 1030/83, 307.

42. Telegram from R. Black to J.B. Johnston, 4 August 1956, CO 1030/83, 314.
43. After Lim's suppression of the Chinese students' movement, the colonial government was convinced that Lim would be the ideal man to support, bolstering the image of an effective Singapore government to face the threat of communist agitation in the city-state, see Lau, "Decolonization", pp. 54–60.
44. Memorandum from Lennox-Boyd to the Cabinet, 30 November 1956, CO 1030/122.
45. Minute by R.H. Scott, 7 September 1956, FO 1091/44, 137.
46. Secret Report, Far Eastern Department, Colonial Office, 24 August 1956, FO 1091/44, 161.
47. Cablegram from New Zealand Government to F.H. Corner (New Zealand High Commissioner), 14 December 1956, DO 35/9873, 629; Cablegram from Australian Government to Australian High Commissioner, 14 December 1959, DO 35/9873, 628.
48. *SS*, 2 Apr 1957, p. 6.
49. Memorandum from E.N. Larmour to W.I.J. Wallace (7 Mar 1958), CO 1030/472, 124–26.
50. Letter from E. Melville to I.M.R. McLennan, 29 November 1956, DO 35/9873.
51. Draft Royal Instructions, CO 1030/469, 18–21.
52. Letter from E.M. West to J.D. Hennings, 12 February 1959, CO 1030/877 and note by the Colonial Office Establishment and Organisation Department, 26 June 1959, CO 1030/877, 13.
53. Telegram from W. Goode to Colonial Office, 19 November 1959, DO 35/9888, 22 and telegram from Colonial Office to Goode, 27 November 1959, DO 35/9888, 32.
54. *SLAD*, Vol. 3, Sitting No. 7, Col. 1695 (26 April 1957).
55. Colonial Office, *Singapore Conference 1957*, pp. 6–7. The Yang di-Pertuan Negara could only be dismissed by Her Majesty, see Government of Singapore, *Singapore (Constitution 1958)*, p. 10. See furher deliberations on this clause in CO 1030/478.
56. Explanatory memorandum by Hennings, 25 May 1959, CO 1030/478, 22.
57. *SLAD*, Vol. 3, Sitting No. 7, Col. 1695 (26 April 1957). Lim, however, had earlier indicated before the 1957 talks that he was fine with British selection of a nominee for the Head of State, see Lau, "Decolonization", p. 49.
58. Comments on the Draft Order-in-Council from E.N. Larmour to W.I.J. Wallace, 7 March 1958, CO 1030/472, 126.
59. Murphy, *Monarchy*, pp. 19–20.
60. Chatterjee, *The Nation*, p. 14.
61. Hack, *Defence and Decolonisation*, pp. 234–50.
62. A.J. Stockwell, "The White Man's Burden and Brown Humanity: Colonialism and Ethnicity in British Malaya", *Southeast Asian Journal of Social Science* 10, no. 1 (1982): 44–68. *The White Man's Burden* is a poem writtten by

Rudyard Kipling to encourage the imperial domination of the West over non-White societies under the pretext of a civilizing mission.

63. Murphy, *Monarchy*, pp. 54–60.

64. CO, *Singapore Conference 1957*, p. 9. On the Federation's position towards the ISC, see correspondences in CO 1030/476.

65. Lim, *Reflections*, pp. 87–89.

66. See Lau, "Decolonization", pp. 47–60 for a more detailed study of attempts by both the British and Lim Yew Hock at reaching a settlement for the constitutional talks.

67. Lim, *Reflections*, p. 89.

68. Colonial Office, *Singapore Conference 1956*, pp. 20–21.

69. Report from Goode to W.I.J. Wallace (14 March 1958), CO 1030/469, 216–18. A comparison of the draft Constitution with the final Constitution would indicate barely any reduction to the mentions of "Crown" or "Her Majesty", but most conspicuously, the oaths for ministers had the clause "truly serve Her Majesty Queen Elizabeth II, her heirs and successors" removed. See CO 1030/468, pp. 82–175 for the draft Constitution.

70. Minute by Lennox-Boyd, 25 July 1956, DO 35/9872.

71. *ST*, 21 February 1959, p. 1.

72. Ibid.

73. *SS*, 6 June 1959, p. 1.

74. Colonial Office, *Singapore Conference 1957*, p. 6.

75. Trocki, *Prince of Pirates*, p. 226. Examples are peppered in pre-colonial texts and are too numerous to be cited here. Nevertheless, it seems that the title was used only by Malay rulers after the establishment of Melaka. The Sultan of Melaka, for instance, was refered to as "Yang di-Pertuan Melaka". For some examples, see A. Samad Ahmad, *Sulalatus Salatin* (Kuala Lumpur: Dewan Bahasa dan Pustaka, 1984), pp. 85, 91, 106, 305; Ahmad Kassim, ed., *Hikayat Hang Tuah* (Kuala Lumpur: Dewan Bahasa dan Pustaka, 1965), pp. 17, 43, 91, 397.

76. Kwa Chong Guan, "Why did Tengku Hussein Sign the 1819 Treaty with Stamford Raffles", in *Malays/Muslims in Singapore*, p. 9 and Virginia Matheson, "Strategies of Survival: the Malay Royal Line of Lingga-Riau", *Journal of Southeast Asian Studies* 17, no. 1 (1986): 5–6. On Raja Kecil's attempt to claim the Johor throne, see Timothy Barnard, *Multiple Centres of Authority: Society, Environment and the Malay State in Siak, 1674–1827* (Leiden: KITLV, 2003).

77. Kwa, "Why did Tengku Hussein Sign", pp. 16, 18.

78. Eric Hobsbawm, "Introduction: Inventing Traditions", in *The Invention of Tradition*, edited by Eric Hobsbawm and Terence Ranger (Cambridge: Cambridge University Press, 1983), p. 1.

79. Ibid., p. 6.

80. Ibid., p. 9.

81. Ibid., pp. 13–14.
82. As quoted in Chew, *President Yusof*, pp. 99–101.
83. The Yang di-Pertuan Agong was in turn modelled after the Yang di-Pertuan Besar of Negri Sembilan, and it was initially named as such, see United Nations Food and Agriculture Organisation, *Report of Malaya Constitutional Commision* (Kuala Lumpur: Government Press, 1957), p. 22.
84. *SFP*, 30 March 1957, p. 1.
85. Graham Saunders, *A History of Brunei* (London: RoutledgeCurzon, 2002), pp. 72, 205. After Brunei's independence from Britain in 1984, the sultan was stylized as "Yang di-Pertuan Negara Brunei Darussalam", see p. xv.
86. *SS*, 25 April 1957, p. 6.
87. *SS*, 18 May 1958, p. 2.
88. Telegram from J.B. Johnston to R. Black, 3 August 1956, DO 35/9872.
89. Hugh Hickling, "Malaysia", in *Sovereigns and Surrogates*, p. 224. For functions of the governors of Penang and Melaka, see Government of Malaya, *Constitutional Proposals*, pp. 123–62. While the 1957 Malayan Constitution is written in English, "governor" was retained in its Malay translation, see Kerajaan Malaya, *Chadangan-Chadangan Perlembagaan Persekutuan Tanah Melayu* (Kuala Lumpur: Jabatan Chetak Kerajaan, 1957), pp. 26–27. "*Gabnor*" was nevertheless accepted as the Malay translation in the normenclature, see *BH*, 3 July 1957, p. 3.
90. On self-governance in Malta and Ghana, respectively see J.D. Krivine, "Malta and Self-Government", *World Affairs* 111, no. 2 (1948): 112–13 and W.E.F. Ward, *A History of Ghana*, 4th ed. (London: George Allen and Unwin, 1967), pp. 322–50.
91. Note from R.C. Ormerod to E.L. Sykes, 5 April 1956, DO 35/9888.
92. Hickling, "Malaysia", p. 224.
93. Chew, *Biography of President Yusof*, pp. 99–101.
94. Letter from R.C. Ormerod to R.W. Newsam, 6 April 1956, DO 35/9888, 1.
95. Note by L.B. Walsh Atkins, 31 August 1956, DO 35/9888, 3.
96. I.M.R. McLennan to E. Melville, 29 November 1956, DO 35/9873.
97. Note from L.B. Walsh Atkins to J. Chadwick and MacLennan, 28 November 1956, DO 35/9873.
98. Gavin McLean, "From Cocked Hats to Designer Frocks—The 'Queen in Drag' in Twentieth-Century New Zealand", in *Exploring the British World: Identity, Cultural Production, Institutions*, edited by Kate Darian-Smith (Melbourne: RMIT Publishing, 2004), p. 979.
99. Clifford Geertz, *Negara: The Theatre State in Nineteenth-Century Bali* (New Jersey: Princeton University Press, 1980), p. 4.
100. See Richard Winstedt, *Dictionary of Colloquial Malay* (Singapore: Marican & Sons, 1957), pp. 44, 161 and Vernon Hendershot and W.G. Shellabear, *A Dictionary of Standard Malay* (Mountain View: Pacific Press Publishing Association, 1945), pp. 131–32. In both these dictionaries, the term "*negara*"

is left out in favour of "*negeri*". "*Negeri*" was used to refer to "settlement" in pre-colonial times but was a term with little emotive value, see Anthony Milner, *The Malays* (West Sussex: Wiley-Blackwell, 2008), p. 59. On the "*negeri*", see Milner, *Invention of Politics*, pp. 104–7. Also, the Constitutions of Johor and Trengganu established respectively in 1895 and 1911 refer to the state as "*negeri*", see Iza Hussin, "Textual trajectories: Re-reading the Constitution and Majalah in 1890s Johor", *Indonesia and the Malay World* 41, no. 120 (2014): 255–72 and Mubin Sheppard, *Papers Relating to Trengganu* (Kuala Lumpur: MBRAS, 1983), p. 54.

101. The Straits Times, *Buku Merdeka: Tanah Melayu Menjadi Negara* (Singapore: The Straits Times Press, 1957).

102. Indonesia has referred to itself as a "*negara*" since independence, see Majelis Pemusyawaratan Rakyat Republik Indonesia, *Undang-undang Dasar Negara Republik Indonesia Tahun 1945* (Jakarta: Sekretariat Jenderal MPR RI, 2011), pp. 17–58.

103. The Tunku publicly signalled his openness to Singapore's entry into the Federation during a Foreign Correspondents Association of Southeast Asia meeting in May 1961, where he outlined the idea of "Greater Malaysia", see Sopiee, *Malayan Union*, p. 129.

104. *SB*, 23 July 1958, p. 6.

105. A similar point is made in Stanley Bedlington, "The Singapore Malay Community: The Politics of State Integration" (PhD thesis, Cornell University, 1974), pp. 66–71.

106. Lee, *Singapore*, pp. 191–212. Also see Lee Kuan Yew's radio talks in Lee Kuan Yew, *The Battle for Merger* (Singapore: Straits Times Press, 2014), pp. 4–84 and arguments made in Thum Ping Tjin, "The Fundamental Issue is Anti-colonialism, Not Merger", *Asia Research Institute Working Paper Series*, no. 211 (2013).

107. *ST*, 19 September 1958, p. 8; *ST*, 17 October 1958, p. 9.

108. *ST*, 19 September 1958, p. 8.

109. *BH*, 7 October 1958, p. 2; *BH*, 18 October 1958, p. 7; *BH*, 28 October 1958, p. 2.

110. Sahid Sahooman, *Oral History Interviews*, Reel 1.

111. *BH*, 11 October 1958, p. 7 and *BH*, 18 October 1958, p. 7.

112. Letter from W. Goode to Colonial Office, 27 October 1958, CO 1030/476, 76.

113. Ibid.

114. *BH*, 28 October 1958, p. 1.

115. *ST*, 28 October 1958, p. 5.

116. Ibid.

117. Sahid Sahooman, *Oral History Interviews*, Reel 1.

118. Letter from Tengku Muda Mohamed to Queen Elizabeth II, 10 February 1958, FCO 141/15022, 3A.

119. Telegram from W. Goode to Colonial Office, 14 March 1959, FCO 141/ 15022, 3.
120. *BH*, 5 March 1959, p. 2.
121. *SS*, 12 May 1959, p. 5.
122. *BH*, 18 April 1959, p. 4.
123. Letter from Singapore Pan-Malaya Islamic Party to Buckingham Palace, 21 October 1959, CO 1030/633, 109.
124. Letter from the Colonial Office to the Yang di-Pertuan Negara, 18 November 1959, CO 1030/633, 98.
125. Cannadine, *Ornamentalism*, pp. 101–20.
126. See the thematic chapters in Jan Morris, *The Spectacle of Empire* (London: Faber and Faber, 1982).
127. Ibid., p. 11.
128. Cannadine, *Ornamentalism*, pp. 58–59.
129. See Amoroso, *Traditionalism*.
130. Ibid., pp. 4–12.
131. Ibid., pp. 78–83.
132. There has been no academic endeavour that has compiled and critically analysed such ceremonies in the Singaporean context. But for examples, see the unveiling of the Raffles' statue on Centenary Day in *The Singapore Free Press and Mercantile Advertiser*, 28 January 1919, p. 10; officiation of memorials and plaques in *ST*, 10 December 1948, p. 7 and *ST*, 26 September 1921, p. 10; launch of infrastructural projects in *ST*, 20 March 1912, p. 7 and *ST*, 25 August 1913, p. 8.
133. Cannadine, *Ornamentalism*, p. 32.
134. Ibid., p. 105.
135. *BH*, 13 June 1959, p. 1.
136. *SS*, 14 June 1959, p. 1.
137. See reactions to the Yang di-Pertuan Negara's speech: *SFP*, 2 July 1959, p. 1; *SS*, 2 July 1959, pp. 1, 4; *SS*, 3 July 1959, p. 9 and *ST*, 3 July 1959, p. 1.
138. Ibid. For Goode's full speech, see Ministry of Culture, *Towards a More Just Society* (Singapore: Government Printing Press, 1959).
139. *ST*, 1 July 1959, p. 1.
140. Julie Summers, *The Colonel of Tamarkan: Philip Toosey and the Bridge on the River Kwai* (New York: Simon and Schuster, 2016), pp. 8–9.
141. *ST*, 30 September 1959, p. 9.
142. While the parade on the morning of 3 June 1959 was cancelled because of wet weather, events planned for the day were still graced by the Yang di-Pertuan Negara: *ST*, 3 June 1960, p. 1.
143. Cannadine, *Ornamentalism*, pp. 101–20.
144. Amoroso, *Traditionalism*, pp. 73–96. Also see the same transformations of the British monarchy in Cannadine, "The Context, Performance and Meaning of Ritual", pp. 108–64.

145. Kelly and Kaplan, *Represented Communities*, pp. 9–13.
146. Ibid., pp. 140–41.
147. *ST*, 18 January 1960, p. 7.
148. Ibid.
149. Ibid.
150. Ibid.
151. *ST*, 1 February 1960, p. 4.
152. Ibid.; *ST*, 18 January 1960, p. 7; *SFP*, 15 February 1960, p. 12.
153. *ST*, 31 May 1959, p. 4.
154. *BH*, 15 February 1960, p. 1.
155. On the ambivalent project of developmental technologies and infrastructure in the colonial period, see Daniel Headrick, *The Tools of Empire: Technology and European Imperialism in the Nineteenth Century* (Oxford and New York: Oxford University Press, 1981); Mrázek, *Engineers of Happy Land*; John Broich, "Engineering the Empire: British Water Supply Systems and Colonial Societies, 1850–1900", *Journal of British Studies* 46, no. 2 (2007): 346–65. For a historiographical review of technology, infrastructure and empire, see David Arnold, "Europe, Technology and Colonialism in the 20th Century", *History and Technology* 21, no. 1 (2005): 85–106 and Jonan van der Straeten and Ute Hasenöhrl, "Connecting the Empire: New Research Perspectives on Infrastructures and the Environment in the (Post)colonial World", *NTM Journal of the History of Science, Technology and Medicine* 24, no. 35 (2016): 355–91.
156. Milner, *Kerajaan*, pp. 66–75.
157. *ST*, 4 January 1961, pp. 10–13 and *BH*, 4 January 1961, p. 7.
158. *ST*, 4 September 1960, p. 1.
159. *BH*, 31 January 1962, p. 5 and *BH*, 1 February 1962, p. 1.
160. Jan Morris, *The Spectacle of Empire*, pp. 92–95.
161. *BH*, 9 June 1959, p. 1.
162. In 1951, the Tunku managed to galvanize support to pressure for the lightening of their death sentences, see Syed Muhd Khairudin Aljunied, *Colonialism, Violence and Muslims in Southeast Asia* (London and New York: Routledge, 2009), pp. 41–42; for the cirucmstances behind the riots, see pp. 15–24.
163. *SLAD*, Vol. 11, Sitting No. 8, Col. 482–520 (14 August 1959).
164. Ibid.
165. *ST*, 4 December 1959, p. 1.
166. Carolyn Strange, "Introduction", in *Qualities of Mercy: Justice, Punishment, and Discretion*, edited by Carolyn Strange (Vancouver: UBC Press, 1996), pp. 3–20.
167. Ibid.

4

COMMONER, OR PRIVILEGED ELITE?

High Births and Hierarchies

The PAP government touted the Yang di-Pertuan Negara as an egalitarian symbol in spite of the pseudo-royal persona which had become inextricable in the performance of his duties. Returning to Yusof's swearing-in ceremony on 3 December 1959, Prime Minister Lee conveyed to the people of Singapore:

> From tribal chiefs to Kings and Emperors through the ages down to present day dictators and presidents it was the individual leader that personified the State. But our Yang di-Pertuan Negara is no such potentate … It is not his high birth which has commended him for this high office, for he is a commoner.[1]

This rhetoric sought to bankrupt the idea of given privileges of birth, consecrating the office's significance as an egalitarian symbol in a new self-governing Singapore. Later during the ceremony, thousands of businessmen, unionists and students marched in unison to give salute to the titular embodiment of the state in a grand display of a socialist utopia.[2]

Lee also alluded to the Yang di-Pertuan Negara's function as an emblem for the "commoner". Pitched in rather condescending terms, the prime minister asserted that the people were unable to fully comprehend abstract concepts like "the State" or "collective leadership"; a more physical symbol like the Yang di-Pertuan Negara was therefore more suited for their simple minds.[3] The highest office in this new Singapore was therefore meant to connect intimately with ordinary people. The PAP leaders who were at the ceremony also donned their signature white shirts and slacks to keep to a socialist aesthetic, supposedly making them appear a little more down-to-earth. This was in sharp contrast to the haughty dress of opposition lawmakers and other dignitaries who were in their ties and business suits.[4] In these symbolic displays of style, the Yang di-Pertuan Negara carried the PAP government's vision of a Singapore free from the stratifying practices of class distinctions.

The colonial order under British rule had entrenched the existence of hierarchies and class distinctions. Historian David Cannadine has argued that in their encounter with societies outside of Britain and Europe, British imperialists viewed other races and cultures not solely through the lens of difference but also through similarities.[5] More specifically, they recognized that other forms of human communities also consisted of different social classes, not unlike British society back home. In imagining and managing their overseas territories, British imperialists therefore emulated stratifying practices of social distinctions in Britain through the imperial honours system, the promotion of visual displays of ceremony and the recognition of ranks held by indigenous elites. The British therefore reinforced local hierarchies and integrated them into a larger imperial one in which the British Crown reigned at its apex. From this perspective, British society was still seen as the best of human civilization, not only through the ideology of Anglo-Saxon racial supremacy, but also through the lens of class.

In British Malaya, descendants of the Malay aristocracy and royalty were often favoured in terms of education and employment opportunities in the colonial bureaucracy. Titles and exalted positions tied to the indigenous hierarchy carried prestige and access to exclusive social privileges. Singapore was part of this socio-political ecosystem. The previous chapter has discussed how the colonial governor was responsible for bestowing honours and ranks to locals who displayed loyal service to the empire. Colonial officials also glorified themselves with pageantry to become White "aristocrats", lifting them up to the highest strata of the social hierarchy. If the social order under empire continued to segment society according to class, Cannadine has suggested that decolonization, as the mirror image of British imperialism, entailed a social revolution, or a flattening of class distinctions.[6] This sense of change, however, needed representation. Upon winning the 1959 elections, the PAP declared in immodest terms that their success in the polls signalled a "new era", a compelling shift from the status quo.[7] The message was simple: the rise of the PAP's nationalist regime meant that it was no longer business as usual for the colonial order in Singapore.

After coming into power, the PAP government had promoted the party's socialist vision through its policies. At the very core of this vision was the aspiration to live up to the party's claim as an advocate for the working class, standing for the eradication of all forms of inequalities in society.[8] The party was therefore in direct opposition to the embedded colonial order of hierarchy and class distinctions. Yusof's perceived distance from aristocracy or "high birth" became a meritorious basis for his eligibility as Yang di-Pertuan Negara. He personified a Singapore where barriers of class did not seem to matter.

The egalitarian signification of the office was especially important for the PAP government to uphold. Even before its rise to power, the party had consistently maintained its firm belief in the equality between men:

> All men are equal, and no privilege should accompany the accident of birth, race, rank, religion or sex. Rewards and one's place in society should and must correspond to work and ability, a combination of which two factors determines a person's contribution to society.[9]

This professed faithfulness to the principle of equality seemed to be in harmony with the government's choice to nominate Yusof as Yang di-Pertuan Negara. Elected based on its popular socialist platform, the party therefore derived its political legitimacy from an ethos of social justice, fairness and freedom from class discrimination. These claims of bringing about greater equality, however, need further probing. The narrative which follows responds to these driving questions: how did the Yang di-Pertuan Negara evoke the idea of an equal society? And conversely, how did the office continue to reinforce the class distinctions of colonial society? Attempts to construct the egalitarian symbolism of the Yang di-Pertuan Negara, like any other exercise of meaning-making, came with contradictions, ironies and interruptions.

Before the PAP made grand claims of new beginnings, the stratifying nature of class politics was in fact a motivating force behind the creation of the office of Yang di-Pertuan Negara. In 1956, during preliminary talks on a constitutional settlement for Singapore, Chief Minister Lim Yew Hock stood his ground when officials from the colonial office rebutted his insistence for a Malayan governor-general. To him, a non-British, Asian Crown representative would be a symbol of national liberation which would "satisfy the masses".[10] Lim seemed to be under the impression that the ornamental figure of a Malayan governor-general would in some way bolster his image as a nationalist leader in the eyes of the electorate. Governor Black sympathized with Lim's strategy. According to the governor, "it is on the inarticulate and politically unaware sections of the population—the majority in fact—that the appointment of a Malayan governor-general would have the most effect".[11] Black also forecasted the persistent ignorance of normal workaday persons on constitutional affairs as a reason for them to be "deeply impressed by the appointment of a Malayan governor-general and regard it as a clear indication of the decline of British power here".[12]

These sentiments reveal that at the onset, both Lim and British officials conceptualized the future Yang di-Pertuan Negara based on the credulity of the "masses", who could be fooled into thinking that Britain was giving up its status as paramount power in Singapore. The Yang di-Pertuan Negara was therefore imagined as an instrumental accessory built on class prejudices of those in power. They viewed ordinary people as a senseless, unwitting bloc of impressionable minds who lacked the ability to engage with the "high" realm of constitutional politics.

A Royal Proposal

The colonial order ingrained class prejudices of this kind, but these sentiments also manifested in other ways. The previous chapter has explored public attempts by the Singaporean branch of UMNO and the KMS to turn the island into a sultanate and to get a scion from a royal family to fill the post of Yang di-Pertuan Negara. The implied premise of these proposals was that there was merit to the idea of given privileges at birth, that the descendants of patricians whose genealogy could be traced to a precolonial royal family had a sovereign right to lord over others. Besides the series of ill-fated schemes pushed by the KMS and UMNO, there was a similar plan taking place behind the scenes when the PAP government took office following the 1959 elections. According to ex-PAP minister Rahim Ishak, the Tunku had pushed for his elder half-brother, Tunku Ya'acob, to become Singapore's first Malayan-born Yang di-Pertuan Negara. Rahim even claimed that the Tunku made a personal appeal to the Queen to nominate Tunku Ya'acob, who like the Federation prime minister was also a prince from Kedah.[13]

Declassified correspondence within Whitehall confirms the existence of a plan to promote Tunku Ya'acob's candidacy. On 5 October 1959, J.D. Smith, a senior official in the Commonwealth Relations Office, notified the Colonial Office of ongoing attempts to nominate Tunku Ya'acob as Singapore's Yang di-Pertuan Negara. Smith had learnt from a team of Malayan journalists visiting London that support was actively being canvassed in the Federation for this purpose.[14] Tunku Ya'acob was then the high commissioner of the Federation to the United Kingdom, having served previously as an exemplary civil servant in British Malaya. Under the "member system", which was first introduced in 1951 as a limited measure for self-government in the Federation, the British appointed him as the member in charge of agriculture and forestry, a position equivalent to a minister. Tunku Ya'acob was also temporarily made regent of Kedah later in the same year when his elder brother, who was the reigning sultan, went on a leave of absence.

As sterling as he was in the colonial system, Tunku Ya'acob was not directly involved in the Federation's party politics. He did however take up the role as UMNO's advisor on agricultural affairs and was even tipped to be Onn Jaafar's replacement as party chief ahead of his younger brother. In spite of his popularity, Tunku Ya'acob did not mount a leadership bid, allowing Tunku Abdul Rahman to rise as UMNO leader and later on as the prime minister of the Federation. Dedicating his career to agrarian development and public service, Tunku Ya'acob decided to stay clear from elections and party politics. He nevertheless remained a revered figure, particularly amongst the rural communities in the Federation.[15] On the eve of the Federation's independence in August 1957, the Alliance government appointed him as Chairman of the Federation's Public Service Commission before posting him to London as Malayan high commissioner in 1958.[16]

Considering Tunku's Ya'acob's stellar curriculum vitae, his appointment as Yang di-Pertuan Negara of Singapore would engender several political implications. As a prince, he would cement the royal allusions already attached to Singapore's titular office. Tunku Ya'acob's main appeal nevertheless lay in his direct link to the ruling elites of the Federation which might understandably enhance Singapore's ties to the central government in Kuala Lumpur. He boasted connections with the highest offices in the Federation government and Whitehall, serving as a close associate of UMNO, a Kedah royal and a senior diplomat.

His perceived distance from party politics would have further contributed to his suitability for a supposedly apolitical office. His popularity as an agrarian reformer might even blunt notions of pomp and circumstance usually associated with someone of princely standing, making him more palatable to the popular egalitarian platform of the PAP government. Since the city-state's constitutional future as part of the Federation remained uncertain, any strategy to encourage closer association between Singapore and the Federation could make a difference. This attractive proposition might also alleviate the well-known suspicions that the Federation prime minister harboured towards "Chinese-dominated" Singapore. Having someone whom Kuala Lumpur trusted to preside over the city-state's affairs could therefore relieve any misgivings Federation leaders may have towards the left-wing PAP government. Tunku Ya'acob's candidacy would have been a seductive prospect to the proponents of merger.

The person responsible for lobbying Tunku Ya'acob's candidacy for the post of Yang di-Pertuan Negara was probably Lee Kuan Yew. This statement disputes Rahim Ishak's earlier account that it was Tunku Abdul Rahman who was behind the plot. In August 1959, two months before the Commonwealth Relations Office caught wind of Tunku Ya'acob's possible candidacy, Goode, the former governor of Singapore, approached Lee to ask for potential candidates. The ex-governor was then serving in the joint office of British commissioner and interim Yang di-Pertuan Negara. His term of office would expire on 2 December 1959, six months after the Constitution's implementation, to make way for a Malayan-born person. Writing to the Colonial Office, Goode described his meeting with the Singaporean prime minister:

> I have spoken to the prime minister about my successor as [Yang di-Pertuan] Negara. His view, which I agree, is that he will recommend a name to me for submission to Her Majesty through the secretary of state. Should the secretary of state be unable to support the recommendation, he would so inform the prime minister and ask for another recommendation. But I hope we could avoid this embarrassment by my warning you informally in advance before sending a formal recommendation. The prime minister has in mind to recommend a member of one of the Federation royal families but has not yet made any real progress in getting down to individuals. I shall press him not to delay in getting on with this.[17]

This anecdote, besides confirming Lee's intentions to appoint a member of a Malayan royal family, is further evidence for an earlier point from the previous chapter: the selection of the Yang di-Pertuan Negara was ultimately within the discretion of the colonial secretary and by extension, the British government. Notwithstanding the asymmetrical relationship between the British and Singaporean governments, Goode appealed to the Colonial Office to maintain a sense of goodwill with Lee. A rejection of Lee's chosen candidate needed careful management to avoid prejudicing British relations with PAP leaders, thus the preference for informal consultations with the Singaporean prime minister.

Lee's plans initially raised eyebrows in London. Officials in both the Colonial Office and Commonwealth Relations Office had not expected Lee to even consider nominating someone of royal heritage. They were under a mistaken impression that the prime minister was an uncompromising left-wing ideologue. In fact, they even lauded the Singaporean prime minister for his ingenuity. British officials appreciated his intentions to nurse closer ties with members of the Federation government and believed this particular idea would "hasten close association" between both territories.[18] According to the Constitution, the only qualification clearly stipulated for the office of Yang di-Pertuan Negara was that candidates must be "Malayan-born". This satisfied officials in the Colonial Office because it covered the legal basis for the appointment of someone from the Federation to fill the post because "Malayan-born" must necessarily refer to someone who was born in either Singapore or the Federation.[19]

While impressed with Lee's decision to seek a royal personage to serve as Yang di-Pertuan Negara, British officials still refrained from getting dragged into the matter. It was likely that they feared possible diplomatic repercussions. Any indications of Whitehall orchestrating a secret plan for merger might sour relations with Federation leaders, who saw any expansion of Malaya's federative arrangement as their exclusive sovereign right to determine. While the final decision on the Yang di-Pertuan Negara was ultimately up to the discretion of the colonial secretary in London, the initiative to find a suitable candidate belonged to the Singaporean government. The timing of Lee's declared intention to seek someone from a Malayan royal family suggests that it was the Singaporean prime minister who was behind the move to efffect Tunku Ya'acob candidacy as Yang di-Pertuan Negara, contrary to Rahim Ishak's allegations.

Lee's machinations, however, eventually fell through. On 26 October 1959, Goode wrote to the Colonial Office and informed them about the Singaporean prime minister's naming of Yusof as his chosen candidate for Yang di-Pertuan Negara.[20] British officials recognized that Yusof was the next best alternative since the prime minister's plans to find a willing member of Federation royalty "had drawn a blank".[21] There was another compelling reason why it was unlikely that Tunku Abdul Rahman had advocated for his elder brother's candidacy. The Federation prime minister was ardently opposed to any attempt at leveraging the Yang di-Pertuan Negara's appointment as a means to pressure the Federation government into accepting merger with Singapore. Goode further disclosed that Lee had repeatedly tried to meet the Tunku to discuss this appointment, but his attempts to reach the Federation prime minister were unsuccessful.[22] This was consistent with the Tunku's anti-merger position at this time.

Even though he tried to distance himself from the issue of the Yang di- Pertuan Negara's appointment, the Tunku was livid when he heard of Lee's plans to nominate Yusof. In his opinion, Lee's intention to appoint the brother of Aziz Ishak, a member of the Federation Cabinet, as Yang di-Pertuan Negara was a conniving move to politick Singapore's entry into the Federation via a back door. The Tunku regarded Aziz as the most "difficult" member of his Cabinet and viewed him with apparent scorn.[23] He sharply spelt out to the British high commissioner in Kuala Lumpur, Sir Geofroy Tory, that Yusof's nomination would make Lee look "ridiculous" and "would not further merger in any way".[24]

The issue of Singapore's entry into the Federation, however, was not the only reason for the Tunku's misgivings. The Federation prime minister complained about Yusof's lack of public service experience and firmly believed that both Ishak brothers were "dangerously left-wing and personally untrustworthy".[25] According to the Tunku, shareholders of the *Utusan* newspaper removed Yusof as managing editor precisely because of his involvement in "dangerous" politics. The premier went further to even allege that Yusof had misused the newspaper's funds, although he had no proof to support this claim. Yusof's activities as managing director of the Utusan deserves careful scrutiny and will be examined later.

On 30 October 1959, Lee broached the subject of the Yang di-Pertuan Negara to the Tunku when the latter made a brief stopover in Singapore en route to Australia. While refusing to comment on the appointment, the Tunku assured Lee that he would send a delegation to the swearing-in ceremony.[26] The salient point here is that the Yang di-Pertuan Negara's egalitarian symbolism, premised on Yusof's background as a "commoner", appeared to have been an afterthought. Lee did not merely fail in getting a royal personality appointed to the office. By putting forward Yusof's name as Yang di-Pertuan Negara, he also struck a raw nerve by naming someone whom the Tunku regarded as deplorable.

As much as he was hostile towards Yusof's candidacy, the Tunku nevertheless declared to Tory in no uncertain terms that he did not want to get involved because the appointment was a matter for the Colonial Office and the Singaporean government. He also refused to name an alternative candidate. The Tunku was exceedingly cautious because further entanglements might drag him down a rabbit hole and set an unwelcome pretext for merger. Perhaps a harbinger of future politicking between the Alliance government in Kuala Lumpur and the PAP government in Singapore, Tory also highlighted that the Tunku seemed to "enjoy" the thought of using this controversial appointment as a way to cast the PAP in an "unfavourable light".[27]

Goode was particularly troubled by the Tunku's reaction. With agreement from the Colonial Office, he insisted that some measure of acknowledgement of Yusof's appointment from the Tunku was necessary. This was both diplomatic courtesy and a legal fallback because Yusof was after all a citizen of the Federation. The Tunku or any other Federation leader could make a future claim that there were no formal consultations between Whitehall and Kuala Lumpur about Yusof's appointment.[28] This situation might cast an unfavourable light on the British, particularly among other Commonwealth leaders. It would portray the British as having little regard for the sovereign status of a former colony by appointing one of the latter's citizens to an imperially sanctioned post. The Commonwealth Relations Office shared Goode's cautious posture. Officials recognized that by taking up the office of Yang di-Pertuan Negara, Yusof would need to declare his allegiance to the British sovereign. Federation leaders might subsequently use this as evidence of Yusof's disloyalty, giving them an excuse to deprive him of his citizenship.[29] For the British, a stateless man occupying the dignified office of a Queen's representative would be a mortifying scenario because they were already bending over backwards to preserve whatever little prestige they still had as a great imperial power.

In November 1959, the Commonwealth Relations Office tasked Tory with acquiring some sort of formal acknowledgement from the Federation government in regard to Yusof's nomination. Since the Tunku was away in Australia, Tory discussed the matter with Razak, who was serving as acting prime minister. The latter, however, abstained from making any promises about letting Yusof keep his citizenship because such a matter was for a collective decision by the Federation Cabinet. But Tory insisted— he argued that rescinding Yusof's citizenship would be unreasonable because Federation leaders had seen the draft of Singapore's Constitution and had not expressed any reservations towards the appointment of a "Malayan-born" person to the office. The British government had taken this signal in good faith that Kuala Lumpur would have no problems if the Singaporean government was to nominate a Federation citizen as Yang di-Pertuan Negara.

Realizing that the Federation's consistent abstention in Singaporean affairs had backfired, Razak gave in and agreed to urgently consult the Tunku. On 10 November 1959, Tory updated the Commonwealth Relations Office on the Tunku's response. The Malayan premier had given his word that if he was asked about Yusof's appointment, he would simply send out this official statement: "The Federation government have been informed of the appointment of the Yang di-Pertuan Negara of Singapore but had no comment to offer since it is no concern of the Federation".[30] The statement seemed satisfactory for Whitehall officials, at least for now.

An Oath to the Sovereign Protector

The back-and-forth correspondence between Kuala Lumpur and London on the future Yang di-Pertuan Negara delayed any public announcement on the identity of Goode's successor. Although Lee had formally submitted Yusof's name as his chosen candidate in October 1959, the Singaporean people were kept on a knife-edge about the nomination. This mystery generated public restlessness as the swearing-in ceremony drew closer. Even after preparations for the ceremony were well underway, the PAP government refused to disclose any details to the press.[31]

There was also no official debate on candidate selection in the Assembly. The Yang di-Pertuan Negara's royal appointment would take place when the British colonial secretary officially nominates a candidate to the Queen. While the former was legally bound to consult the Singaporean government, there was no clause in the Constitution which stipulated that endorsement by the Assembly was necessary at any time during the nomination process.[32] This did not sit well with opposition lawmakers. They complained that if the Yang di-Pertuan Negara was truly a symbol of unity divorced from party politics, then the elected representatives of the people—whether in opposition or in government—should at least be involved in the deliberations regarding his appointment.[33] The PAP government unsurprisingly did not entertain their protests.

The prolonged, uneasy silence on the identity of the future Yang di-Pertuan Negara was also probably due to the Colonial Office's strict directive forbidding any mention of Yusof's nomination until there was formal approval from the Queen.[34] The public embargo of this information dragged on as the Colonial Office, out of courtesy rather than formality, waited for the endorsement of Prime Minister Harold Macmillan before sending Yusof's name for royal assent. The British prime minister finally cleared the appointment on 20 November 1959.[35] Three days later, the Colonial Office brought up the subject of Yusof's appointment to Sir Michael Adeane, the Queen's private secretary, who indicated that Her Majesty would be happy to appoint Yusof as Yang di-Pertuan Negara but could only do so after a formal letter of recommendation from a member of the British Cabinet.[36] Colonial Secretary Ian Macleod then took another three days to send a formal recommendation to Her Majesty.[37]

The process sounds tedious enough as it is. Yet there was another problem—the Queen was away at her country home in Sandringham, and because of that, "boxes [took] a little longer to travel".[38] As the man on the ground, Goode had to directly manage pressure from an increasingly restless PAP government and deter imconvenient questions from the Singaporean public. The poor ex-governor did not hide his annoyance when he telegrammed the Colonial Office on 27 November, grumbling that "continued delay in announcement becomes increasingly embarrassing and will soon be ludicrous".[39] The Queen gave an official approval only on 30 November, a mere three days before the swearing-in ceremony.

Yet, the Commission of Appointment, the legal document that was to legitimize Yusof as Yang di-Pertuan Negara, still required the colonial secretary's countersignature. Exasperated officials gave Goode instructions via emergency telegram to proceed with the long-delayed public announcement on Yusof's appointment. And after so much dithering, the Singaporean press released the identity of the new Yang di-Pertuan Negara on 1 December 1959 at 9.30 pm local time—a little less than 36 hours before the swearing-in ceremony. A day later, the Colonial Office sent word to Goode that true copies of the Commission would not reach Singapore in time for the ceremony but instructed him to continue with the legal procedures. For the appointment to be valid, a copy of the Commission's text must be read aloud as if it was already counter-signed.[40] This Kafkaesque situation is worth recounting to show how that the entire process of appointment was a highly exclusive affair bordering absurdity, confined to the interactions of a few souls in the highest offices of Singapore and the imperial metropole. For all the talk about the Yang di-Pertuan Negara being a symbol for ordinary people in an enlightened era of representative politics, the public was deliberately kept in the dark about the man who was supposed to represent them.

In the public announcement, the PAP government portrayed Yusof as a man dedicated to public service. He had been serving as Chairman of the Public Service Commission (PSC) in Singapore for six months prior to his appointment. His name was therefore already recognizable to the public, with the *Straits Times* claiming that "the choice came as no shock" because there were longstanding rumours that Yusof was going to be the Yang di-Pertuan Negara.[41] Whether these rumours were widely circulated or not, tittle-tattle was still no substitute for an official government announcement.

On top of his time in the civil service, the PAP government further publicized Yusof's credentials as the founder of the *Utusan Melayu*, probably the most prominent Malay newspaper in both Singapore and the Federation. The paper was known for its anti-colonial leanings and had a reputable standing among trade unions.[42] According to the official statement:

> For the Yang di-Pertuan Negara, Inche Yusof Bin Ishak himself, it marks not the achievement of personal ambition but the realisation of the very ideals of progress, elevation of human dignity and nationalism which he has sincerely set out in his long career as a Malayan journalist.[43]

This statement invoked his conviction as an anti-colonial nationalist who wanted to uplift the status of those deemed inferior in the colonial order. A biographical write-up published by the Singaporean government further accentuated his distance from social privileges, specifying that "the attainment of such high office had normally been reserved for those long favoured by the metropolitan power" and that "Yusof could never possibly acclaim such privilege and he has never pretended or tried to".[44]

The official write-up also pointed out that Yusof had brief stints in public service.[45] He was a member of the Films Appeal Committee from 1948 to 1950 and was also part of the Nature Reserves Committee. Perhaps most importantly, Yusof, together with other notable nationalist personalities like Minister for Culture S. Rajaratnam, was a member of the Malayanisation Commission. The Marshall government tasked this body with ascertaining the scope and pace of the drive to replace expatriate civil servants with local-born officials. When the Commission submitted its 1956 report, it was so controversial that the British predicted a total collapse of the civil service should the Singaporean government implement all of its aggressive recommendations.[46] By highlighting Yusof's anti-colonial credentials and the absence of his social privilege in the colonial order, the PAP government not only conveyed Yusof's perceived distaste towards the hierarchies of the imperial system but also attempted to relieve the colonial contours of the Yang di-Pertuan Negara. Indeed, the PAP government was determined to cleanse the lingering memory of the office's previous occupancy by the last colonial governor.

This drive to cultivate a humble persona for Yusof even played out during the nomination process. The Colonial Office was unsure about the inclusion of *"inche"* or "mister" in the official salutation for Yusof. Its inclusion in official correspondence from Singapore suggests an attempt by the PAP government to inflate his disposition as a "commoner", as opposed to using "tuan" meaning "sir" or other fancy salutations. Since it was not a formal title, the British eventually dropped *"inche"* in the royal instructions which confirmed Yusof's appointment.[47] Beyond the corridors of officialdom, Yusof's friends sang further praises for him when interviewed by the press. Although he was moving into the Istana, they were confident that the building's "past associations of grandeur" would not affect Yusof.[48] His ascendency as Yang di-Pertuan Negara was as much a celebratory affair as it was an effort to exorcise the hierarchical order of empire.

Meanwhile, over in Kuala Lumpur, Yusof's confirmation as Yang di-Pertuan Negara did not quell the festering apprehension Federation leaders harboured towards his appointment. To the horror of British officials, their fears about the dangers of Federation "indifference" on the new Yang di-Pertuan Negara came true. On the day of the swearing-in ceremony, High Commissioner Tory frantically sent a dispatch to London from Kuala Lumpur to recall his distressing experience of having to deal with the Federation leadership. Both Razak and the Federation interior minister, Dato' Suleiman Abdul Rahman, were determined to nullify Yusof's citizenship because they interpreted the Yang di-Pertuan Negara's oath of allegiance to the British monarch as an act of disloyalty towards the

Federation. Razak then clarified that he and the Tunku had earlier agreed to maintain official apathy only in regard to the appointment—the issue of Yusof's citizenship was an entirely different matter. In the Federal Constitution of Malaya, dual citizenship was not recognized. One of the requirements of federal citizenship was the renunciation of loyalty to other countries, and thus a failure to do so might result in the revoking of one's citizenship.[49] Suleiman also opined that as ministers, their hands were tied; should a lawmaker bring the matter up in parliament, the Federation government had to be consistent in its stance on divided national loyalties.

An increasingly flustered Tory demanded a direct meeting with the Tunku the following day. The former counselled the Federation prime minister about the absence of any clause in the Federal Constitution which stated that an oath of allegiance to another sovereign amounted to disloyalty. Such an oath was therefore not equivalent to taking up citizenship from another country. Moreover, at the time of his appointment, Yusof neither relinquished his current citizenship nor was he a registered citizen of Britain or Singapore.[50] Tory was stern. He warned the Tunku that depriving the Yang di-Pertuan Negara of his citizenship was insulting to the Queen because Yusof was now Her Majesty's representative. Since Federation leaders were already aware of Yusof's appointment, any move to humiliate the Yang di-Pertuan Negara was a deliberate move to implicate the Queen in their politicking.

The Tunku was caught in a bind. While he initially stuck with his cabinet colleagues, Tory's cautionary advice about the potential damage to the British monarch pushed the premier towards an epiphany:

> ... the Tunku said that the last thing he wanted to do was to cause embarrassment to the Queen and that I could rest assured that he would take no action that would have this effect. He was always anxious to uphold the dignity of the Queen, and this was why, against his better judgement, decided to send a representative delegation to the installation at Singapore ... He added, characteristically, that this was also why he sent them in a RMAF (Royal Malayan Air Force) aircraft and had told them to wear suits to make them respectable in contrast to Singaporean representatives.

In contrast to the PAP leadership, the Tunku clearly venerated social hierarchies tied to royalty, attaching great value to sartorial choices as a form of deference. His background as a prince did not determine otherwise. The Tunku then gave Tory a personal guarantee that if the Federation Cabinet deprived Yusof of his citizenship, he would keep the matter so secret that even Yusof himself would not know about it. This hypothetical scenario was so baffling that Tory called the Tunku's bluff. Reporting to the Commonwealth Relations Office, Tory was confident that Federation leadership had backed down and would "not make mischief out of this".[51] It was therefore ironic that the Yang di-Pertuan Negara's allegiance to the British Crown became *both* a reason to embarrass Yusof as a stateless person and a reason to spare him from this embarrassment. In spite of the office's supposed signification of a new, egalitarian Singapore, the Yang di-Pertuan Negara's dignity was preserved only due to his privileged position as Crown representative in the British imperial system.

The socio-political hierarchy of the imperial system continued to entrap Yusof's appointment in a chronic state of ambivalence. About a month after the new Yang di-Pertuan Negara assumed office, British officials further deliberated on the conundrum of his citizenship status to prevent another incident similar to Tory's ordeal. Walter Ian James Wallace, the assistant secretary in the Colonial Office, undertook closer investigations into the clauses of the Malayan Federal Constitution. He came to the conclusion that the Federation ministers had from the very beginning no right to deprive Yusof of his citizenship. Since he was a native of Perak, one of the constituent states of the Federation, Yusof was the subject of the state's ruler. Upon the Federation's independence on 31 August 1957, all subjects of the peninsular rulers were automatically recognized as federal citizens.[52] In contrast, naturalized citizens needed to forfeit their loyalties to any other foreign country when registering for federal citizenship, but this issue was moot in Yusof's case because he was not a naturalized citizen. Under the Article of 28(2) of the Federal Constitution, any person born in the Federation cannot have his federal citizenship taken away on the basis of his retention of foreign citizenship.[53]

Perhaps more importantly, Wallace conceded that this entire episode arose from the conventions of the imperial system. Historically, Crown representatives were British subjects and did not hold the citizenship of the territories where they were deputizing for the British monarch. After the establishment of the postwar Commonwealth, however, this became a problem. Former colonies enacted their own constitutions, each with separate jurisdictions and different stipulations on citizenship. The category of "British subject" subsequently became obsolete. Still insistent on maintaining some semblance of imperial unity, the British enacted the 1948 British Nationality Act, which treated the category of "Commonwealth citizen" as equivalent to a citizenship of the United Kingdom and the Colonies.[54] Since the Federation remained a member of the Commonwealth, the British had little issue with a Federation citizen swearing an oath of allegiance to the Crown since it kept to the long-established convention of imperial subjecthood.

The controversy arising from Yusof's citizenship status, however, was indicative of strained norms in the imperial system during the global era of decolonization. Yusof's inauguration as Yang di-Pertuan Negara has to be seen in this context. On the one hand, it exposed the increasing contradictions in what was left of the British Empire, but on the other, Yusof was renewing the practices of imperial subjecthood when taking his oath of loyalty to the Crown. Despite conjuring an image of disruption, the installation of the Malayan-born Yang di-Pertuan Negara had in fact refreshed the socio-political hierarchy of empire.

Narrowing the Power Distance

Renewed practices of the imperial system did not preclude the performance of change. After Yusof assumed office, opposition assemblymen began to scrutinize the privileges of the new Yang di-Pertuan Negara. In response, Lee informed the Assembly that Yusof had made the enlightened decision not to stay in the Istana. This appeared, at least on the surface, in conformity with the sacrosanct principle of equality held by the nationalist regime of the PAP. While the image of forgoing residence in the former Government House was an ostensible gesture of humility and a break from the norms of colonial Singapore, the Assembly was also told that Yusof would instead reside in a bungalow situated within the Istana grounds. The upkeep for the bungalow would be deducted from his annual salary of $42,860, although his earnings would still be exempted from income tax.[55] The initial gusto seemed inhibited in what appears to be some sort of strange socialist foreplay—as he moved out of one colonial manor, Yusof was to move into another manor on the same property and would pay rent with his untaxable salary.

This exercise may be symbolically significant, but even the merit of this claim is questionable. Yusof was still housed behind high walls and surrounded by the Istana's spacious 40-hectare compound, secluded from the governed similar to how the colonial governors of Singapore once were. The Istana also remained the exclusive location for dignitaries and officials to convene. Even though entry was largely denied to the public, this social distance was overlooked during certain occasions. On New Year's Day in 1960, the Yang di-Pertuan Negara opened the Istana compound to the public for the first time in history. 2,000 curious souls, all of whom were probably in wonder about the secrets behind the Istana's walls, turned up for the monumental event. Their expedition into uncharted public grounds was however confined to the compound's majestic lawn since the Istana building itself was still out of bounds.[56] Till today, on selected holidays, this tradition has persisted.[57] The mystique of the old Government House was now lifted for the people, seemingly bringing the Yang di-Pertuan Negara closer to them, even though the exercise remained an ambiguous gesture undertaken only during special circumstances.

The image of the Yang di-Pertuan Negara as benefactor for the "commoner" was accepted by the public up to a certain degree. After taking over the government, the PAP inherited a chronic problem of unemployment in Singapore left behind by Lim Yew Hock's administration. In August 1959, Byrne, the minister in charge of labour, described the employment situation in Singapore as "grim" because the number of jobless residents was reaching a point of saturation.[58] The PAP government admitted that its policies would need at least two years to effectively rectify the situation.[59] Some segments of the unemployed population in Singapore, however, were more proactive in their search for jobs. On 29 December 1959, a group of them stirred trouble at the Ministry of Labour building, forcing Byrne to descend from his office and threaten the rabble-rousers with police action.[60] Following the commotion, a group of forty unemployed men marched in a procession from Orchard Circus to the Istana. They demanded a meeting with Yusof to plead for jobs. The police, however, turned the men away.[61]

Later, in March 1960, a group of former servicemen announced that they would submit a petition to the Yang di-Pertuan Negara to express their dissatisfaction towards the freezing of their allowances. In the same way, a group of retrenched seamen petitioned the Yang di-Pertuan Negara two months later to demand for employment.[62] These cases only provide a cursory glance at the numerous petitions submitted to Yusof during his time as Yang di-Pertuan Negara. Although he was largely absent from making direct interventions, the actions of the unemployed men illustrate that Yusof's appointment had strengthened a certain interpretation of the Yang di-Pertuan Negara's powers and significance—he was expected to address the problems of the people, particularly the aggrieved members of the working class.

For centuries, petitions have been a medium for popular politics. Through them, political subjects seek redress for injustices or demand some kind of action from the powers that be. For the ruling elites, it would be in their interests not to deny the submission of requests or complaints from their subjects. Their legitimacy to rule, particularly during the post-Enlightenment era of popular politics, is partly based on the myth of subjects having direct access to them.[63] But the right to petition does not mean that there would be subsequent policies or favourable directives in response to the petitioners. Petitions are furthermore inherently deferential to the ruling elites because they are appeals for intercession.[64] This performative political act therefore becomes a device to consolidate the prevailing state of ruler-subject relations, even if the contents of the petitions may seem overtly critical of the power structure.

It is worth mentioning that as the representative of the Crown in Singapore, it was the constitutional role of the Yang di-Pertuan Negara to accept petitions to the Queen.[65] This was faithful to the norms of the colonial order, a context in which the colonized lacked representative institutions. Disgruntled colonial subjects would submit petitions to the imperial parliament or the colonial governors, but in doing so, the petitioners also deferred to the governing structure of the British Empire. These petitions were nevertheless largely met with aloofness or objection in London as compared to petitions from constituents in the British Isles. In other words, the universal right to petition for British subjects led to unequal outcomes. The metropole treated the concerns of non-White peoples in imperial dependencies as provincial and merely secondary.[66]

Revolutionary situations, like that in a decolonizing Singapore, are also often accompanied with an increased intensity in petitioning due to a perceived readjustment of power relations.[67] In a promising new era which had supposedly transcended the oppression of colonial rule, petitions to the Yang di-Pertuan Negara should thus be seen as an important symbolic practice to reaffirm Yusof's image as a benign representative of the people. They provided ordinary people with a means of approach to a higher state power beyond their elected ministers and political representatives. To the petitioners, the apotheosis of state power, now embodied in a man whose background exuded a distaste towards exploitation, would better relate to their problems. The Yang di-Pertuan Negara could then presumably pull the mysterious levers of modern government to appease his downcast subjects.

As the physical embodiment of the State, Yusof, like the governors of colonial Singapore, provided legitimacy for modern institutions and organizations. He was patron to several community organizations, like the Saint John's Ambulance Brigade (SJAB) and sports bodies like the Singapore Government Services Football Association (SGSFA), most of which were institutional legacies of British rule. Yusof also took on the governor's former role as Singapore's Chief Scout.[68] He participated actively in the ceremonies of these organizations, thereby bestowing them with the character of state institutions. To further reinforce his accessibility to the people, the Yang di-Pertuan Negara started to host events in the Istana for selected members of the public, such as inviting scouts and athletes as guests for tea. They were no doubt a different audience from the usual dignitaries and premiers.[69]

Yusof and his wife, Noor Aisha, graced all sorts of public events, whether it was for welfare causes or public interest. For instance, a colonial-era sports festival, the New Year's Water Sports Games, had the Yang di-Pertuan Negara as its new guest-of-honour. Colonial officials of Singapore had graced this annual event since 1823.[70] With the conspicuous display of state flags blending with Yusof's dignified presence, the event became another example of colonial-era rituals being adapted for the nationalist cause. His attendance injected an official atmosphere into these ceremonies, bequeathing them with a sense of legitimacy. These ceremonies were not value-free displays. With their own proprieties and protocols, they played an important role in sanctifying relations of authority.[71]

The structure of meaning in these ceremonial practices went both ways. With officiation from the representative of the sovereign, they provided a type of lawful authorization for the institutions and organizations which hosted them. These ceremonies also sealed a mode of behaviour characteristic of modern institutions through the disciplining of human bodies and actions; the ceremonies and parades all require precision, drilling and physical performance to visualize power.[72] Through salutes and flattering displays, they elevated the Yang di-Pertuan Negara to a stately figure of prime importance while denoting those who were part of the "masses". Simply put, they manifested hierarchy through pageantry. These ceremonies instilled a form of symbolic authority in Yusof, affirming his distinguished status within the existing socio-political hierarchy.

These ceremonies were forms of invented traditions. To project a sense of change under the new nationalist regime, the familiarity of these practices were reinterpreted while novel elements were selectively adopted. Moreover, they fostered a sense of connectedness between the people of Singapore for the PAP's nation-building project. Public tours by the Yang di-Pertuan Negara were part of these ritualistic practices, carrying precedents undertaken by the colonial governors and modern monarchs, as described earlier with respect to Yusof's Southern Islands tour. Amongst his other numerous tours, Yusof visited rural Bukit Panjang in May 1961. The villagers received him with the familiar ceremonial trappings. They welcomed him with firecrackers as well as a choreography of Javanese *kuda kepang* and Chinese lion dances. They were also generous with their cries of "*merdeka*". In his own words, Yusof told the villagers that he wanted to learn their "way of life with (his) own eyes and ears".[73]

At the turn of the new year in 1960, the Yang di-Pertuan Negara continued with the tradition of colonial governors by reading a New Year's Day message over *Radio Singapura* to express his well-wishes for Singapore. The practice was reminiscent of the Royal Christmas Broadcast undertaken since 1932 to bring the monarch closer to the vast territories of the British Empire. This imperial tradition was once again put to the service of nationalist aspirations.[74] Yusof's 1960 New Year message was effectively a call for merger:

> I need not emphasise the fact that by history, geography and many other ties, including family connections, we are part and parcel of Malaya. In light of this important we cannot but show the most friendly attitude and treat the problems of the Federation as our own.[75]

Later in March that year, the Yang di-Pertuan Negara emulated another similar tradition instituted for the Yang di-Pertuan Agong: the Hari Raya Address. It was a wish come true for the writer mentioned in the previous chapter, who had turned to the Berita Harian to air his hopes for a similar practice in Singapore. Yusof's Hari Raya Address wove the anti-colonial message into celebratory sentiments ushered by the end of Ramadan. He reminded listeners about the "true significance of Hari Raya", which was to remember the plight of the less fortunate, especially "Muslim countries which (were) still colonised".[76] His message emphasized gratefulness for Singapore's new self-governing status. Through the medium of sight and sound, these traditions reduced the perceived distance between the Yang di-Pertuan Negara and the people. They gave him credence as an egalitarian symbol while creating a platform of shared experiences for those who were fortunate enough to have caught a glimpse of him or to have heard his voice.

The Repentant Radical?

Beyond traditions and ceremonial performances, Yusof's personal history added a humanized complexion to his office, further shaping the symbolic meanings of the Yang di-Pertuan Negara. The PAP government had a firm basis when invoking Yusof's nationalist credentials as a Malayan journalist. The *Utusan* was an important vehicle for modernist ideas in Singapore and Malaya.[77] Yusof was both the paper's managing director and chief editor and had steered its journalistic team since its founding in 1939. In order to seek venture capital to start the *Utusan*, a young

Yusof had to find small-time investors in Malay kampungs, appealing to working people to buy shares. He had envisioned the Utusan as the first of paper of its kind, owned by the Malays for the Malays.

One of its driving aims was to "modernize" the intellectual orientations of the Malays. The *Utusan* encouraged them to welcome the changes brought about by the capitalist economy and new technologies of the twentieth century, and in the process, they should strive to advance their socio-economic conditions. The paper also urged the community to abandon "archaic" values averse to these changes.[78] The *Utusan*, at least in its incarnation before the Second World War, lived up to its mandate. Under Yusof's leadership, it became a prominent mouthpiece which represented and relayed the socio-economic grievances of the Malays. *Utusan* journalists depicted the Malays as victims of unfair economic practices by immigrants but were careful enough not to overtly criticize the economic policies of the British, dodging charges of sedition from the colonial government.[79] Together with its contemporaries in the world of Malayan journalism, the *Utusan* came to be an important component of a "public sphere"—a discursive arena where modern ideas of community and citizenship were exchanged, contested and disseminated amid dramatic shifts engulfing colonial society.[80]

During the Second World War, the Japanese expropriated the paper and its publishing equipment. This, however, did not mark the death of the *Utusan*. Its temporary Japanese-sponsored incarnation, the *Berita Malai*, continued to offer reading material for the public and took on an anti-British character due to its faithful airing of wartime propaganda in a bid to stir anti-colonial sentiments in its readers.[81] Yusof helmed the *Berita Malai* for about a year before retiring quietly. More than a decade later, his complicity with the Japanese military continued to taunt him even after his nomination as Yang di-Pertuan Negara. The British conservative newspaper, *The Daily Telegraph*, plastered an unfavourable report on Yusof following his nomination. It highlighted that "he is no friend of Britain" and called attention to his background as a Japanese collaborator.[82]

In the era of decolonization, however, being branded as unfriendly to Britain was not a curse but a badge of honour for most in Singapore. Yusof later secured new loans to resuscitate the paper after the war and managed to re-build the *Utusan* as a respectable newspaper which stayed true to its egalitarian roots. Although Yusof incurred great personal embarrassment when seeking these loans, the postwar *Utusan* eventually managed to sustain itself financially.[83] He was therefore not only a determined champion of social change, but his resolve to jumpstart the paper also demonstrated his sense of enterprise as a businessman.

Working under tight conditions as a result of the Malayan Emergency, the *Utusan* manoeuvred official constraints to undertake a left-leaning platform under the influence of A. Samad Ismail, its star journalist. Samad was also one of the founders of the PAP, although his stint in the party was short-lived.[84] Both he and Yusof formed a formidable team: Samad was the intelligent mind behind the Utusan's contents, while Yusof was the taskmaster who put things into order.[85] It was therefore no surprise that the paper was well-disposed to the anti-colonial movement in Singapore and the Federation. It aired columns sympathetic to the cause of students and strikers, criticizing the colonial power for exploiting the oppressed segments of colonial society irrespective of their race or class identifications. Samad himself was an intellectual leader within anti-colonial circles in Singapore.[86]

In trying to understand the ideological inclinations of the *Utusan* and its journalists, the difference between "right-wing" and "left-wing", or radical and conservative, can admittedly be quite arbitrary.[87] Ideologies are often flexible enough to be repurposed to suit different circumstances. Without focusing on specific issues, it would be difficult to understand the intellectual nuances behind the actions of certain groups. Historian Firdaus Haji Abdullah, however, offers a helpful, historicized description of the "radical" brand of Malay politics in which Yusof was deeply involved:

> A main feature of the radical nationalist group was its unwillingness to cooperate with, and a deep distrust of the British. Thus, members of this group took pride in their *non-co politik* (politics of non-cooperation with the British). Couple with their distrust of the British, was a disenchantment with the British-groomed bureaucratic elites, along with traditional aristocratic elites.[88]

Firdaus's words quoted here needs to be treated as more descriptive rather than prescriptive. Under Yusof's watch, the Utusan invited some resentment from the ruling class in Malaya since it held a critical stance against the traditional hierarchy tied to royalty, even though the paper generally supported the aristocrat-led UMNO in the party's pursuit of Malayan independence.[89] Yusof's intimacy with the "radical" brand of Malay politics during the postwar years was probably the main reason why he incurred the Tunku's wrath following his nomination as Yang di-Pertuan Negara. Based on his career as a journalist, Yusof had accumulated a reputation as an abolitionist of social inequalities in the hierarchical order of empire.

Yusof's flirtations with revolutionary anti-colonialism were more intimate than what was revealed to the public. Samad was a high-ranking member of the Singapore People's Anti-British League (ABL), an illegal group affiliated with the MCP. Like its communist parent organization, the ABL aimed to abolish British colonial rule through tactics which included violence and terror.[90] Other ABL members included prominent personalities in the anti-colonial revolutionary movement in Malaya such as Devan Nair and Lim Chin Siong. While neither an official member of the ABL nor the MCP, Yusof became entangled with communist elements through Samad. A now declassified Special Branch report records disputed accounts that Yusof "expressed pleasure at the successes of Chinese Communists", but it confirms that he paid a $10 monthly subscription fee to the MCP in 1950.[91] The report further states that because of this "communist taint", Yusof was not allowed to enter the United States in 1951 for a study visit. A year later, Yusof even received unsolicited Malay-language communist material.

But was the man who would become the first Malayan-born Yang di-Pertuan Negara really a communist? The Special Branch made a critical observation that Yusof's involvement with the MCP was a result of him being "too weak-minded" to resist Samad's influence rather than his faith in communism, claiming that Yusof's politics had "mellowed" after he resigned as managing director of the *Utusan*.[92] The only person who would know the true extent of his personal affinity with the MCP was probably Yusof himself.

When the British detained Samad in 1951 under counter-insurgency measures, Yusof, as a responsible friend and employer, enlisted Lee Kuan Yew's legal services to help free the *Utusan*'s star journalist from detention.[93] His relationship with Lee blossomed from then on.

A few years after their first meeting, Lee personally persuaded the already retired Yusof to serve as Singapore's Yang di-Pertuan Negara.[94] It might not come as a surprise that Yusof revealed, at least in private, that his political views were very much aligned to the PAP's.[95] When deliberating his appointment in October 1959, British officials initially dissuaded Lee from selecting Yusof. They cited Yusof's "security background" and branded him as a "PAP sympathizer", although they appreciated the political capital his appointment might offer to the Singaporean government.[96] Perhaps after Samad's close brush with prolonged detention, Yusof had renounced his earlier zeal in supporting the MCP and committed himself instead to the socialist ideals of the PAP in the realm of constitutional politics.[97]

Due to his shifting political leanings, the British judged his personality as elusive. The Colonial Office acknowledged that Yusof was "politically educated" and "intellectually alert", while Goode predicted that as Yang di-Pertuan Negara, Yusof would "not necessarily always submit to ministerial pressures".[98] Nominating him as Yang di-Pertuan Negara was therefore a strategic move on Lee's part. Amid the PAP's desire to instill a sense of sovereignty in Singapore, having a recognizable personality in anti-colonial circles installed to the highest office in the land seemed to be a victory for self-determination. The party would also attain potential acclaim from the trade unions and communist-inspired elements within the party. Furthermore, Yusof's rise conveyed a triumph for the downtrodden segments of Singaporean society due to the *Utusan*'s well-known advocacy for their plight. But perhaps the most important reason was his friendliness with Lee and the PAP. Yusof's tacit support for the party made him a worthy ally (if not a coincidentally compliant one) to work with in order to push through the PAP government's socialist vision for Singapore.

Colonial Elites in British Malaya

The familiar, mildly heroic narrative recounted above which underpinned the Yang di-Pertuan Negara's tribulations against the authoritarian order of colonial rule falls apart upon further scrutiny of Yusof's background. An unmistakable element of privilege haunted his passage to the office, one that was symptomatic of the indigenous elites of British Malaya. Further scrutiny would reveal that Yusof was from no mere family of commoners, but on the contrary, was of the lineage of an aristocrat from Minangkabau named Datuk Jenaton, a younger sibling to the sultan of Pagar Ruyong. In the late eighteenth century, he migrated to the Malay Peninsula together with his followers to escape a brewing civil war. The Sultanate of Pagar Ruyong was later dissolved following the encroachment of Dutch colonial rule over the East Indies. Thanks to his highborn heritage, Datuk Jenaton attained asylum easily from the Sultan of Kedah and was even bestowed a piece of 100-hectare land in Penang to settle in.[99] His descendants, proud of their nobility, often attempted to salvage the purity of their bloodline in order to preserve the mythical "blue blood" of Minangkabau royalty; since Syeds and Syarifahs were supposedly descendants of the Prophet Muhammad, Jenaton's heirs were fond of marrying Arabs as an alternative to marrying the declining numbers of individuals who could claim royal Minangkabau ancestry.[100]

Generations of Jenaton's descendants continued to prosper upon the advent of British rule in the peninsula. Instead of making English-medium education available to all, the British only encouraged members of the Malay aristocratic class to enter the colonial education system.[101] This kept to the principle of colonial governance which entrenched social distinctions in indigenous societies, as elaborated earlier.[102] The aristocratic class had been gradually inhibited from their traditional occupations as tax collectors and as pirate adventurers following the consolidation of the colonial economy and modern public administration.[103] By co-opting the members of the aristocratic class, colonial administrators in Malaya managed to reassign the displaced members of the traditional aristocracy into new roles in this new British-dominated order.

Yusof's father, Ishak bin Ahmad, was to benefit from this socio-political reconfiguration. Like other descendants of Malay aristocracy, Ishak received an English-medium education and joined the clerical ranks of the civil service. He was eventually promoted to a senior position in the Fisheries Department of the Federated Malay States and the Straits Settlements. When his superior officer went on leave, Ishak was even appointed as Acting Director thereby making him the first Malay to (temporarily) head a government department.[104] The British even made him a Member of the Order of the British Empire (MBE) in 1939 for his illustrious service to the colonial administration.[105] Like other affluent people of his time, Ishak became part of a property-owning class and could afford to buy a piece of land in Singapore. The road leading to this tract of land was later named Jalan Ishak in his honour.[106]

As he treaded the footsteps of his father, Yusof was denied a place in the Malay College of Kuala Kangsar (MCKK), also known as the "Eton of the East", because he was not royalty.[107] Yusof nevertheless received a prestigious English education, first in Victoria School and later in Raffles Institution—both of them located in Singapore, with the latter becoming the nest for the most privileged and able in the colony.[108] Yusof's biographers celebrate him as the only Malay of his cohort in Raffles Institution.[109] It must however be emphasized that education was in itself a marker of privilege and luxury. While Yusof's academic trajectory was an impressive feat, it validated the class privileges that he and his three brothers had enjoyed relative to the other Malays in Singapore, who by this time had formed the underclass of colonial society.[110]

While initially aspiring to be a lawyer, Yusof later settled on being a police cadet after failing to attain the grades needed to read law under a Queen's scholarship. But his dreams of establishing a career in the police force were later dashed upon his realization that only descendants of royalty in Malaya could become gazetted officers. Having a genealogical claim as a descendant of the defunct Pagar Ruyong sultanate only got him second-rate prestige amongst the aristocratic class tied to the royal houses of Malaya which endured due to British patronage. In what was perhaps the genesis of his anti-hierarchical fervour, Yusof even stood up against a fellow cadet who was a descendant of Malay royalty after the latter had mistreated a member of staff.[111] The future Yang di-Pertuan Negara later withdrew from the Police Academy due to his frustrations. While he had benefitted from class privileges available to the elites of colonial society, Yusof did not get to enjoy the full premiums afforded to those at the peak of the socio-political hierarchy.

Having failed to achieve his ambitions, Yusof chose the path of journalism—a path which gave him an effective platform to challenge the asymmetries of colonial society. His contributions to journalism eventually earned him an honour, the *Johan Mangku Negara* (J.M.N.), bestowed by the Federation government. The J.M.N., however, did not come with a title, not even a "Datuk-ship".[112] In his interview with researcher Bruno Lopez, Samad pointed out that Yusof made the decision to move the *Utusan*'s headquarters from Singapore to Kuala Lumpur in 1957 because it was close to the source of titles bestowed by the ruling class of the Federation, and that Yusof had desired such a recognition. But Lopez, in his critical assessment of the interview, treats Samad's allegation as mere discontentment of an ally-turned-adversary.[113]

This dismissal is premature. In his memoirs, Aziz Ishak reveals that as a member of the Federation cabinet, he had appealed to his ministerial colleagues to award his older brother an honour for contributions to the field of journalism. Aziz's retrospective account makes a point about how Razak and the Tunku had failed to appreciate Yusof who, by the date of the autobiography's publication in 1977, had passed on and was fondly remembered as the inaugural president of an independent Singapore. A careful reading of Aziz's memoirs, however, supports Samad's rather denigrative allegations that Yusof had a personal desire for titles; he tells of his older brother's disappointment with the J.M.N. and expectations of a higher honour.[114] But Aziz assures his readers of a happy ending to the saga. Yusof was later vindicated when he was awarded a more "deserving" title of *Tun* after Singapore's merger with Malaya.[115] Many, including the PAP government, have peddled the narrative that Yusof agreed to be the Yang di-Pertuan Negara neither for selfish reasons nor out of spite for the Malay ruling classes, but was answering the noble call of duty at personal sacrifice.[116] Indeed, for someone whose anti-colonial and egalitarian ideals became a selling point, Yusof still held a personal desire for aristocratic titles and honours.

This revelation about Yusof's desire for titles casts a more human light on Yusof's acceptance of his appointment as Yang di-Pertuan Negara. It suggests that his sense of service was mixed with a need to salvage his personal pride and to uphold his own *nama* (name, title or reputation) at a level which befitted his standing and legacy.[117] Many might relate to this human need to save one's pride. Yusof's life story could after all be seen as a series of failures—a failure to enter the MCKK, a failure to be a gazetted police officer and a failure to get a title commensurate with his contributions. These setbacks were a result of the socio-political order short-changing him. It is no wonder that Yusof later became a full socialist convert, espousing an eradication of class distinctions. Accepting the appointment of Yang di-Pertuan Negara provided Yusof with an opportunity to recover his own reputation. Furthermore, the bestowal of honours is not a neutral, pedestrian practice because they were hallmarks of hierarchical orders. By accepting these titles, recipients tie themselves to an existing social scale.[118] Similar to his father's linkages with the imperial hierarchy through the MBE, Yusof's acceptance of the J.M.N. was a submission to Malaya's hierarchical order. It confirmed his standing within a structure steeped in social distinctions based on an aristocratic legacy. Yusof might have been an egalitarian idealist but rejecting the J.M.N. or other more desirable titles might have been a little too "socialist" even for him.

While it is undeniable that Yusof's and his father's careers were a result of some measure of personal effort, their life trajectories remain emblematic of the class privileges enjoyed by indigenous elites under British rule. Ishak and his forefathers had benefitted from the opportunities which became available to them with the coming of the colonial order, allowing them to maintain their esteemed status as part of the aristocratic-bureaucrat class.[119] Another marker of these privileges was access to an English-medium education, something also enjoyed by Ishak's sons. Indeed, privilege often stays in the family. This, however, did not preclude them from holding onto egalitarian beliefs. Yusof's ideological leanings corresponded with his father's—Ishak was an advocate of education as a means to improve the dignity of the Malays (on top of his recommendation that they eat more fish).[120] The salient point here is that both Yusof and his father were beneficiaries of the imperial social hierarchy, even though they might distance themselves from the pomp of class distinctions whenever it was advantageous for them. Their access to prominent positions legitimized the inequalities of the colonial order.

Aristocratic heritage still carried prestige in the post-independence Federation. Even as the PAP emphasized Yusof's background as a "commoner", he was not unlike the many UMNO politicians who dominated the political landscape in the Federation. Leaders like the Tunku, Deputy Prime Minister Razak and Home Affairs Minister Tun

Dr Ismail were from families in the upper crust of the Malayan socio-political hierarchy. Favoured as the new political elites in the postwar Federation, they became elected representatives to replace Malay royalty as the arbiter of politics in the era of constitutional politics. The significance of Yusof's appointment communicated his affiliation with the struggles of ordinary people while also affirming his resonance with the class distinctions in the socio-political order of British Malaya. It would be disingenuous to admit otherwise. Yusof's appointment as the Yang di-Pertuan Negara therefore came with this baggage of privilege.

In tandem with Yusof's class identity was his access to social networks that may have been invaluable to his rise as Yang di-Pertuan Negara. Aziz Ishak revealed in an interview with Bruno Lopez that the Tunku had taken on one of his five sisters as a wife, making Aziz and Yusof related to the Federation prime minister by marriage.[121] It is, however, difficult to verify when the marriage transpired or whether there was even such a marriage in the first place because it concerns a particularly intimate aspect of his family. Melanie Chew and Norshahril Saat, both of whom have built their biographical studies of Yusof on Lopez's work, did not investigate this claim further, although Chew notes that Yusof's family denied the existence of the marriage.[122] It is worthwhile to mention that this denial of Yusof's familial ties to the Federation prime minister would have been convenient for the PAP government in the context of post-separation, when it began its nation-building project of distancing Singapore from Malaysia.[123]

This familial link needs further contemplation. The Tunku was publicly known as a "playboy" who had his generous share of romantic adventures.[124] He had at least four wives whom he married at different points of his life; based on public information, none of the four women were sisters to Yusof and Aziz. The Tunku's first wife, Meriam Chong, was a Thai of Chinese descent who tragically died after contracting malaria. He then had a short-lived marriage to Violet Coulsen, his former landlady in England, but their marriage was initially kept secret from the public due to disapproval from the regent of Kedah.[125] His fifty-year marriage to a third wife, Sharifah Rodziah, is well-known, but the Tunku later wedded a Chinese woman named Bibi Chong in secret. This fourth marriage is redacted in his official biography and till today, unmentioned in the official site of Malaysia's Prime Minister's Office.[126]

Aziz's revelation to Lopez is provocative. Could it be possible that the Tunku had married one of Yusof's sisters in secret, as he did in the case of his second and fourth wives? Did Aziz accidentally let slip a piece of information known only to members of his family—a secret to safeguard the reputation of a sister? Lopez has gone even further to record Aziz's claim that Yusof was unhappy with how the Tunku had treated his sister, suggesting an unpleasant turn to this marriage.[127] For a supposed delusion on his part, it is interesting to note that Aziz had gone to such detail. The insinuations made through this line of questioning are speculative. While no definitive conclusion could be drawn with regard to this "secret marriage" at this moment of writing, this historical trace posits a possible familial relationship between Yusof and the Tunku. The Yang di-Pertuan Negara's kinship ties, or "social capital", were not divorced from his class identity. When looking at Yusof's life story, the recurring figure of Aziz, a member of the Tunku's cabinet until 1963, is a further reminder of how one's connectedness to ruling circles paves the way to power. In spite of his strained personal relationship with the Tunku, Yusof's access to exclusive networks, whether real or perceived, may have been a factor in PAP government's decision to nominate Yusof as Yang di-Pertuan Negara. Appointing a personality who was intimately connected to members of the Federation Cabinet could presumably be useful in influencing Singapore's cause in the Federation—a possible ace up the PAP's sleeve.[128]

The Lord of Singapore

Selected details of Yusof's life story sanctified the Yang di-Pertuan Negara as a symbolic testament to egalitarian aspirations, but beneath these overt invocations, the office was also guilty of perpetuating the class distinctions of the colonial era. The official tasks of the Yang di-Pertuan Negara were still based on the privileged practices of the colonial elites, in spite of the humble, non-elitist demeanour that the office was supposed to bear. These activities included fraternizing with members of high society. Exclusive occasions of cocktail and garden parties for dignitaries and political leaders were regularly patronized or even hosted by the Yang di-Pertuan Negara.[129] When he needed to get around for his official duties, Yusof was chauffeured in the state car, which was a Rolls-Royce.[130] By the 1950s, the Rolls-Royce was not just a British luxury but also an automotive ambition. It was an eblem of upper class privilege; owning such a vehicle was a statement of wealth in British society.[131] It is no surprise that the Rolls-Royce also became the choice car for colonial governors and kings.[132]

Although such practices may be defended as "innocent" traditions for the sake of diplomatic hospitality or official duties, the projection of grandeur exclusive to a privileged group of people were stratifying habits that continued to materialize and enforce class divisions in Singaporean society—they mark concrete, visible differences between the lived experiences of the ruler and the ruled, the governing class and the "commoner". The "new" Singapore State continued to be a patron of the parties and banquets which had been a staple of the rich and powerful since the island's establishment as a British colony.[133] The era of self-government, in spite of overt displays of reforms, perpetuated class stratifications of colonial society through overt displays of social privilege.

Yusof was not an innocent bystander to these stratifying practices. The former secretary-general of the Singaporean branch of UMNO, Tan Sri Syed Esa Almenoar, provided a critical perspective into the day-to-day execution of the office of Yang di-Pertuan Negara. He revealed in an oral history interview that Yusof revelled in certain acts which projected class exclusivity. The National Archives of Singapore interviewed Almenoar in 1984, over a decade after Yusof's passing and almost twenty years since the establishment of the Republic of Singapore. In the excerpts cited below, Almenoar mixes the terminologies of the office of president and Yang di-Pertuan Negara, but this mistake is understandable due to the sequence of memory. He refers to Yusof as "president" since it was the last office that the latter held before his death in 1970. In the context of expressing UMNO's reservations towards the 1958 Constitution, the interview provides a rare, critical window into Yusof's personal interactions in his official capacity. Almenoar shared, "UMNO was not very happy.

I'm talking about UMNO Singapore was not very happy because we had a governor who acted just like a Sultan. And that, UMNO was not very happy".[134]

If Singapore UMNO's dream was to re-establish a sultanate in Singapore as discussed in the previous chapter, the Yang di-Pertuan Negara had indeed fulfilled this dream, but not in the manner which the party had imagined. Almenoar went on to detail how Yusof had acted "like a Sultan":

> And of course, UMNO Singapore felt that the appointment of—as I said—the Governor or President whatever it may be, should be something different. They wanted it to be something like the Governor of Melaka or something like that. But the rank of the President in Singapore, according to them appears to be like a Sultan, see? And there have been comments on the words used by our first President. You know, only Sultans used the word "*beta*", the Malay word "*beta*" ...
>
> ... When he was appointed as President, the President himself really made him appear himself like a Sultan [sic]. The way he speaks to the people. So that sort of double enforced what they [UMNO] are worried about.[135]

In these excerpts, Almenoar points out that by acting as if he was Malay royalty, Yusof had defied the expectations held for a non-royal post, which was understood to be similar to that of a mere ceremonial governor and had used the term "*beta*" in conversations when referring to himself. This is significant. Members of Malay royalty have used this pronoun to exclusively refer to themselves in first person, particularly when addressing their subjects.[136]

In this interview, Almenoar dwelled upon an ancient curse, which was probably an allusion to the *daulat* (sovereignty), a type of the supernatural power possessed by Malay royalty as a sign of their right to rule. When the Yang di-Pertuan Negara acted "like a Sultan" in the performance of his duties, he had transgressed the *daulat*, and thus a curse befell him. To demonstrate his point further, Almenoar made rhetorical comparisons to Devan Nair, the incumbent Singaporean president during the time of the interview:

They [UMNO] felt it [the office] should be lower than the Sultan. But they felt he [Yusof] should act as a Governor, and particularly, a Muslim, how can you be a Sultan? If Nair want to behave like that, they wouldn't worry. Now, but if some Muslims behave like that then they worry. Because there is a curse. They believed there is a curse, that if you are not Sultan, you want to be a Sultan, you'll get it.[137]

This comment has irreverent undertones because it was probably hinting at Yusof's untimely death in 1970 while in office, implying that the late president had died because of the curse.

Almenoar proceeded to recount the displeasure within the rank and file of the Singaporean branch of UMNO towards Hamid Jumat, who was party leader and a senior member of Lim Yew Hock's government. Party members blamed Hamid for failing to use his good offices during the constitutional talks to clearly spell out that the ceremonial office of Crown representative should not be mistaken for royalty.[138] Internal party dissent even culminated into an attempt to oust Hamid in 1959, but the Tunku intervened just in time to calm the rebellion.[139] Seen in this context, UMNO's sultanate proposal was a solution to completely cast away the Yang di-Pertuan Negara's association with royalty, but having failed to further the proposal, their worst fears came true: a Yang di-Pertuan Negara who was not royalty but held pretentions that he was.

Almenoar's recollections are intriguing. Although he may seem overtly critical, there are some details which could make his account compelling. First, the interview was not specifically about Yusof. Almenoar's descriptions about the Yang di-Pertuan Negara's conduct was from a segmented part of the interview focused on the 1957 constitutional talks. He shared his vivid opinions as a subsidiary point to vindicate UMNO's doubts towards the outcome of the negotiations. It was only after further probing by the interviewer that Almenoar elaborated his qualms towards the late president's behaviour. The tangent, therefore, was unlikely a result of any deliberate plan on Almenoar's part to insult Yusof personally but came about as an authentic, unplanned real-time reaction towards UMNO's marginalization during the conference.

Second, Yusof's demeanor as Yang di-Pertuan Negara seemed to be sharply etched in his memory. Granted, the details he provided was a result of retrospection, hence the lack of precision in his recollections. But considering the degree to which Almenoar passionately conveyed his displeasure, the conduct of the Yang di-Pertuan Negara must have had a striking impression on him. Yusof's adoption of royal habits in spite of the fact that he was not a sultan would have been provocative for UMNO members since the political party prided itself as the defender of Malay sovereignty and customs. As staunch supporters of restoring the sultanate of Singapore, a royal pretender appointed to the island's titular office was insulting to their cause. It is also significant that during the time of the oral history interview, Almenoar was already a senior politician halfway into retirement.[140] The platform of the interview provided him an opportunity to freely express himself. Even if we exercise a strong hermeneutic of suspicion by assuming that Almenoar was securing his political legacy for posterity, smearing Yusof's reputation by adding rich elaboration on hexes, unhappiness and hubris to a secondary point was an unconventional strategy. He could have spent more effort and time to recall his many other substantive contributions and that of UMNO's, which he eventually did share.[141] And finally, when recalling their service as pioneer journalists of the *Utusan*, Almenoar had in fact shown great respect for Yusof and his brothers. This suggests that he was reasonably even-handed, confining his personal disdain to Yusof's term as Yang di-Pertuan Negara.[142]

Almenoar's account is one of the rare critical opinions about a celebrated former president. His comments could be rejected in toto as that of an indignant politician from a fledging political party. To do that, however, would be intellectually dishonest. At the very least, what could be accepted as true was that not everyone received the Yang di-Pertuan Negara as an undisputed testament of the breaking down of hierarchies in self-governing Singapore. Like any other symbol, the office's meanings were not absolute but inherently contested. Almenoar and his party colleagues had the *perception* that Yusof inflated his social standing in a pretentious manner, and in that sense, the Yang di-Pertuan Negara was an amplifier of class distinctions. The ambiguous design of the office had given sufficient latitude to its appointee to perform what he considered to be proper conduct for the office. This engendered an unresolved contradiction when the appointee took it upon himself to execute the decorum which he thought was personally befitting for his class status. If Almenoar's recollections hold a kernel of truth, then it becomes evident that Yusof was not completely faithful to the egalitarian message of his office. Yusof's journey to restore his armour propre had reached poetic ending when he became Yang di-Pertuan Negara. A descendant of a petty aristocratic family who was constantly reminded of his subordinate place in the socio-political hierarchy could now act like royalty. At least for Yusof, barriers along the lines of class ironically did break down with the coming of the PAP nationalist regime.

After Yusof's ascendency as Yang di-Pertuan Negara, the office's egalitarian symbolism did not preclude its role in stratifying society according to class. At the onset of the office's establishment were prejudices held by the ruling elites towards the subject classes in Singapore. The former conceived the office as a potentially potent distraction to seize the imagination of ordinary people. The Yang di-Pertuan Negara was a tangible totem embodying the city-state's new sense of being in the age of decolonization, veiling the city-state's continued existence as a subordinate territory of Britain. The PAP's rise to power in 1959 only fanned the flames of social revolution. The party's socialist vision aimed to create a more equal society—a radical break from the discriminatory practices of class distinctions perpetuated during the colonial order. Yusof's appointment as Yang di-Pertuan Negara was meant to manifest this bold vision. His image as a "commoner" represented the collapse of class hierarchies because now an individual who appeared so distant from social privileges was able to occupy a high office previously reserved for the White aristocrats of colonial Singapore. By revising ceremonies and traditions from the colonial order, the Yang di-Pertuan Negara was also made more accessible to the people, demonstrating the shrinking of power distance between the rulers and the ruled.

Beyond this distracting gust of change, the socio-political hierarchy entrenched during the days of British Malaya still had its bite. The trappings of lavishness and ceremonial splendour continued to preserve social asymmetries in Singapore. In the hopes of engendering merger, the Singaporean prime minister also attempted to make a deal with the devil by searching for a candidate who was from a royal Malayan bloodline. It was only because of Lee's failure to find a spare prince or lord that Yusof became a substitute. After Yusof accepted his appointment and swore allegiance to the British Crown, it inadvertently almost caused a major rift in the triad relationship between Singapore, Britain and the Federation. It was the renewed practice of imperial subjecthood—another reminder of the reinvigorated structure of the imperial system in Singapore—that protected Yusof from the scheming of Federation leaders. A Malay journalist committed to the revolutionary ideals of anti-colonial nationalism became a rich well for the PAP government to tap into as they hoped to solidify the egalitarian message of the Yang di-Pertuan Negara. But conversely, Yusof's background as a colonial elite and his subsequent execution of the Yang di-Pertuan Negara's functions seemed to also harden the burdens of class in colonial society. The next chapter tells this story and unmasks how the Yang di-Pertuan Negara represented the breaking down of racial barriers ingrained in the colonial order.

Notes

1. Speech by Lee Kuan Yew, 3 December 1959, CO 1030/480, 42.
2. *SFP*, 4 December 1959, p. 1 and *ST*, 4 December 1959, p. 1.
3. Speech by Lee Kuan Yew, 3 December 1959, CO 1030/480, 42.
4. *Times*, 4 December 1959, DO 35/9888, 47.
5. See Cannadine, *Ornamentalism*, pp. 5–6.
6. Ibid., pp. 153–54
7. PAP, *Petir*, 2, 5 (May 1959), p. 1.
8. The PAP's first policy address promised a "social revolution" to achieve "a more just society". See Ministry of Culture, *Towards a More Just Society*.
9. PAP, *Petir* 2, 3 (February 1959), p. 1.
10. Letter from J. Chadwick to R. Black, 3 August 1957, DO 35/9872.
11. R. Black, "Memorandum on the course to be followed in future constitutional negotiations", 8 October 1956, FO 1091/44, 95.
12. Ibid.
13. Chew, *President Yusof*, pp. 99–101 and Bruno Lopez, "Yusof Bin Ishak: Journalist and Head of State" (Academic Exercise, Department of History, National University of Singapore, 1987), p. 60.
14. Letter from W.J. Smith to J.D. Hennings, 5 October 1959, DO 35/9888, 5.
15. *ST*, 13 May 1951, p. 4.
16. See Tunku Ya'acob's curriculum vitae in DO 35/9821.
17. Letter from W. Goode to E. Melville, 18 August 1959, DO 35/870, 265.
18. Letter from W.J. Smith to R.C.C. Hunt, 9 September 1959, DO 35/9888, 4.

19. Ibid.
20. Telegram from W. Goode to Colonial Office, 26 October 1959, CO 1030/633, 139.
21. Note from J.D. Hennings to W.I.J. Wallace, E. Melville, J. Martin and H. Poynton, 28 October 1959, CO 1030/633, 4.
22. Letter from W. Goode to W.I.J. Wallace, 12 October 1959, DO 35/9888, 6.
23. Ibid.
24. Telegram from G. Tory to Commonwealth Relations Office, 21 October 1959, CO 1030/633, 141.
25. Ibid.
26. Telegram from W. Goode to Colonial Office, 30 October 1959, CO 1033/633, 129.
27. Telegram from G. Tory to Commonwealth Relations Office, 21 October 1959, CO 1030/633, 141.
28. Telegram from W. Goode to Colonial Office, 28 October 1959, CO 1030/633, 130.
29. Telegram from Commonwealth Relations Office to G. Tory, 2 November 1959, DO 35/9888, 17.
30. Telegram from G. Tory to Commonwealth Relations Office, 10 November 1959, DO 35/9888, 20.
31. *ST*, 1 December 1959, p. 1.
32. Government of Singapore, *Order in Council 1958*, p. 10.
33. *ST*, 24 November 1959, p. 4.
34. Telegram from Colonial Office to W. Goode, 26 November 1959, CO 1030/633, 78.
35. Letter from D. Stephens to J.T.A. Howard Drake, 20 November 1959, CO 1030/633, 88.
36. Letter from M. Adeane to D.L. Pearson, 24 November 1959, CO 1033/633, 81.
37. Letter from I. Macleod to Buckingham Palace, 27 November 1959, CO 1030/633, 62.
38. Telegram from Colonial Office to W. Goode, 30 November 1959, CO 1030/633, 60.
39. W. Goode to Colonial Office, 27 November 1959, CO 1030/633, 75.
40. Colonial Office to W. Goode, 2 December 1959, CO 1030/633, 45.
41. *ST*, 2 December 1959, p. 1.
42. Chew, *President Yusof*, pp. 87–89.
43. *ST*, 2 December 1959, p. 1.
44. "Biography of the First Malayan born Yang di-Pertuan Negara, Enche Yusof bin Ishak", 30 November 1959, CO 1030/633, 37–40.
45. Ibid.

46. On the composition and terms of reference of the Malayanisation Commission, see *Indian Daily Mail*, 29 June 1955, p. 1. For the assessment of British officials on the Malayanisation Commission, see Report from R. Black to A. Lennox-Boyd, 19 March 1956, CO 1030/122; Report from R. Black to the Colonial Office, 22 October 1955, DO 35/6289. For a historical analysis on Malayanisation, see Yeo, *Political Development*, pp. 68–86.

47. See exchange of correspondences in CO 1030/ 891. Also see Norshahril, *Yusof Ishak*, pp. 56–57.

48. *SFP*, 2 December 1959, p. 1.

49. See Colonial Office, *Constitutional Proposals for the Federation of Malaya* (London: H. M. Stationery Office, 1957) and United Nations, *Report of Malaya*.

50. Telegram from W. Goode to Colonial Office, 4 November 1959, CO 1030/633, 107.

51. Minute and telegram from G. Tory to Commonwealth Relations Office, 3 December 1959, CO 1030/699, 25–27.

52. Colonial Office, *Constitutional Proposals*, p. 37. Also see Government of Malaya, *The Federation of Malaya Agreement* (Kuala Lumpur: Government Press, 1952).

53. Colonial Office, *Constitutional Proposals*, p. 43.

54. Patel, *Immigration and the End of Empire*, pp. 56–57.

55. *SLAD*, Vol. 11, Sitting No. 15, Col. 905–907 (11 December 1959).

56. *BH*, 2 January 1960, p. 1.

57. President's Office, "Istana Open House", https://www.istana.gov.sg/Visit-And-Explore/Istana-Open-House (accessed 1 June 2019).

58. *SFP*, 12 August 1959, p. 5.

59. *ST*, 15 June 1959, p. 1.

60. *BH*, 29 December 1959, p. 1.

61. Ibid.

62. *ST*, 4 March 1960 and *BH*, 21 May 1960.

63. Lex Heerma van Voss, "Introduction", in *Petitions in Social History*, edited by Lex Heerma van Voss (Cambridge: Cambridge University Press, 2002), p. 1.

64. Ibid., pp. 2–3.

65. Government of Singapore, *Order in Council 1958*, p. 12.

66. See Richard Huzzy and Henry Miller, "Colonial Petitions, and the Imperial Parliament, ca. 1780–1918", *Journal of British Studies* (2021): 1–29.

67. van Voss, "Introduction", p. 5.

68. *ST*, 3 January 1960, p. 11.

69. For example, see *ST*, 24 December 1959, p. 4; *ST*, 24 August 1960, p. 14.

70. *BH*, 30 December 1959, p. 4; *ST*, 2 January 1960, p. 8.

71. Hobsbawm, "Introduction", p. 9.

72. Michel Foucault, *Discipline and Punish: The Birth of the Prison*, translated by Alan Sheridan (New York: Vintage, 1995), pp. 187–89.

73. *ST*, 8 May 1961, p. 9.
74. Murphy, *Monarchy*, pp. 22–23.
75. *ST*, 1 January 1960, p. 7.
76. *ST*, 29 March 1960, p. 1.
77. The discussion on the *Utusan* throughout this book is with reference to its second incarnation under Yusof's leadership from 1939. On the *Utusan* under Eunos Abdullah, see Milner, *Invention of Politics*, pp. 89–110. On the flourishing of Malay journalism in the 1930s, see Mark Emmanuel, "Viewspapers: the Malay press of the 1930s", *Journal of Southeast Asian Studies* 41, no. 1 (2010): 1–20.
78. Zainuddin Maidin, *Di Depan Api, di Belakang Duri* (Kuala Lumpur: Utusan Publication, 2013), pp. 12–25 and Zahairin Abdul Rahman, "Utusan Melayu: Origin and History, 1939–1959" (Academic Exercise, Department of History, National University of Singapore 1988), pp. 14–16.
79. Roff, *Malay Nationalism*, pp. 176–77 and Abdul Latiff Abu Bakar, *Abdul Rahim Kajai: Wartawan dan Sasterawan Melayu* (Kuala Lumpur: Dewan Bahasa dan Pustaka, 1984), pp. 207–48 and Henk Maier, "The Writings of Abdul Rahim Kajai: Malay Nostalgia in a Crystal", *Journal of Southeast Asian Studies* 41, no. 1 (2010): 77–81.
80. Milner, *Invention of Politics*, pp. 129–30.
81. Maidin, *Di Depan Api*, pp. 36–37 and A. Samad Ismail, *Memoir A. Samad Ismail di Singapura* (Bangi: Penerbit Universiti Kebangsaan Malaysia, 1993), pp. 202–3.
82. *Daily Telegraph*, 2 December 1959, DO 35/9888.
83. Lopez, "Yusof Bin Ishak", pp. 31–35.
84. Cheah Boon Kheng, "Introduction", in *A. Samad Ismail: Journalism and Politics*, edited by Cheah Boon Kheng (Kuala Lumpur: Singamal, 1987), p. xvi.
85. Lopez, "Yusof Bin Ishak", pp. 35–37 and Chew, *President Yusof*, pp. 88–89.
86. Zahairin, "Utusan Melayu", pp. 57–58. Samad was also good friends with Devan Nair, one of the PAP's preeminent unionists, see Cheah Boon Kheng, "Introduction", p. xxiv.
87. David Scott, *Refashioning Futures: Criticism After Postcoloniality* (Princeton: Princeton University Press, 1999), p. 19.
88. Firdaus Haji Abdullah, *Radical Malay Politics: Its Origins and Early Development* (Petaling Jaya: Pelanduk Publications, 1985), pp. 6–7.
89. Maidin, *Di Depan Api*, pp. 74–79.
90. Bilveer Singh, *Quest for Political Power: Communist Subversion and Militancy in Singapore* (Singapore: Marshall Cavendish Asia, 2014), pp. 112–17.
91. Special Branch Dossier on Yusof Bin Ishak, undated, item MAL 53/312/1 (6), DO 35/9888.
92. Ibid.
93. Lee Kuan Yew, *The Singapore Story: Memoirs of Lee Kuan Yew* (Singapore: Marshall Cavendish, 2004), pp. 156–57. Lee was to play a part during

controversial junctures of the *Utusan*'s history, see Maidin, *Di Depan Api*, pp. 73, 95.

94. Tan, *Noor Aishah*, pp. 53–54.
95. Lopez, "Yusof Bin Ishak", pp. 46, 63–64.
96. Minutes by R.C. Ormerod, 19 October 1959, DO 35/9888.
97. Maidin attributes Yusof's conversion to socialism to Samad's influence, see Maidin, *Di Depan Api*, pp. 73, 95.
98. Letter from D.L. Pearson to T.J. Bligh, 18 November 1959, CO 1030/ 633, 92.
99. Aziz Ishak, *Mencari Bako* (Kuala Lumpur: Adabi, 1983), pp. 14–16.
100. Ibid., pp. 17–19.
101. Amoroso, *Traditionalism*, pp. 60–63. For education structure in early colonial Malaya and Singapore, see Turnbull, *A History of Modern Singapore*, pp. 206–10. On the types of Malay education available from the twentieth century onwards, see Roff, *Malay Nationalism*, pp. 100–13, 127–57.
102. Cannadine, *Ornamentalism*, pp. 58–70.
103. Amoroso, *Traditionalism*, pp. 50–59.
104. *ST*, 15 May 1937, p. 12.
105. *ST*, 20 February 1939, p. 12; *Malaya Tribune*, 20 February 1939, p. 12.
106. Tan, *Noor Aishah*, p. 33.
107. Chew, *President Yusof*, p. 59. Social distinctions played a vital part in the MCKK's structure, see Roff, *Malay Nationalism*, pp. 100–13.
108. Turnbull, *A History of Modern Singapore*, pp. 208, 244.
109. Chew, *President Yusof*, p. 68; Norshahril, *Yusof Ishak*, p. 14; Lopez, "Yusof Bin Ishak", p. 3.
110. Roff, *Malay Nationalism*, pp. 178–84, 188–97.
111. Lopez, "Yusof Bin Ishak", pp. 7–8.
112. Aziz Ishak, *Special Guest: The Detention in Malaysia of an Ex-cabinet Minister* (Singapore: Oxford University Press, 1977), p. 20.
113. Lopez, "Yusof Bin Ishak", pp. 53–54.
114. Aziz, *Special Guest*, p. 20.
115. Ibid., pp. 21–22.
116. Chew, *President Yusof*, pp. 102–3; Norshahril, *Yusof Ishak*, p. 60; Lopez, "Yusof Bin Ishak", pp. 57–62.
117. This is a play on the ideology of the *kerajaan*, see Milner, *Kerajaan*, pp. 167–72.
118. Cannadine, *Ornamentalism*, p. 100.
119. Amoroso, *Traditionalism*, pp. 142–43 and for the reinvention of the Malay raja, see pp. 67–97.
120. *ST*, 21 May 1933, p. 10 and *ST*, 16 May 1937, p. 8.
121. Lopez, "Yusof Bin Ishak", pp. 55, 63.
122. Chew, *President Yusof*, p. 102.

123. See Lily Zubaidah Rahim, *Singapore in the Malay World: Building and Breaching Regional Bridges* (London and New York: Routledge, 2009).

124. *ST*, 31 August 1957, p. 10 and *BH*, 12 May 1966, p. 1.

125. Ranjit Gill, *Of Political Bondage: An Authorised Biography of Tunku Abdul Rahman, Malaysia's First Prime Minister and His Continuing Participation in Contemporary Politics* (Singapore: Sterling Corporate, 1990), pp. 11–14. On his marriage to Bibi Chong, see Zaain Zin, "Tunku Abdul Rahman pada Mata Puterinya", *Utusan Malaysia*, 5 August 2018, https://www.utusan. com.my/mega/rona/video-tunku-abdul-rahman-pada-mata-puterinya-1.743081 (accessed 8 June 2019).

126. Perdana Leadership Foundation, "Biography of Tunku Abdul Rahman (English)", http://www.perdana.org.my/index.php/pms-of-malaysia/tunku-abdul-rahman/tunku-abdul-rahman (accessed 8 June 2019).

127. Lopez, "Yusof Bin Ishak", p. 55.

128. Lopez makes a similar point in ibid., p. 63.

129. For example, see *ST*, 4 June 1960, p. 14; *ST*, 5 July 1960, p. 4; *SFP*, 20 July 1960, p. 6; *ST*, 20 August 1960, p. 4; *SFP*, 22 August 1960, p. 3; *ST*, 21 January 1961, p. 4; *ST*, 23 April 1961, p. 9; *ST*, 3 May 1961, p. 4.

130. *SFP*, 2 December 1959, p. 1.

131. James Taylor, *British Luxury Cars of the 1950s and '60s* (Oxford: Bloomsbury, 2016), pp. 15–23.

132. The British high commissioner of Malaya used a similar car, see *ST*, 8 October 1951, p. 1. The Yang di-Pertuan Agong and the Shah of Iran was also chauffeured in a Rolls-Royce, see respectively *ST*, 25 September 1959, p. 1 and *ST*, 20 December 1959, p. 3.

133. Turnbull, *A History of Modern Singapore*, pp. 33, 147–49.

134. Syed Esa Almenoar, "Political History of Singapore 1945–1965 Accession No. 000013", Transcript of Oral History Recording, Reel 004, National Archives of Singapore (17 January 1984), p. 37.

135. Ibid., pp. 37–39.

136. Asmah Haji Omar, *Bahasa Di Raja* (Kuala Lumpur: Dewan Bahasa dan Pustaka, 1985), p. 20.

137. Almenoar, "Political History of Singapore", p. 40. On the *daulat*, see Chandrasekaran Pillay, "Some Dominant Concepts and Dissenting Ideas on Malay Rule and the Malay Society from the Malacca to the Colonial and the Merdeka Periods" (PhD dissertation, University of Singapore, 1977), pp. 44–45.

138. Ibid., pp. 40–41.

139. *BH*, 25 April 1959, p. 1.

140. Esa was still active in the political successor of Singapore branch of UMNO, the Pertubuhan Kebangsaan Melayu Singapura (Singapore Malays National Organisation, PKMS), but retired in a year after the interview, see *ST*, 2

May 1985, p. 14. He died about a decade later, see *BH*, 9 November 1994, p. 10.

141. See the 13 reels of his interview in Tan Sri Syed Esa Almenoar, "Political History of Singapore 1945–1965 Accession No. 000013", Transcript of Oral History Recording, National Archives of Singapore (January 1984).

142. See ibid., Reel 001.

5

MULTIRACIAL, OR COMMUNAL ICON?

Breaking Racial Divides

The durability of class privileges in Singapore and the Federation was not totally divorced from the imprints of race. Upon Yusof's appointment as the Yang di-Pertuan Negara, the PAP government trumpeted the idea that he was to be a symbol of unity for all of Singapore, not a parochial figure for any racial community. During the installation ceremony, Lee emphatically broadcasted to the residents and citizens of Singapore that Yusof as Yang di-Pertuan Negara "symbolises all of us".[1] The Yang di-Pertuan Negara, as a national symbol, was therefore meant to transcend race. It is important to note that in the historical context, the difference between race or the physical colour of one's skin, and ethnicity, which connotes the cultural practices beyond the biological referent, was not a relevant distinction. As a legacy of colonial knowledge, the historical actors in late colonial Singapore viewed race as a marker which carried social meaning and was a signifier of cultural attributes. It was also an opaque cloak which obscured deeper structural issues stemming from class contentions, or the social relations of economic production.[2]

This message of transcending racial divisions subdued the status quo of colonial society in two ways. The first could be characterized by a "horizontal" movement. Under colonial rule, the British governed racial communities of Malaya separately, resulting in racialized division of labour and disparate socio-economic outcomes between different racial communities. British officials hardly gave any consideration to the formation of a post-racial sense of fraternity to bond their colonial subjects, at least before the Second World War.[3] The Malayan-born Yang di-Pertuan Negara was thus a corporeal symbol of transition into a more cohesive society. In his speech during Yusof's installation ceremony, the Singaporean prime minister was mindful of how class issues had become potently racialized:

> (t)he racial and cultural conflicts engendered by differing economic status between the indigenous peoples and the Chinese settlers in neighbouring countries are grim reminders to us to accomplish our task of integrating our peoples now and quickly.[4]

The PAP government aimed to eradicate communalism in Singapore. It recognized that the gulf between the socio-economic realities of Singapore's racial communities turned the already visible racial divides material. Furthermore, at the time of Yusof's installation in December 1959, neighbouring Indonesia was in the midst of a violent takeover of Chinese-owned businesses and properties, sparking an exodus of Chinese Indonesians to China.[5] This made interracial conflict a very sobering possibility for Singapore.

In its manifesto for the 1959 elections, the PAP canonized its belief that interracial tensions in Singapore stemmed from economic inequalities, which were the result of divisive colonial policies.[6] Even though the party subscribed to the idea that class divisions were the main impediments to a united society, it acknowledged that the people were still thinking in communal terms.[7] To remedy this situation, the party prescribed its "Malayan orientation of socialism", designed to outstrip material divides and converge the people towards a cohesive, "mass-based" society.[8] The PAP effectively melded its ethos of social equality with its outlook on race. Through socialist policies such as the creation of public housing, technical training and a fairer distribution of income, the PAP government hoped to equalize income positions of different racial groups, thereby vanquishing inequalities based on skin colour.

Although it was predominantly Chinese in composition, the PAP's membership also reflected this non-communal orientation. Cadres and leaders hailed from different racial backgrounds with the party opposing the classification of "Malayan-Chinese", "Malayan-Indians" or "Malayan-Malays" because it would undermine the formation of truly egalitarian society.[9] The PAP proclaimed:

> Divisions and loyalties based on race, colour and creed have no meaning for us. We do not worship at communal altars. We cannot be prey to old communal antipathies and prejudices. We cannot deviate from the high road of national unity and progress and lose ourselves in the blind alleys of communal chauvinism, whether they be of Malay, Chinese or Indian variety.[10]

This poetic message of transcending racial divisions clearly appealed to the electorate in Singapore, judging from the PAP's decisive victory during the 1959 elections. In his Mandarin speech to the Assembly in July 1959, Minister of Home Affairs Ong Pang Boon reiterated that the PAP government prioritized the building of a united community based on the principles of socialism, which centred on mass appeal as opposed to communal orientations.[11] To represent the dismantling of communal barriers, the PAP government launched a symbolic struggle towards a post-racial social order.

The Yang di-Pertuan Negara also subverted the racialist order of colonial society by way of a more "vertical" movement. The appointment of an individual who was not of Caucasian descent sought to invalidate any sense of inferiority attached to one's race. As much as empire was a hierarchical order along the lines of class, there was also the coexistence of a racial hierarchy.[12] This hierarchy upheld the supremacy of Whites, referring to those with Caucasian or European descent and relegated those from "coloured" racial backgrounds as lesser counterparts. Throughout much of the nineteenth and early twentieth centuries, the world system was organized along this racial hierarchy. European and American imperial states dominated the international system while subjugating territories with majority non-White populations. Even after the entrenchment of sovereign equality through the League of Nations and the UN, non-White countries continued to struggle against the global colour line and correct inequalities of wealth and power between them and former imperial states.[13]

This cross-territorial racial hierarchy was also reproduced in the social realities of colonized peoples. A "rule of colonial difference" sustained the rationale of White imperial rule over coloured societies, differentiating the colonizer and the colonized on the basis of skin colour.[14] Since Singapore's existence as part of the British Empire, the rulers of the island were "civilized" White men, except during the brief interlude of Japanese imperialism. By succeeding the colonial governor, Yusof heralded an unprecedented moment in Singapore's history since 1819, signalling a social revolution which the nationalist regime had hoped to engender. Indeed, Minister of Culture S. Rajaratnam announced to the people of Singapore that a Malayan-born Yang di-Pertuan Negara would be "rooted in this country" and "identified much closely to the aspirations and hopes of the people".[15] With Yusof as a symbol, the PAP government attempted to inculcate a sense of dignified confidence based on the idea that non-White peoples were as capable at governing themselves. This mood was not exclusive to Singapore but resonated with the spirit of nationalist movements throughout the larger Afro-Asian world.

To attest to the breakdown of racial divides, a distinct "multiracial" flair accompanied Yusof's installation as the first Malayan-born Yang di-Pertuan Negara. The parade following the swearing-in ceremony saw the participation of peoples from a myriad of different communities.[16] Commentaries of the event were also aired in four languages on *Radio Singapura*.[17] Religious institutions even took the initiative to commemorate the occasion in their own ways: a *chettiar* temple had a mass feeding session for the poor; Magain Aboth Synagogue held a special service; church bells rang throughout the island.[18]

In conjunction with Yusof's appointment, grand celebrations of Loyalty Week showcased the diversity of Singapore's racial communities and in doing so, promoted a sense of inclusive belonging to the State. The week-long festival was mirthful. It featured cultural performances, sporting events and exhibitions in a bid to flaunt the kaleidoscope of cultures inherited by residents of the city-state.[19] *Semai* dancers were even brought in from Pahang and Perak, while Chinese film stars from Hong Kong made their glittering appearances alongside acclaimed Malay film star, Kasma Booty.[20] There was a similar display planned for Singapore's first

National Day celebrations in June 1960. In one parade, floats displayed the values of this new Singapore, with two girls from each of the island's main racial communities standing on the "unity" float.[21] Mosques and churches organized special prayers to commemorate the occasion.[22] On that day, Yusof addressed the people of Singapore:

> ... more and more people are becoming conscious of getting down to the task of breaking down racial barriers, of forging ahead towards a better life of cultivating a sense of loyalty and belonging to the State and above all, of making a success of the various responsibilities which each and every one of us must carry in our private and public lives.[23]

With the lifting of the stifling colonial screen, the office generated a celebration of diversity. It became the task of the Yang di-Pertuan Negara to support the projection of a colourful yet unifying sense of identity.

Towards a Malayan Nation

For the PAP government, the endeavour to unify a diverse Singapore was inseparable from the efforts to further merger with the Federation. This important task required proactive intervention. To provide a guiding hand, Rajaratnam's Ministry of Culture spearheaded most of these nation-building initiatives to elucidate the enigma of what being "Malayan" actually meant.[24] Artists, literati and other practitioners in Singapore's cultural scene reciprocated the government's enthusiasm. During the 1960 Yang di-Pertuan Negara's Address, the government announced the formation of a "National Culture Brigade" to promote a common Malayan identity, inviting praise from Singapore's artists.[25] Ho Kok Hoe, president of the Singapore Art Society, further called on his fellow artists to form a "localized" artistic community devoted to the creative production of artworks which could both capture and inspire a sense of rootedness to Malayan life.[26] The PAP government also established the People's Association (PA) in 1960 to promote the bonding of the Singapore's racial communities through sports and recreation.[27]

In parallel to these initiatives, the PAP government enhanced the status of Malay, the lingua franca of the region, as Singapore's national language. It had already deployed the language to substantiate a sense of change during state rituals like the Yang di-Pertuan Negara's Address.

More ambitious than ever, the PAP government also rolled out a large-scale effort to promote Malay as a common medium of communication for the different racial communities by amending school curriculums and organizing evening classes for working adults.[28] It encouraged policemen, many of whom were Malay, to teach the language on a voluntary basis during these evening classes in order to make up for the shortfall in teachers, attesting to the intensity of this effort.[29] The growing use of the language would not only serve as a bridge between the racial communities, but it would also demonstrate Singapore's seriousness in merging with the Federation, where Malay had become the sole official language recognized by the Federal Constitution.[30] These efforts encouraged the residents of Singapore to abjure any other national loyalties and to identify themselves as individual parts of a united Malaya.

Yusof was not merely a symbolic generator of racial harmony, but through the embodied performance of his office, he also became an active participant in these government-led efforts. Part of his duties was to officiate ceremonies that were of "civic" character. These events involved organizations that were established based on varied causes, whether national, humanitarian or simply passionate in nature. The previous chapter has explored Yusof's role as patron to community organizations like the SJAB and the Scouts. Also on his long list of engagements were events of similar "racially neutral" character like sports meets and charity drives.[31] By officiating these events, the Yang di-Pertuan Negara encouraged a shared sense of community which blocked out overt communal features. He injected this message of post-racial fellowship wherever possible. To take a case in point, during the launch of a 1960 National Day carnival, Yusof declaimed:

> A national carnival which is as all-embracing as this is unprecedented in the history of Singapore. I would go so far as to say that this mighty effort is only possible because the people are thinking and organising along the national lines and for the national cause.[32]

On the surface, this racially sanitized movement to build a shared national character did not seem to contradict the concurrent strategy of celebrating the assortment of cultures in Singapore. For the PAP government, they were two prongs of the same effort to disempower racial divides under the new nationalist regime.

The Yang di-Pertuan Negara galvanized the acceptance of racial diversity, but at the same time, he encouraged a sense of racial transcendence. Yusof regularly officiated events which were deliberately choreographed to blunt any racial bearings which he might have carried. In May 1960, Yusof attended the International Bazaar for the School of the Blind, a clearly non-communal event. Children sang *Rasa Sayang*, *Ma-Ma-how* and *Linden Lea* in a multi-lingual recital to welcome the Yang di-Pertuan Negara, after which he echoed again the message of uniting communities.[33] Later in July, he attended a Red Cross fundraising ball as guest of honour. This dinner, held in a Chinese restaurant, advertised a multiracial guest list.[34] Yusof also inaugurated a cross-cultural heritage festival which featured performances in four languages in September that year.[35] While Malay in terms of his racial heritage, he symbolically challenged communal divides by simply being conspicuously present in these events.[36] In these outward displays of unity in diversity, the Yang di-Pertuan Negara, as the embodied representation of the nation, was the principal conductor who synthesized multiple medleys of different racial identities into a grander Malayan symphony.

While these events were largely dignified and symbolic, at times, they carried a potent political charge to confront the tenacious force of communalism. On National Day in 1961, the Yang di-Pertuan Negara made an unusually antagonistic speech at the Padang in front of the 15,000-strong crowd, directing his attacks against "the communalist":

Although the communalist has had a lean time during the last two years, we must not underestimate his power of evil … the communalist hopes to come to power by exploiting the latent prejudices of people who have not learnt to think in terms of Malayan nationalism.[37]

Framing the battle against communalism as a moral battle of "good versus evil" amplified the need to transcend parochial boundaries of race, providing a persuasive yet simplistic dichotomy of black and white.

The Yang di-Pertuan Negara occasionally fused his impassioned calls for a common post-racial Malayan identity with personal anecdotes. During a visit to his alma mater in June 1961, Yusof proudly revealed that it was during his time in Raffles Institution that he began to consider himself "a Malayan first, second a Malay".[38] He correspondingly spoke of "hopeful signs" that a Malayan identity was forming in Singapore during a dinner hosted by the Old Rafflesian Association that same month. In his address to the illustrious alumni of the school, Yusof urged his audience to pay due respect to Sir Stamford Raffles as "the first Malayan" and a "true friend of the Malays" because the colonial adventurer had shown a keen interest in the customs and history of the region.[39] In his eagerness to convey the value of a localized "Malayan" identity beyond the bounds of race, the Yang di-Pertuan Negara—Singapore's most exalted anti-colonial symbol—had ironically revealed his admiration for the man who had brought the colonial enterprise to the island in the first place.

While the Yang di-Pertuan Negara was a signifier of the breaking of racial barriers, he did not isolate himself from events that were overtly religious or specific to one community. During these occasions, Yusof reliably infused the message of racial transcendence which he was entrusted with. In September 1960, he had dinner with Muslim leaders, most of whom were Malay, at the Raffles' Hotel to commemorate the Prophet Muhammad's birthday. Yusof once again repeated the message of getting past parochial identifications despite the event being a religious gathering. He persuaded the guests to take the Prophet as an example of "mutual tolerance", while proclaiming:

> We have lived together in peace and tranquillity and it is a source of pride to the people of Singapore that the process of building a nation is being pursued in the spirit of mutual tolerance and harmony among the many races in this country.[40]

In his 1961 Hari Raya message, Yusof called upon Muslims in Singapore to contribute towards building a more united Singapore. He reminded listeners that Islam wanted its followers to be "free from prejudice and ignorance".[41]

The Yang di-Pertuan Negara further directed distinctive racial identities towards a more cosmopolitan orientation in an attempt to lighten the weight of communalism. During an event to celebrate the contributions of Singapore's Scottish community, Yusof remarked in jest that while he found the "mysterious haggis" perplexing, the government was serious about Scots joining the "Malayan" nation and playing their part in forming a "world culture".[42] In April 1961, the Yang di-Pertuan Negara opened an exhibition of Malay art and commended Malay artists for their work. He confessed to the crowd that the best artworks at the exhibition were those that incorporated "what was good and healthy from other sources".[43] This exhibition, however, stirred tensions within the local artist community. About two months later, a veteran Malay artist complained to the *Berita Harian* that he was deliberately side-lined by fellow artists. According to him, the artworks displayed during the April exhibition were in no way "national" but were rather "Western". Sharing his experience as a visitor to the exhibition, he claimed that the Yang di-Pertuan Negara had (sarcastically) asked "which sultan's palace is that?" when looking at one of his student's artistic works, probably hinting at its rustic features.[44] Through Yusof's social interactions, the Yang di-Pertuan Negara prodded the demolition of "backward" racial loyalties and spurred a "progressive" cosmopolitan outlook.

Festering Anxieties of Colonial Rule

The colourful overtones associated with Yusof's appointment and duties camouflaged the racialist discourse which was institutionalized by his office. One only needs to scrape the symbolic and temporal layers of the office to understand how the Yang di-Pertuan Negara maintained a fragile façade—a tenuous symbol which concealed the spectre of race within Singapore's new constitutional arrangements. During the global age of decolonization, British officials stationed all over the empire often interpreted the increasing demands for self-determination as a swelling of uncontrolled passions among colonized peoples—Whitehall correspondences often conflated what was "anti-colonial" and "anti-European". To establish themselves as superior based on racial origins, the British perpetuated a deep-rooted colonial discourse as an "apparatus of state power". [45] This entailed an "othering" of the colonized, or the creation of essentialized divisions between the White colonial rulers and the non-White colonial populations when thinking, representing and managing the latter.

In Singapore and the Federation, the British continued to repeat the colonial discourse even as they began to reluctantly comprehend that their colonial subjects could be capable of modern governance, resulting in an ambivalent attitude towards the entire project of decolonization.[46] To take a case in point, the British high commissioner in the Federation, Sir Donald MacGillivray, played up the idea of "Pan-Asian solidarity" in March 1956 when advising the Colonial Office about self-determination in Singapore. Expressing his sentiments just six months after the Bandung Conference, he prepared a lengthy memorandum detailing the different political aspirations of nationalist leaders in Singapore and the Federation. But in spite of the nuances, MacGillivray reminded the colonial secretary that "although Singapore is predominantly Chinese and the Federation is politically Malay, both Chinese and Malays are 'Asian', a word that is having an increasingly emotional content".[47] There was a simplistic basis underlining his framing of decolonization. It stiffened the idea that despite varied circumstances of both territories, ultimately it came down to a facile dichotomy of Whites against non-Whites—a rhetoric of "us against them".

With this image of a restive bloc of coloured peoples, the British genuinely felt their power slipping and questioned the loyalties of their subjects. MacGillivray's memorandum only fed into the prejudices of Whitehall officials when they were drawing contingency plans to deal with possible unrest should the constitutional talks with the Marshall delegation fail. A report from the General Headquarters (GHQ) of the Far Eastern Land Forces made chilling claims that if riots were to become widespread, the governor in Singapore would have insufficient security personnel at his disposal. The report outlined that in Singapore, the "police rank and file [were] Malays from the Federation whose loyalty could not be guaranteed in all circumstances".[48] To back the police, there were only two companies of British military troops on the island, one of which was the Singapore Guard Regiment, a unit comprised mainly of Malay soldiers.

Governor Robert Black stood behind these worries. He explained to the colonial secretary that the loyalty of Malay police officers and soldiers in Singapore were "passing to UMNO" following the party's ascendency in the Federation.[49] The oaths of loyalty which the Malay security personnel had undertaken as well as their years of service to the Crown all amounted to nothing. These suspicions were not at all novel but stemmed from long-standing fears of native revolt. In the empire, a sense of insecurity was chronic among the paper-thin strata of White inhabitants in non-settler colonies. Since the non-White population vastly outnumbered them, it gave the impression that colonial subjects could easily rise up against their White colonial masters. Violent episodes of colonial uprising by non-White imperial troops like the 1857 Indian Rebellion and the 1915 Singapore Mutiny continued to haunt Whitehall's institutional memory, feeding these fears.[50] While the Malays were posing one problem, the same GHQ report forewarned that the Chinese in Singapore would transform the island into a satellite of either the Kuomintang or Communist China upon British withdrawal.[51] British officials saw decolonization as the gradual takeover of their colonies by coloured peoples who caballed along the lines of racial loyalties. These prejudices thus mangled with the security imperatives used to justify prolonged colonial rule in Singapore.

Their racial prejudices also fattened British scepticism towards the future office of Yang di-Pertuan Negara. When Lim Yew Hock refused to give up on the idea of a Malayan governor-general in the lead up to the 1957 talks, British officials began collating a list of repercussions which might arise from the creation of the proposed office. What was disturbing for them was the possibility of a non-White person ranking higher than any other White official in the hierarchy of a colony.[52] This challenged the very fundamentals of the imperial project, which sought to maintain the image of British paramountcy. Governor Black even tried to offer the possibility of "an Englishman who was a political figure" as Crown representative in the hopes of persuading Lim to agree to a dignified White appointee with political clout rather than a detached White bureaucrat.[53] This same line of thinking went into the selection of a governor-general for Ghana earlier that year. Whitehall officials believed that Crown representatives in the non-White colonies should not only be "mentors" for local political leaders but also have experience as political insiders in the United Kingdom.[54]

Chief Minister Lim categorically refused Black's offer. The most valuable premise of the Malayan governor-general was the idea of a local personage serving as the common receptacle of loyalty for the people of Singapore. Moreover, there was also very little effort to distinguish anti-White or anti-European animosities from demands for independence. When Colonial Secretary Alan Lennox-Boyd recounted Lim's position on the Malayan governor-general to the British Cabinet, he stated that a local-born appointee would have "the ground cut away from under the feet of the current anti-European and anti-colonial agitators".[55] His rhetoric leaned on the simplistic idea of an Asian pied piper mesmerizing other Asians to placate bitterness against White people, trivializing the manifold grievances which constituted anti-colonialism.

Another worrying prospect was the demoralizing effect a non-White Crown representative might have on expatriate civil servants in Singapore, particularly those who occupy the higher echelons of the security forces. After coming into power in 1955, the Marshall government launched an aggressive drive to Malayanize the civil service, rattling Whitehall circles. British officials warned local ministers that the hasty removal of expatriates in favour of local-born officers would compromise the efficiency of the entire civil service.[56] Yusof, the future Yang di-Pertuan Negara, was part of the Malayanization Commission, the official body that recommended extensive efforts to phase out expatriate manpower from the Singaporean civil service. In March 1956, Governor Black notified the colonial secretary about the Commission's anti-European stance because it comprised of people who held "extreme views", describing their public hearings as "bitter and unscrupulous attacks on European officers and the Public Service Commission".[57]

The representative of the Crown in Singapore had always been the head of the colony's civil service. If he was a local-born (non-White) appointee, the British presumed that expatriate officers might no longer feel secure about their jobs and would deliberately hasten their retirement plans, precipitating a collapse of Singapore's defence, internal security and state services. British Commissioner-General in Southeast Asia Robert Scott piled on Black's wariness. He was not sure if the Malayan Crown representative would be competent enough to oversee the smooth running of the State. According to him, "a new, untried, inexperienced—and most certainly not very competent—Malayan in Government House would be to take a great risk indeed".[58] With no clue about the eventual identity of the Malayan Crown representative, Scott was already doubtful of the appointee's capability to preside over the state. These sentiments reeked of the racial prejudices which Singapore's colonial rulers continued to harbour against the Asians whom they governed.

Even though Whitehall eventually settled on the office of Yang di-Pertuan Negara during the 1957 constitutional talks, doubts about the unpredictable nature of an Asian Crown representative still persisted. In May 1958, when the foundations of the Yang di-Pertuan Negara were still relatively fluid, British officials reckoned with the potential powers and scope of the future office. One thread of discussion concerned the ability of the Asian Crown representative to pardon British soldiers sentenced to death row by court martial. D.R.E. Hopkins, an official in the War Office, articulated his concerns to his colleagues from the Colonial Office about possible issues with a "non-British person" assenting to the execution of British soldiers.[59] Under the provisions of the 1881 Army Act, all executions conducted in a British colony would require the approval of the governor. Hopkins clarified that the Army Act mandated the governor's approval for an execution because the powers of clemency was invested in him as the local Crown representative.

With the reconstitution of the governorship into the office of Yang di-Pertuan Negara, these powers now lay in the hands of a non-White, Malayan-born person. Hopkins further underscored that when the provisions of the Army Act were first enacted, the idea of an Asian Crown representative was simply unfathomable.[60] In response, the Colonial Office assured him that the new constitutional arrangements circumvented this problem. Executions of soldiers took place in military prisons, and since the defence of Singapore firmly remained the responsibility of the British government, any sentence dispensed under court martial would fall under British jurisdiction.[61] Whatever went on in British military installations was strictly British business.

There was nevertheless a nervous sense of liberal self-righteousness towards this issue. Out of respect to local authority, officials agreed that military authorities stationed on the island should inform the Yang di-Pertuan Negara about executions carried out on Singaporean soil, even though he would not be able to veto them.[62] The War Office even suggested inserting an extraordinary clause into the Constitution to exempt the Yang di-Pertuan Negara from pardoning British military personnel. Officials in the Colonial Office nevertheless resisted this move because there was no precedent in other self-governing colonies. They were particularly worried that a discriminatory clause on the basis of race would result in a parliamentary backlash should British lawmakers in Westminster catch wind of the plan.[63] This situation demonstrated that even at the tail end of imperial rule, the "rule of colonial difference" still actively shaped the decision-making processes concerning decolonization. The ambivalent colonial discourse employed here was not just racialist, but it also came with a distinct tinge of racism. It perpetuated a deference to a racial hierarchy and the "otherness" of the Asian Crown representative. The ability of the Malayan-born Yang di-Pertuan Negara to decide the fates of White men remained a petrifying prospect for the official mind in London. Rather than accepting shifting mores which came with the age of decolonization, the British refused to confront the discomforting challenges to imperial pride, choosing instead to circumvent the issue using a legal technicality.

Minority Woes

Besides the colonial colour bar, local interracial tensions harrowed the symbolic meanings of the Yang di-Pertuan Negara. The celebration of racial transcendence attendant to the office in fact carried traces of disquiet felt by the Malays throughout British Malaya, not just in Chinese-majority Singapore. Under British colonial rule, the exploitative system of capitalism had resulted in unequal development among the different racial communities.[64] British capital enjoyed special treatment due to the intervention of the colonial state in the economy. Exclusive laws ossified the Malay peasantry, while British and Chinese capital interests remained largely unchecked, resulting in structural impediments for Malays to own the means to produce wealth.[65] Over time, Malay socio-economic dislocation began to trouble the British, who feared a full-blown Malay revolt against colonial rule. To ensure that the colonial enterprise remained lucrative, the British enshrined Malay indigeneity into the laws of the colonial state, guaranteeing the "special position" of the Malays while enshrining the colonial state as protector of indigenous Malay interests.

Things, however, were much worse for the Malays in Singapore. With the island serving as a primary node for both Chinese and British economic activity, the racial community held a precarious socio-economic position with little of the "protection" accorded to Malays of the peninsula. The lack of local indigenous leadership on the island further compounded on the community's sense of vulnerability. In the Malay states, the British institutionalized the rulers as representatives of their Malay subjects, but in Singapore, there was no such insurance; with the demise of the British-sponsored sultanate in the colony, there was no Malay personage who could speak for Malay interests with authority. Considering this void, wealthier non-Malay Muslims—many of whom were of Arab and South Asian descent and were more dominant in the colonial elite class— began to position themselves as leaders of all Muslims in Singapore.[66] It was in this context that Malay leaders in Singapore formed the KMS in 1926 with the aim of advocating for Malay rights and welfare in the colony. But while the political organization made inroads to push for the upliftment of the racial community, the crippling effects of the Great Depression and the Second World War inhibited any significant change.

During the initial postwar decade, it was clear that the Singaporean Malays were suffering from long-term socio-economic marginalization. London-trained economist Dr Goh Keng Swee, who was to be a key ally of Lee Kuan Yew in the future PAP government, published a 1954 report on incomes and housing in Singapore. One of his key findings was that destitution did not recognize the boundaries of race.[67] But claims of Malay socio-economic marginalization become apparent after a careful reading of other sections of the data. While the Malay working class was performing slightly above average in terms of income, other economic parameters did not provide an encouraging picture. The racial community was significantly underrepresented in the elite income strata and had lower levels of disposable wealth. As a result of the colonial education policy, the Malays were a generation behind in establishing an English-educated professional class in comparison to the Chinese.[68] Comprador capital also remained dominant in the economies of both Singapore and the Federation, but the Chinese formed an overwhelming portion of local capitalists.[69] In their attempts to legitimize themselves as most deserving to inherit power, Singaporean leaders had to wrestle with the socio-economic marginalization of the Malays.

Developments taking place north of Singapore turned concern into exigency. In the Federation, elites of the different racial communities achieved a political settlement through a constitutional guarantee of the special position of the Malays as the country's indigenous people, upholding the privileged status of their language, religion and culture. As a further instrument to safeguard Malay political dominance, the rulers were additionally given constitutional roles as guardians of Malay rights and customs.[70] Singapore remained constitutionally untethered to these constitutional developments taking place in the Federation. For the Singaporean Malays, the appearance of British withdrawal thereby incited feelings of insecurity towards the uncharted prospect of a Chinese-dominated government ruling the island.

Fears of a Chinese-dominated government, however, were not exclusive to the Singaporean Malays. In January 1957, representatives of other minority groups in Singapore came together to discuss the impending constitutional talks between the Colonial Office and the all-party delegation led by Lim Yew Hock. The convention's attendance list was colourful. Leaders from the Eurasian Association, the Malayan Indian Congress, the Straits Chinese Business Association, the British-European Association as well as the KMS signed a joint petition addressed to the colonial secretary. Going against the demands of the all-party delegation, they expressed their lack of faith in party politics to truly represent the different communities in Singapore and wanted a safeguard in the form of reserved seats in the future legislature. The signatories claimed that the petition was not one instigated by "frightened minorities" but was a serious effort to institutionalize "non-racial, non-party interests" as adjuncts to the system of elected representation.[71] Proposing to work together in a non-political alliance, the organizations intended to recommend names for these reserved seats.

The tenor of this "minority memorandum" was not peculiar. In their more socially diverse colonies, the British entrenched a racialized format of reserved representation for minority groups, honouring the "enlightened" liberalism of the imperial project.[72] What was particularly jarring was that the KMS smuggled itself into the convention even though it was effectively a political party which had participated in previous elections. The KMS party leader, Tengku Muda Mohamed, no doubt capitalized on his prestige as a descendent of Singapore's former royal family to fashion his political image as the most eminent spokesperson for the Singaporean Malays. But in a blow to Tengku Muda's ambitions, a coalition of Malay community organizations formed the Malay National Congress a month later to denounce his cooperation with other minority communities. The Congress sent a counter-petition to the colonial secretary to treat the "minorities memorandum" as "unrecognised and most unwarranted by the Malays".[73] Delegates then settled on a mandate to "strengthen and unite" the Malays in Singapore and strive for British recognition of "Malay ownership of the island".[74] A segment of the Malay community clearly did not see their positions as equal to other minorities, insisting that as Singapore's indigenous people, the Malays were deserving of exclusive rights. Despite their demands, the scope and form of these rights remained vague. This backlash was not only a strong indication of Malay restiveness towards greater self-government in Singapore, but also proof of the heterogenous aspirations within the racial community.

Due to the divisions within the community, there was a heavy contest for the right to speak for, defend and represent the Malays in Singapore. An array of organizations and parties championed for the welfare and exclusive privileges for the racial community, but the most prominent among them had to be the Singaporean branch of UMNO. The party was after all the junior coalition partner in the Marshall and Lim Yew Hock governments, and its president, Hamid Jumat, was deputy chief minister. The party's parent organization in Kuala Lumpur was furthermore the leading force of the Alliance government in the Federation. UMNO's political weight allowed the party to posture itself as the authoritative voice of the Singaporean Malays. In 1957, during preparatory discussions for the constitutional talks in London, UMNO presented its shopping list to other members of the all-party delegation: a Malay as head of state, Malay as the sole official language and Islam, the predominant faith of the Malays, as the state religion.

While these demands were a clear gesture towards merger by mimicking the clauses of the Federal Constitution, other members of the all-party delegation rejected them. In retaliation, UMNO threatened to withdraw from the talks. Other members of the all-party delegation, however, recognized that they would lose credibility should UMNO follow through with its threat. The British could simply cite the lack of minority representation to deny any further constitutional concessions. Consensus was achieved only after the Tunku made a day trip to Singapore to mediate the dispute. To appease UMNO's concerns and put up a cohesive front, the all-party delegation came to a gentlemen's agreement to appoint a Malay as the first Malayan-born Crown representative.[75] Later during the talks, the all-party delegation accepted the inclusion of an "indigenous clause" in the preamble of the proposed Constitution. This was a constitutional guarantee which legally bounded the future Singaporean government to improve the lives of Malays in the city-state.[76] Besides recognizing the "special position of the Malays, who are the indigenous people of the island", the clause also tied the government "to protect, safeguard, support, foster and promote their political, educational, religious, economic, social and cultural interest and the Malay language".[77] But as extensive as this sounded, a few sections of the Malay community were not satisfied.

It was amid this incendiary state of affairs that the woes of the Singaporean Malays latched onto the symbolic meaning of the Yang di-Pertuan Negara. In May 1958, after the all-party delegation and the Colonial Office agreed on the main points of the new Constitution, Hamid blazoned the earlier gentlemen's agreement on a Malay Yang di-Pertuan Negara and made a personal pledge to fulfil it, portraying himself as the long-awaited saviour of the Malays.[78] He reiterated this commitment to party colleagues after UMNO passed the resolution to restore the Sultanate of Singapore in October that year. For a significant section of the party, a sovereign Malay ruler in Singapore would provide a firmer warranty of the privileged position of the Malays.[79]

Expectations of a Malay titular figure soon began to gain traction in the run-up towards the 1959 elections. Hoping to chisel away UMNO's monopoly over Malay political representation, other Malay-based parties, like the island branch of the PMIP and the KMS, also called for a Malay Yang di-Pertuan Negara.[80] In February 1959, the Tengku Muda submitted a petition to the Queen, which was cited earlier in a previous chapter. The petition demanded that Her Majesty appoint a descendant of Hussein

Shah as Crown representative. It then proceeded to inflame fears of a Chinese-dominated PAP government in Singapore:

> The removal of the Union Jack and the disbandment of the mace from City Hall are again attributable to the concern of the people of Singapore. The Malays have no confidence that the PAP will maintain and reserve the rights of the Malays when it become [sic] the government. In view of this, the Malay Union advises Your Majesty's government to be more careful and cautious in its dealing with the Singapore constitutional reforms particularly in regard to the privileges and rights of the Malays as the rightful owner and sons of the soil of the island of Singapore.[81]

This petition as well as the sustained attempts to push for a Malay titular figure—whether in the form of sultan or Yang di-Pertuan Negara—casted aspersions on the PAP's ability to protect Malay interests.

While the PAP enjoyed a handsome electoral victory in the 1959 polls, UMNO still won comfortably in three Malay-majority constituencies, embedding the party as the PAP's main rival in providing a political voice for the Singaporean Malays. Even though UMNO lost power and was no longer part of the Singaporean government, segments within the party continued to actively campaign for their earlier plans to restore the Sultanate of Singapore.[82] These initiatives aggravated the perception of a deficit in the Constitution and sowed further distrust towards the PAP government in the Malay community.

Diluting Chineseness

Well aware of the Chinese image of the city-state, Singaporean leaders saw the appointment of the Yang di-Pertuan Negara as a critical instrument to advance merger and to appease the Singaporean Malays. Even as far back as 1956, Lim Yew Hock had indicated to British officials that he wanted a Malay as the Crown representative, hoping that the appointment would quell the Federation's suspicions towards a Chinese-dominated Singapore. In August 1956, Governor Black enquired if the Singaporean chief minister would consider Marshall for the office as a way to turn a Malayan anti-colonial personality into a symbol of self-determination. Knowing full well of his predecessor's erratic behaviour, that possibility was particularly repulsive for Lim. Marshall was also a Sephardic Jew. According to Lim, Marshall's appointment would not be as valuable as an "old Malay" or a "Malay from the Federation" when it came to the cause of merger.[83] Black further suggested Sir Han Hoe Lim, former Chairman of the Public Service Commission, but Chief Minister Lim resisted the idea and postulated that he would "prefer not to have a Chinese".[84]

As Lim sketched premature plans to appoint the future Yang di-Pertuan Negara, the PAP was having a particularly difficult battle against its "Chineseness". Although the party held onto an ideology that presumably transcended boundaries of race, religion and gender, it failed to arrest claims that it was under the control of Chinese chauvinists.[85] In 1958, a group socialist-leaning UMNO members defected to the PAP in frustration over their former party's failure to uplift the socio-economic position of the Malays.[86] The defection seemingly moderated the PAP's Chinese image and supplemented the party with a crew of Malay grassroots activists. In its 1959 election manifesto, the PAP tried to attenuate demographic anxieties in the Federation.[87] It admitted that Chinese chauvinism was plaguing its party brand and that this image could have regional implications as it played into feelings of indignation harboured by the indigenous communities in Indonesia and the Federation towards their more affluent Chinese citizens.[88] Recognizing that the appearance of a Chinese-dominated government was a liability for the city-state, the PAP promised to take steps to allay Malay fears both in Singapore and the Federation as a means to advance merger.[89]

The party's electoral victory in June 1959 became testament to this promise. Seven out of the PAP's forty-three elected lawmakers were Malay.[90] One of its most significant post-election moves was to staff the Cabinet with ministers from different racial communities in a bid to dilute the party's Chinese-ness; of the nine PAP ministers, six were Chinese while the other three were Malay, Eurasian and Malayali respectively.[91] In one of his first speeches to the Assembly as prime minister, Lee Kuan Yew disclosed his personal determination to tackle Chinese chauvinism:

> I hope, if there is nothing else that we have achieved in the course of
> the next five years, we will at least have achieved one thing—prove
> conclusively in a Chinese-dominated city that to play the Chinese

Chauvinist line is not the way to power, that a Party which carries with it the majority of the Chinese can act in a way which fits into the context and pattern of a Malayan society, and not a Chinese society.[92]

Immersed with post-election euphoria, the premier went on to confidently contrast the PAP's mass appeal against the MCA's communal-based ideology, making a clear jibe at the governing formula of the Alliance in the Federation.[93] If anyone should be accused of Chinese chauvinism, it was the MCA—UMNO's traditional coalition partner—not the "racially blind" PAP. This political posturing, however, did little to build trust with the UMNO-led Alliance government. The Tunku later characterized the PAP government's political thought as "alien to Malay ideas" and "were based more or less on Chinese ideas".[94] In trying to rebrand itself as a non-Chinese party, the PAP plunged even further into the depths of communal politics.

Following the 1959 elections, political skirmish between the UMNO branch in Singapore and the PAP went into full swing. Goode, as interim Yang di-Pertuan Negara, delivered the PAP government's first Yang di-Pertuan Negara Address in July 1959 to the Assembly. During the subsequent debate on the Address, Ali Alwi, the UMNO assemblyman for Kampong Kembangan, deplored Goode's silence on the special position of the Malays.[95] For Ali, the PAP government had failed to spell out its plans to translate the "indigenous clause" enshrined in the Constitution into policy. He played up the PAP's nonchalance towards Malay sensitivities:

I say this because what struck me most recently when the PAP gained its overwhelming victory and introduced its successful election candidates at the City Hall, was the use of symbols ... If we were to visit that building now we can see that all the symbols are unintelligible to the Malays. This is a source of concern and fear to the Malays.[96]

Ali was probably referring to the PAP's lightning bolt insignia and election banners in Mandarin, alleging that they seemed foreign and "communist".[97] The conjoined twins of Chinese-ness and communism was alive and well. Displaying a party's symbol might not seem too controversial, but Ali was embittering the existing sense of dislocation amongst the Singaporean Malays. Adding further bite to his criticisms, he flagged problems in the government's promotion of the Malay language. On the surface, it seemed favourable to use Malay as the common medium of communication among different racial communities since it would ensure the dignified status of the language. Despite this, Ali predicted that the increasing number of Malay-speaking non-Malays would compete with Malays who were in their jobs because of their command of the language.[98] These assessments only aggravated class-based racial anxieties.

The PAP, however, defended the party's concern for the Malays. Minister Ahmad Ibrahim assured the Assembly of the PAP's faithfulness to the "indigenous clause" by pointing out that the government's socialist policies would help all, regardless of race.[99] Malay lawmakers from the PAP then launched a concerted rebuke against UMNO, accusing the latter of doing little to help the Malays when it was part of government.[100] But UMNO was not a lone wolf in howling the cries of dislocation. Ali's criticisms correlated with complaints published in the Malay-language press, expressing uneasiness towards increasing airtime for *"Tionghua"* programmes on the local radio channel, *Radio Singapura*, with some claiming that the Malays were being treated like *"orang menumpang"* or temporary tenants.[101] This rhetoric was forceful. Being recognized as indigenous to the island while having to witness creeping signs of their cultural displacement would only foment resentment among Singaporean Malays.

The PAP government was hardly any different from ex-Chief Minister Lim when it came to racializing the Yang di-Pertuan Negara for the purpose of merger. In September 1959, there were rumours about the PAP government's plans to appoint the recently retired Federation Finance Minister and MCA politician, Tun Lee Hau Shik, as Singapore's first Malayan-born Crown representative. The news caught many by surprise, even Tun Lee himself.[102] As a close ally of the Tunku and a key figure in the Federation's independence movement, Tun Lee as Yang di-Pertuan Negara would presumably help Singapore advance the cause of a united Malaya. But his appointment would also be parlous. The Malays in Singapore might read it as the PAP's attempt to seal the Chinese character of the city-state, breaching the 1957 gentlemen's agreement on a Malay Crown representative.

These rumours notwithstanding, correspondence between Goode and the Colonial Office provides a different picture. When Lee Kuan Yew first indicated his intention to appoint a scion from a Malayan royal family as Yang di-Pertuan Negara, British officials praised the Singaporean prime minister. They believed that appointing a Malay from a prestigious royal background would not only accelerate merger but also relieve interracial anxieties in Singapore.[103] For Lee, a Malay occupying the highest office of the state to balance off the Chinese-dominated Singaporean government was a step towards the racially blind society which his party had envisioned. Since the formation of the PAP government, the composition of senior offices of the State adhered to this vision: the prime minister was Chinese, the chief justice was British, the speaker of the Legislative Assembly was Eurasian, and the head of the Public Service Commission was Malay.[104] By nominating a Malay candidate as Yang di-Pertuan Negara, the PAP government would hit the nail on the coffin, taming the incessant accusations of latent Chinese chauvinism mounted against the party.

British officials, however, were more restrained when Lee nominated Yusof as Yang di-Pertuan Negara in October 1959. As discussed in the last chapter, they were not too keen on the latter because of his dealings with Samad and MCP elements. But after failing to find a willing royal personality, Lee's options were constrained. Goode reported to the Colonial Office that the Singaporean prime minister "was set on having a Malay" because "the Malay community as a whole (was) generally hostile to the PAP government".[105] The former governor cited UMNO's continued push for a Singaporean sultan and the imperative to temper the PAP's Chinese bearing in preparation for merger as reasons for Lee's resolve to find a suitable Malay candidate. Lee had little room to manoeuvre. Should he breach the 1957 gentlemen's agreement on a Malay Crown representative, the PAP leader would most likely enrage the Singaporean Malays who were already suspicious of his government. In doing so, he would also worsen the chances for merger since it might offend the Tunku, the broker of the gentlemen's agreement.

Lee was adamant that the future Yang di-Pertuan Negara must not only be Malay, but he also had to be respectable enough in the eyes of the Chinese, who were after all the PAP's main support base. According to

Goode, Lee was fully aware that the Chinese would not respect anyone who bore any "signs of financial or moral laxity or who would not impress his dignity onto them".[106] Among other contenders of standing was Dato' Suleiman, the minister of interior from the Federation. In fact, it was the Federation's Deputy Prime Minister Razak who had recommended him as a possible candidate to Lee. Not wanting to turn the office of Yang di-Pertuan Negara into a retirement post for politicians from the Federation, Lee politely turned down Razak's suggestion.[107]

After further deliberations, the British began to sympathize with Lee's conundrum and gradually adopted a more amenable position towards Yusof's nomination. Among the most senior officers of the State, Sir George Oehlers, the speaker of the Legislative Assembly, was the Colonial Office's preferred choice as Yang di-Pertuan Negara. British officials nevertheless recognized that Oehlers's Eurasian heritage "count[ed] against him" and that he was no match for a "full-blooded Malay".[108] An alternative choice was Chief Justice Sir Alan Rose. He carried a dignified impartiality that was ideal for the office but did not qualify because he was not Malayan-born.[109] Evidently, the British did not mind the appointment of a non-Malay as Yang di-Pertuan Negara. The move to appoint a Malay as Yang di-Pertuan Negara was therefore a deliberate strategy on Lee's part to accumulate political capital for the PAP government.

Besides Yusof, there were still other prominent Malay personalities in the city-state. One of them was Tengku Muda, the most senior member of the former royal family of Singapore. As recounted in a previous chapter, the KMS leader had effectively put himself forward when submitting the February 1959 petition to the Queen, which demanded the appointment of a descendant of Hussein Shah as Crown representative.[110] The British, however, were relieved that Lee kept his distance from Tengku Muda. They labelled the troubled prince as "politically, personally, financially persona non grata".[111] He never won a single electoral contest, and as evidenced by the backlash towards the "minorities memorandum", Tengku Muda was a divisive figure in the Singaporean Malay community. In November 1959, he became a bankrupt after failing to pay a debt of $696.62 owed to an Indian moneylender.[112] Tapping into whatever remnants of his royal prestige was not worth embarrassing Singapore and the PAP government.

Hamid Jumat, the UMNO party leader and ex-deputy chief minister, was another obvious choice. Although Hamid was re-elected as an assemblyman during the 1959 elections, the British understood that a ghost from a discredited former regime would only be a hazard for the PAP, which came into power by laying claim to a clean slate. In addition to that, UMNO was hostile to the PAP and was a political competitor. It seemed that for the Singaporean prime minister, Yusof was the only logical choice given the circumstances. Initially, Lee's strategy to racialize the Yang di-Pertuan Negara reaped some dividends. Upon his appointment as Yang di-Pertuan Negara, newspapers in the Federation circulated the fact that a Malay was now occupying Singapore's highest office.[113] The move to appoint Yusof nevertheless exposed the difficulty of looking beyond racial identifications in spite of the proselytization of a "mass-based" ideology by the PAP government.

A Malay man to personify Singapore—this was not objectionable to the Singaporean branch of UMNO considering Ali's earlier demand for a recognizable symbol for the Malays, not to mention the party's undying demands for a Malay titular figure. The *Utusan*, by this time firmly affiliated with the central UMNO branch in Kuala Lumpur, lauded the Singaporean government's decision to appoint its former boss as Yang di-Pertuan Negara, who was purportedly a Malay through and through.[114] Once Yusof's appointment became public knowledge, the Singaporean branch of UMNO had a change of heart and reversed its earlier intention to boycott the installation ceremony. This short-lived plan was initially undertaken as a protest to the presence of political flags during the ceremonial marchpast. UMNO saw this as a clear violation of the Yang di-Pertuan Negara's unifying and non-partisan spirit.[115]

According to Aziz Ishak, one of the reasons why his elder brother agreed to the appointment was because he believed in the need to soften the PAP's Chineseness and to convey the government's commitment to a non-communal Malayan nation—a task which Yusof was happy to oblige in further testament to his private support for the party.[116] Although this symbolic move alone may not be enough to persuade the Tunku to agree to merger, it illustrated the PAP's seriousness in tempering with its alleged links to Chinese chauvinism. Lee chose Yusof precisely because of his racial identity. He offered the Malays in Singapore a visible symbol of inclusivity through the dignification of someone from the racial community. While promoted as a symbol of the breakdown of racial barriers and an emblem of communal transcendence, the Yang di-Pertuan Negara in actuality consolidated the racialist mould of the colonial order. Race continued to matter in this "new" Singapore.

It was also difficult to shatter racial divisions in the midst of ad nauseum state-sponsored attempts to parade the diversity of Singapore's racial communities. Despite fashioning the Yang di-Pertuan Negara as a conduit to channel a new "Malayan" identity, even the PAP government was not too sure about what really was "Malayan".[117] Did the label stand for a post-racial fraternity based on cultural fusion, or a mere coexistence of different racial communities under a grand multiracial umbrella?[118] When celebrations of Loyalty Week kicked off following Yusof's appointment, political pressure began piling on Rajaratnam. He had to face the Assembly and decipher what the government meant by a "Malayan" culture:

> No one has the intelligence, the imagination and the breadth of knowledge to indicate precisely what the nature of Malayan culture should be ... It is not a matter for any one person to determine, because that will be decided by the people who create the culture—the artists, the dramatists and the painters—and nobody can lay down the law either by administrative actions or by speeches ... I believe that the first step towards the creation of a Malayan consciousness ... is to create what I would call an awareness of and respect for the cultures of other communities.[119]

The PAP government seemed to favour a rather democratic approach towards defining what it saw as "Malayan", but this sparked more questions than answers.

In a rebuttal, Ali went on a scathing diatribe to bring the PAP's hypocrisy out into the open. The UMNO assemblyman shared how he felt isolated when Chinese lawmakers from the PAP spoke in Mandarin amongst themselves, pointing out that the government's earlier plans to have Mandarin lessons for non-Chinese lawmakers had not taken off.[120] Ali then grumbled about how the prime minister had toyed with racial sentiments when Lee accused UMNO of planning to get all Malay-speakers to convert to Islam and "get circumcised".[121] Seow Peck Leng, an SPA assemblywoman, went on to hilariously lampoon government's choreographed efforts at drumming the idea of a "Malayan" culture by asking Rajaratnam: "if an Indian troupe dances an Indian dance depicting a Chinese legend, which has taken place in the Victoria Theatre, and if it is done to continental music played by Malay instruments, is that a step towards Malayan culture?".[122]

The basic principle of expressing mutual tolerance to difference did not sufficiently settle the shape and form of a "Malayan" culture. In 1960, Malay cultural organizations openly called for Malay culture to be the basis of a common Malayan culture for all in Singapore.[123] The idea was quite perplexing, even for UMNO. Ali was himself sceptical since the Malays were a minority community but went against his better judgement by urging the government to carefully study this suggestion in order to demonstrate Singapore's loyalty to the Federation.[124] He further stressed that while there were ostentatious cultural efforts by the government to mitigate racial identifications, such efforts may fall short since Malays still needed more help in improving their education levels and living conditions. Hamid later echoed the sentiments of his party colleague by speaking about unfair treatment that the Malays were facing when applying for jobs in commercial firms.[125] These conundrums demonstrated the seemingly impossible endeavour to define a national culture. Most pertinently, disparate material realities between racial communities inhibited the growth of the government-induced post-racial identity, making the PAP government's cultural efforts more theatrical rather than substantial.

It was also clear that Yusof's rise as Yang di-Pertuan Negara did not pacify the tit-for-tat exchange between UMNO and the PAP: UMNO would blame the PAP for neglecting the Malays in one way or another, while the PAP would denounce UMNO for brandishing the communal card. Just days after Yusof's installation, Prime Minister Lee warned against the use of communal slogans, calling UMNO's harping on racial issues as a full-play on "animal instinctive responses".[126] Hamid replied that such a label would cheapen any criticism of government polices concerning the Malays, especially since the racial community needed special advocacy due to their marginalized socio-economic positions.[127] When Yusof recited his first Yang di-Pertuan Negara Address to the Assembly in July 1960, the PAP government ensured that there was no repeat of the previous year's mistake; this time, Yusof was explicit in acknowledging the indigenous status of the Malays.

UMNO lawmakers, however, were still unsatisfied. Ali once again complained about how the government was trivializing the indigeneity of the Malays.[128] He lectured the Assembly about the historical rights of the racial community over Singapore by reading extracts from the *Sulalatus Salatin*, a text on the genealogy of kings from the precolonial Melaka sultanate. This earned him a chiding from the speaker for dragging on the debate. Ali somehow managed to pull a remarkable feat by linking the *Sulalatus Salatin* to his demand for more concrete policy actions to help Malays in education.[129] The fierce contest between PAP and UMNO for the political allegiance of the Singaporean Malays stretched out in the years to come.

A Malay/Muslim Ambassador for Merger

As the struggle to win over the political allegiance of the Singaporean Malays became protracted, the Yang di-Pertuan Negara did somewhat soften the Chinese appearance of the PAP government, especially when it came to staking Singapore's place in a united Malaya. Yusof was the city-state's pre-eminent representative in the drive to accumulate goodwill from its Malay-dominated neighbours, boosting the diplomatic and policy overtures of the PAP government. Besides his ceremonial immersions with the other rulers from the Federation, the Yang di-Pertuan Negara also hosted a flagship event in the form of grand banquets in the Istana during every National Day from 1960 till 1963. Representatives from each *negeri* of the Federation as well as ministers in the central government in Kuala Lumpur were exclusive guests. Yusof cajoled them into embracing Singapore's rightful place in the Federation and the region. During the inaugural banquet, the Yang di-Pertuan Negara went on a charm offensive:

> They [Federation citizens] are certainly in a happy mood because all members of the Singapore cabinet come from the Federation. Many of

our officers in the public service are also from the Federation. I, too, come from the Federation. It seems as if we are governing Singapore on behalf of the Federation.[130]

The linkages between Singapore and the Federation were intimate, and Yusof became the living icon to manifest this intimacy.

In September 1960, Yusof headed to Brunei in his first official visit outside Singapore and the Federation. The Bruneian sultan, Sir Omar Saifuddin, gave Yusof a pompous welcome fit for a king, complete with a 17-gun salute.[131] Following the visit, the sultan awarded Yusof with the First-Class Order of the *Darjah Kerabat*, Brunei's highest award for a foreign dignitary.[132] The Yang di-Pertuan Negara served as the crucial nexus that bridged Singapore with its closest neighbours. Through his active engagement with the powerful and influential from the region, he cultivated a sense of fellowship with proximate states and tightened Singapore's historical claim as part of a united Malaya and the larger Malay world.

While impassioned communal overtones were verbally absent in these engagements, Yusof's display of Malayness was vivid. The Yang di-Pertuan Negara often appeared in his traditional Malay clothes, in *Baju Melayu* and *songkok*, during most of his ceremonial appearances, whether they were rituals of the State or cultural events of the Malay community, and most importantly, on occasions when representatives from neighbouring countries were present.[133] Yusof's sartorial choices were at odds with his personal image when he was the *Utusan*'s managing editor. Among their fellow journalists, both he and Samad were known for their hatred of the *songkok* and saw it as "a badge of slavery", probably because the headdress was part of the formal attire in Malay royal courts.[134] Noor Aisha, the wife of the Yang di-Pertuan Negara, also remembered that her husband disliked wearing the *songkok*.[135] Apparently, times had changed.

To be generous to Yusof, it seemed that he was willing to forfeit his own fashion tastes to fulfil his official duties, but in doing so, there was a deliberate assertion of his racialized image in representing Singapore. Yusof's choice of style echoed the wearing of "oriental exotica" by the Malay rulers when they undertook public appearances, a practice implemented at the behest of colonial officials—avoid suits and ties, the more elaborate the native dress, then all the better.[136] Flamboyant costume displays were indispensable ingredients in British imperial culture. This feature turned indigenous rulers into nakedly racialized figures to reflect the motley composition of the imperial hierarchy under the Crown's reign. In September 1961, Yusof made a special call to fellow Muslims in the city-state, majority of whom were Malays, in what seemed to be bordering an appeal to communal sentiments for a political cause. He asked fellow Muslims to "spread brotherhood" to their Muslim brothers in the Federation in order to promote the Tunku's Malaysia Plan.[137] When it was politically expedient for the PAP government, there was a tolerance of communal sentiments. Yusof carried the role of a luminary to inspire a sense of cultural affinity among the Malays in Singapore as the island staked its place in the Federation. The fog of Chineseness enveloping the Singaporean government appeared to be thinning.

Yusof's invocation of a Muslim brotherhood is a reminder that Malay and Muslim issues were often conjoined both in Singapore and the Federation. The Malays in both territories were, and still are, predominantly Muslims. The historical entwinement of the Islamic faith and the notion of Malayness is therefore unsurprising.[138] Following the traumatic violence of the 1950 Maria Hertogh riots, Muslim issues in Singapore were less politicized, often mired with the tide of racial politics, while incidents of violence in the city-state throughout the rest of the 1950s were generally associated with communist and anti-colonial agitation.[139] With the rise of a new nationalist regime, there was greater interest to enhance the administration of Muslim life in Singapore as part of wider initiatives to reform governance. These attempts were inclusive, cautious and sensitive. For instance, there was a strong consultative approach between lawmakers and Muslim organizations during Select Committee hearings in 1960 to ascertain the scope of reforms to the 1957 Muslim Ordinance. The law was subsequently amended to ensure greater checks on polygamous Muslim marriages, adhering the spirit of the Women's Charter.[140]

Later, in late 1960 and January 1961, security forces unearthed and foiled a plot by the *Angkatan Revolusi Tentera Islam Singapura* (The Revolutionary Islamic Forces of Singapore, or ARTIS), a clandestine group which aimed to overthrow Chinese rule in the city-state. The group planned to use a combination of inflammatory pamphlets, religious regalia and mystical charms blessed by a *bomoh* (a Malay witchdoctor) to encourage Malays in Singapore to take violent action against the Chinese. Through the collaboration of PAP and UMNO leaders as well as Muslim organisations, there was a massive outreach to calm the public.[141] Further demonstrating the interweaving of religious sentiments with racial politics, Rajaratnam framed the entire affair as a reminder of the dangers posed by "racial carnage".[142] Aside from these rare occurrences of religious incursion into public politics, Muslim affairs in Singapore carried only benign political tints.

Yusof's racial and religious identifications, however, shaped the Yang di-Pertuan Negara into a precarious figure. As the highest-ranking Muslim official in Singapore, he now had to delicately balance his association with the faith and his role as the unifying symbol of a diverse society. During the discussions on the Malaysia Plan, Lee agreed to model the administration of Islam in Singapore in accordance with the Federal Constitution once the city-state becomes part of the Federation, meaning that Yang di-Pertuan Agong would be the ultimate authority on Islam in the city-state.[143] The other peninsular rulers were also constitutionally recognized as custodian of Islamic affairs in their respective states. Before merger, however, it was the Yang di-Pertuan Negara who performed this role in Singapore, although this was not specifically stipulated in the island's Constitution. In his official capacity, he was nevertheless responsible for appointing members of the Muslim Advisory Board, a statutory body that advised the Singaporean government on matters relating to the administration of Islam.[144]

Yusof also made public appearances during religious events, like celebrations of the Prophet Muhammad's birthday, as recounted earlier. During Islamic holidays, the press reliably reported his attendance at congregational prayers and religious processions.[145] Another case in point was the annual Qur'an Reading Competition organized by the Muslim Advisory Board. During the competition's iteration in February 1961, Yusof, like a dutiful and pious patriarch, reminded fellow Malays to read more of the Qur'an during the upcoming fasting month when he presided over the competition.[146] Moreover, in further validation of his role as a quasi-Malay ruler, he would concur with other peninsular rulers on the sighting of the new moon to mark the start of the holy month of Ramadan based on the Islamic lunar calendar. Yusof also took it upon himself to give Hajj pilgrims a personal send-off.[147] Such instances prove that his identity as a Muslim was largely inseparable from the performance of his official duties as Yang di-Pertuan Negara.

Seen in the context of inequalities along the divisions of race, Yusof served as an important signifier of the rights of Muslims to practise their faith freely in Chinese-majority Singapore. The Yang di-Pertuan Negara generated a sense of assurance to ameliorate interracial anxieties, but the execution of the office itself was much more ambivalent. While personifying a Malayan nation which transcended the boundaries of race, Yusof took on a simultaneous religious persona, serving as the de facto guardian of Islam in Singapore.

The Repentant Communalist?

Yusof's biographical baggage compounded on the fragile symbolism of his office. Though he was now a champion for a post-racial sense of Malayan identity, this fact was somewhat ironic considering his intimate history with the *Utusan*. In an effort to promote Yusof's anti-colonial credentials, the PAP government publicized his stewardship of the Malay vernacular paper, which presumably also watered down the perceived Chinese chauvinism of the party. What the PAP government and Yusof's biographers often tend to downplay, however, was that the *Utusan* was not completely innocent from elements of communalism—sentiments which both the PAP government and Yusof himself sought to demonize with the rise of the new nationalist regime. Due to the influence of Samad's politics, the *Utusan* had adopted a clear socialist and anti-colonial stance after Yusof re-established the paper in the aftermath of the Second World War.

The paper, however, had an earlier incarnation. It had more parochial beginnings, born as a response to the dominance of non-Malays over the economy as well as the overreaching influence of non-Malay Muslims. By the 1930s, affluent Arabs and Jawi-Peranakans had control over multiple prominent papers in the vernacular language and positioned themselves as leaders of all Muslims in Malaya, causing tensions within the Malay community.[148] It was amid this increasing sense of alienation amongst Malays that the KMS became the first Malay-based organization claiming to represent socio-political and economic interests of the Malay community. Wanting to explore the possibility of a paper staffed solely by Malays, the KMS assigned the task to its secretary, a youthful Yusof bin Ishak. This initiative later led to the founding of the *Utusan*, with Yusof becoming the paper's founder and managing editor.

The vision for the paper closely followed the communal-based orientations of the KMS.[149] The *Utusan*'s prospectus forbade non-Malays from holding any shares of the paper whether directly or in trust; its Articles of Association further confined the definition of "Malay" to those of racial stock native to the Archipelago and excommunicated Malay women who married immigrants.[150] Yusof even sued a member of the Straits Settlements' Legislative Council, Captain Mohd Hashim, for defamation after the latter alleged that he was not a Malay. To prove his racial heritage, Yusof further compiled evidence of his own "pure Malay" ancestry.[151] The lawsuit, however, was later settled out of court.[152] It was also confounding that Yusof embraced the *Utusan*'s emphasis on the purity of Malay blood when his own family had for generations a proclivity towards marrying Arabs.[153]

In his canonical study of Malay nationalism before the Second World War, historian Willian Roff describes the *Utusan* under Yusof's leadership as "strongly chauvinistic on the Malay behalf, beyond any other paper of the time, and attacked the Chinese particularly and somewhat less directly the Arabs and other non-Malay Muslims".[154] Norshahril Saat, however, disagrees with Roff based on his interpretation of the *Utusan*'s orientation, while another scholar claims that the newspaper was more anti-exploitation than anti-immigrant.[155] Both these latter authors could hardly make a dent in Roff's arguments. Their claims are based on interviews given by individuals who were personally tied to the newspaper's legacy, and both of their works merely examine a handful of *Utusan* articles with little effort at historicization. They cannot match the calibre of Roff's more detailed and meticulous historical study.

Perhaps the tone of the pre-war *Utusan* could be better understood through its most celebrated journalist, Abdul Rahim Kajai. His legacy was crucial to the idea of the Malay *bangsa* (nation or race), so much so that he has been the subject of nostalgia for later Malay journalists.[156] The paper peddled communal sentiments which in large part contributed to the ideological basis of UMNO's postwar formation. By the 1930s, Kajai had gained a reputation as a celebrity newsman known for fiery editorials on the socio-economic marginalization of the Malays.[157] Yusof had in fact refused to start the *Utusan* without first attaining Kajai's assurance that he would join the paper. Keeping to his word, Kajai joined the *Utusan* three months into its launch.[158]

Kajai's writings were both polemic and influential. He was responsible for coining the derogatory terms of "DKA" (*Darah Keturunan* Arab, or Arab blood heritage) and the DKK (*Darah Keturunan Keling*, or Indian blood heritage) to respectively refer to the Arabs and Jawi-Peranakans, expressing his contempt towards their masquerade as Malays.[159] Through his editorials and his satirical *Wak Ketok* cartoons, Kajai titillated the passions of his readers by regularly appealing to their sense of hardship and by criticizing and mocking immigrants.[160] Rather than depending on substantive socio-economic analysis, his writings were largely emotive. They provoked insecurities and promoted exclusive Malay communalism.[161] Kajai often cautioned the Malays to pull up their socks to avoid getting fooled by exploitative immigrants while also gently pressing the British to accord greater protection for the indigenous community.[162] His influence in the pre-war *Utusan* was so potent that some even equated the newspaper to Kajai.[163]

The point here is that Yusof was a devotee to Kajai's writings and was in fact a close friend.[164] While it would be unfair to say that both men were one and the same, it could be said that Yusof was intellectually aligned with the influential Kajai, or at the very least complicit in the perpetuation of ethno-centric thinking. Although Kajai died during the war, his spirit lived on in Yusof. When Onn Jaafar decided to extend UMNO membership to non-Malay Muslims, the future Yang di-Pertuan Negara strongly disagreed with the move and was instead in favour of restricting party membership to those of pure Malay ancestry. Yusof only backtracked on his opposition years later.[165] His collaboration with Kajai's ideas of exclusive Malay communalism is even more persuasive should we consider the fact that Yusof was an obsessive taskmaster. He was often described as "dictatorial" and micromanaged the *Utusan*—nothing could be published without his vetting.[166] Yusof did not hesitate to dismiss workers who fell short of his expectations and did not tolerate any challenge to his authority. For instance, Hussein Abdul Hamid recounted that he lost his job in the *Utusan* after questioning Yusof's decision to pay Aziz Ishak a higher salary for doing the same job as he had done. Yusof then proceeded to fire Hussein for insinuating nepotism, telling him that the issue was "a family matter".[167]

In spite of its advocacy of exclusive Malay communalism before the war, the ushering of postwar decolonization pushed the *Utusan* to take on a more critical stance towards the British. Indeed, the paper was at the forefront of the anti-colonial movement. It supported the cause of Malayan independence through its endorsement of the UMNO-led Malayan Union protests, the formation of the AMCJA-PUTERA coalition as well as the activities of the left-wing movement.[168] The void that Kajai left was later filled by Samad. It was this postwar incarnation of the *Utusan* under Samad's intellectual direction that was perhaps more accurately described as anti-colonial and anti-exploitation and was in better alignment with the ideology of the PAP.[169] During the Emergency, trouble often looked for the *Utusan*'s journalists due to the paper's anti-establishment stance. Even Yusof found himself drawn into the revolutionary elements of the Malayan independence movement. As the *Utusan*'s managing director, he was often summoned by Sir Gerald Templer when the latter was the British high commissioner of Malaya. This was the same Templer who has often been credited as the man who won the Emergency for Commonwealth forces. Years later, following his retirement, Templer visited Singapore in 1960 and called on the Yang di-Pertuan Negara. Yusof mischievously asked if the retired field marshal still remembered him, to which Templer replied, "Yes, I remember you only too well".[170]

Yusof's time in the *Utusan* continued to be tumultuous throughout the 1950s. In 1957, the *Utusan* moved its headquarters to Kuala Lumpur after UMNO acquired a majority of the paper's shares. The party, uneasy with Samad's radicalism, pressured Yusof to get rid of his star journalist.[171] The managing editor eventually relented and transferred Samad to Jakarta. The Special Branch reported that Yusof had told Lee, "the earlier Samad leaves for Indonesia, the better it is for all concerned".[172] It was later revealed that the Tunku had personally orchestrated this move, but Samad continued to hold onto the impression that the motive behind the transfer was more personal, claiming that Yusof was jealous of his popularity among the *Utusan*'s journalists.[173] The bitter rift between both men eventually pushed Samad to defect to the *Berita Harian*. In 1959, Yusof himself left the *Utusan*. One widely circulated reason for Yusof's departure was that he found it increasingly humiliating to do his job. The Tunku often summoned him in the mornings as if he was some lapdog.[174] But Samad, as always, had a contrary view: Yusof left because he had lost the confidence of the *Utusan*'s socialist-oriented journalists, who were resentful towards his frequent submission to UMNO's demands.[175]

Whatever the circumstances behind his departure, it was Yusof's leading role in the Utusan and his association with the politics of Malay nationalism—first through his work in the KMS and the advancement of Kajai's ideas, and later through his support for the independence struggle and his initial pandering to UMNO—that remained the most prominent segment of his public profile. This made him a favourable nominee for the PAP government, which was already going out of its way to dull its persistent association with Chinese chauvinism. Yusof's affiliation, or more accurately, his dubious relationship with communalism, was a contrast to his more post-racial outlook upon taking office. While all human beings are capable of transformation, it would be misleading to ignore the skeletons that remain in the closet, haunting the performance of the Yang di-Pertuan Negara.

The rise of a Malayan-born Yang di-Pertuan Negara complicated the racialist discourse entrenched during the colonial order. Rather than completely eradicating race as a compelling frame to organize life in Singapore, the Yang di-Pertuan Negara replenished its persuasive value. The racial hierarchy of the imperial project upheld the supremacy of Whites over non-Whites, and these prejudices seeped into the institutional structure of the office. The simplistic assumptions of British officials towards non-Whites plagued their thinking about the future appointee and the decolonization process in general. But after a series of careful speculation and forethought, they successfully defended the image of White supremacy in the colony and ensured that the Asian Crown representative could not impede or supersede the authority of White colonial officials.

British rule not only maintained the existence of an unequal racialist social order, but it also erected divisions between the non-White races in colonial society. When the PAP came in power, Singapore was a racially divided society with material disparities largely falling in line with these divisions. The Malays, the island's indigenous community, were particularly affected. Leaders of the racial community competed with one another to harness suspicions towards a Chinese-dominated government and to demand for special political rights for the Malays. In doing so, they seek political capital for themselves. Their efforts included the campaign for a Malay titular figure to represent Singapore. Upon coming into power, the PAP government actively took advantage of the appointment of the Yang di-Pertuan Negara to thin the perceived Chinese-ness of the party. By installing a man who boasted strong credentials as a Malay nationalist, the PAP sought to consolidate its rule by easing anxieties among Malays in Singapore and the region as a whole, while pushing forward towards merger.

Under the new nationalist regime, the Malayan-born Yang di-Pertuan Negara represented the dismantling of racial barriers and a sense of racial transcendence in line with the ideology of the PAP. But the execution of the office, along with Yusof's past as a conspirator of Malay communalism, provide a mixed picture to the symbolic meanings of the office. It seemed that race—whether seen in terms of its value or disvalue—was a flexible apparatus for competing projects and personal ambitions to amass dominance.

Notes

1. Speech by Lee, 3 December 1959, CO 1030/480, 43.
2. Stephen Spencer, *Race and Ethnicity: Culture, Identity and Representation*, 2nd ed. (London and New York: Routledge, 2014), pp. 40–64.
3. Lee, *Singapore*, pp. 21–49. For the list of works consulted on race in British Malaya, see *Bibliography*.
4. Speech by Lee, 3 December 1959, CO 1030/480, 43.
5. Taomo Zhou, *Migration in the Time of Revolution: China, Indonesia, and the Cold War* (Ithaca and London: Cornell University Press, 2019), pp. 115–31.

6. PAP, *The Tasks Ahead I*, pp. 14–15.
7. PAP, *Petir* 3, 3 (September 1959), p. 6.
8. See the statement by the detained PAP leaders upon their release in 1959, reproduced in Lee, *Battle for Merger*, pp. 184–88.
9. PAP, *Petir* 2, 2 (February 1959), pp. 1, 4.
10. PAP, *Petir* 2, 3 (March 1959), p. 2.
11. *SLAD*, Vol. 11, Sitting No. 6, Col. 298–301 (21 July 1959).
12. Cannadine, *Ornamentalism*, pp. 5–6, 121–26.
13. See Getachew, *Worldmaking After Empire*.
14. Chatterjee, *The Nation*, pp. 26–34.
15. *ST*, 8 November 1959, p. 1.
16. *ST*, 3 December 1959, p. 1.
17. *SFP*, 2 December 1959, p. 3.
18. *SFP*, 2 December 1959, p. 6; *SFP*, 3 December 1959, p. 1; *ST*, 3 December 1959, p. 1.
19. For the Loyalty Week programme, see Ministry of Culture, *Minggu Kesetiaan Kebangsaan, Negara Singapura, 3-9/12/1959: Chendera-Mata* (Singapore: Government Printing Office, 1959).
20. *ST*, 25 November 1959, p. 9.
21. *ST*, 3 June 1960, p. 9.
22. *BH*, 6 June 1960, p. 5.
23. *ST*, 4 June 1960, p. 7.
24. Ng, *Singapore Lion*, pp. 301–30 and Lee, *Singapore*, pp. 165–70.
25. *SFP*, 25 July 1960, p. 5.
26. *SFP*, 4 April 1960, p. 8.
27. *ST*, 14 May 1960, p. 4. A National Theatre Fund was also launched during Yusof's installation, receiving enthusiastic support from the community: *ST*, 21 November 1959, p. 16; Ng, *Singapore Lion*, pp. 323–24.
28. Ministry of Culture, *Towards a More Just Society*, p. 5 and *SLAD*, Vol. 11, Sitting No. 4, Col. 179 (17 July 1959).
29. *SFP*, 4 June 1960, p. 8.
30. L.A. Sheridan and Harry E. Groves, *The Constitution of Malaysia* (New York: Oceana Publications, 1967), pp. 209–11.
31. For example, see his patronage of the Spastics Children's Association in *ST*, 9 July 1960, p. 4; Singapore Leprosy Relief Association in *ST*, 13 July 1960, p. 7; Singapore Amateur Athletic Association in *ST*, 20 July 1960, p. 14; Singapore Blood Donors' Association in *SFP*, 1 December 1960, p. 15; Singapore Garden Society in *ST*, 7 April 1961, p. 4.
32. *SFP*, 4 June 1960, p. 1.
33. *ST*, 22 May 1960, p. 4.
34. *ST*, 3 July 1960, p. 5.
35. *ST*, 3 September 1960, p. 4.
36. See for instance *ST*, 24 June 1960, p. 4 and *SFP*, 16 July 1960, p. 5.

37. *ST*, 4 June 1961, p. 1.
38. *ST*, 10 June 1961, p. 4.
39. *SFP*, 29 June 1961, p. 1.
40. *ST*, 10 September 1960, p. 4.
41. *ST*, 18 March 1961, p. 4.
42. *ST*, 26 November 1960, p. 9.
43. *ST*, 22 April 1961, p. 7.
44. *BH*, 10 June 1961, p. 8.
45. Homi K. Bhabha, *The Location of Culture* (London and New York: Routledge, 1994), p. 70.
46. Ibid., pp. 66–84.
47. Memorandum from D. MacGillivray to A. Lennox-Boyd, 30 March 1956, CO 1030/122.
48. Report from GHQ Far Eastern Land Forces to Ministry of Defence, 19 March 1956, CO 1030/122.
49. Report from R. Black to A. Lennox-Boyd, 19 March 1956, CO 1030/122.
50. On the cascading effect of the Indian Mutiny, see Jill C. Bender, *The 1857 Uprising and the British Empire* (Cambridge: Cambridge University Press, 2016).
51. Report from GHQ Far Eastern Land Forces to Ministry of Defence, 19 March 1956, CO 1030/122.
52. Note for discussion prepared by the Colonial Office, July 1956, CO 1030/83, 297A.
53. Letter from R. Black to J.B. Johnston, 9 August 1956, CO 1030/83, 339A.
54. A.J. Stockwell, "Viceregal Crisis in Nkrumah's Ghana", in *Viceregalism: The Crown as Head of State in Political Crises in the Postwar Commonwealth*, edited by H. Kumarasingham (Cham: Palgrave Macmillan, 2020), p. 132.
55. Memorandum from A. Lennox-Boyd to the Cabinet, "Singapore Constitutional Development", 30 November 1956, CO 1030/122.
56. Report from R. Black to A. Lennox-Boyd, 19 March 1956, CO 1030/122.
57. Ibid.
58. Note from R. Scott to J.B. Johnston, 18 September 1956, CO 1030/84, 356.
59. Letter from D.R.E. Hopkins to J. Hennings, 14 September 1958, CO 1030/479, 104–105.
60. Letter from D.R.E. Hopkins to J. Hennings, 12 May 1958, CO 1030/479/145–46.
61. Deliberations are found in CO 1030/479, 78–94.
62. Ibid.
63. Ibid.
64. In Malaya and Singapore, British economic policy pushed Malays to rural living, see Jomo Kwame Sundaram, *A Question of Class: Capital, the State and Uneven Development in Malaysia* (Singapore: Oxford University Press, 1986), pp. 37–124.

65. Ibid., pp. 138–56.
66. Turnbull, *A History of Singapore*, pp. 247–50.
67. Goh Keng Swee, *Urban Incomes and Housing: A Report on the Social Survey of Singapore, 1953–54*, Reprint (Singapore: Government Printing Office, 1958).
68. Ibid., pp. 100, 134 and Tania Li, *Malays in Singapore: Culture, Economy and Ideology* (Singapore: Oxford University Press, 1989), pp. 100–102.
69. J.J. Puthucheary, *Ownership and Control in the Malayan Economy* (Kuala Lumpur: University of Malaya Co-operative Bookshop, 1979), pp. 123–37. Chinese capital had played a major role in economic transformation of the Straits Settlements, see Sundaram, *A Question of Class*, pp. 150–52, 212–13.
70. For a more comprehensive analysis on the constitutional roles of the Malay rulers, see Abdul Aziz Bari, *The Monarchy and the Constitution of Malaya* (Kuala Lumpur: IDEAS, 2013).
71. For a copy of the petition, see FCO 141/7481.
72. See the respective examples of Ceylon and Malaya in Sivasundaram, *Islanded*, pp. 283–317 and Joseph Fernando, *The Alliance Road to Independence* (Kuala Lumpur: University of Malaya Press, 2009), pp. 35–62.
73. Malay National Congress to Alan Lennox-Boyd, 4 February 1957, FCO 141/7481.
74. *ST*, 13 February 1957, p. 7; *ST*, 15 February 1957, p. 5.
75. *Manchester Guardian*, 25 February 1957, DO 35/9873, 661.
76. Rozeman Abu Hassan, *Dasar British Terhadap Hubungan Singapura-Malaysia 1959–1969* (Bangi: UKM Press, 2015), p. 37.
77. Colonial Office, *Singapore Conference 1957*, p. 5.
78. *SS*, 18 May 1958, p. 2.
79. Telegram from W. Goode to Colonial Office, 27 October 1958, CO 1030/476, 82.
80. *BH*, 22 December 1958, p. 4.
81. Petition from Tengku Muda Mohamed to Her Majesty Queen Elizabeth II, 10 February 1958, FCO 141/15022, 3.
82. *ST*, 9 June 1959, p. 7 and Sahid Sahooman, "Oral History Interviews, Reel 1, Accession Number 003210", National Archives of Singapore, 2 August 2007.
83. Savingram from R. Black to Secretary of State for the Colonies, 13 July 1956, CO 1030/83, 297.
84. Ibid. and letter from R. Black to J.B. Johnston, 9 August 1956, CO 1030/83, 339A.
85. *ST*, 3 March 1959, p. 2; *SS*, 20 May 1959, p. 6; *ST*, 19 May 1959, p. 1; *SS*, 26 May 1959, p. 1. Also see Ong, "1959 election", pp. 70–74 and Azhar, "From Self-Government to Independence", p. 359.
86. Sukmawati Haji Sirat, "Trends in Malay Political Leadership: The People's Action Party Malay Political Leaders and the Integration of the Singapore

Malays" (PhD dissertation, Department of Government and International Studies, University of South Carolina 1995), p. 75.

87. PAP, *The Tasks Ahead I*, p. 17.
88. PAP, *Petir* 3, 1 (July 1959), pp. 1, 8.
89. PAP, *The Tasks Ahead I*, p. 17.
90. Sukmawati Haji Sirat, "Trends in Malay Political Leadership", p. 91.
91. All of PAP ministers were also men, see *ST*, 6 June 1959, p. 1.
92. *SLAD*, Vol. 11, Sitting No. 6, Col. 361 (21 July 1959).
93. Ibid. and Cheah, *Malaysia*, pp. 36–39.
94. *Daily Telegraph*, 12 October 1959, DO 35/9865, 79.
95. *SLAD*, Vol. 11, Sitting No. 5, Col. 229–45 (20 July 1959).
96. Ibid., Col. 243.
97. *BH*, 21 July 1959, p. 1.
98. *SLAD*, Vol. 11, Sitting No. 5, Col. 231–32 (20 July 1959).
99. Ibid., Col. 271–76.
100. Ibid., Col. 245–78.
101. *BH*, 18 April 1959, p. 4 and *BH*, 23 July 1960, p. 2.
102. *BH*, 3 September 1959, p. 5.
103. See correspondences in CO 1030/633.
104. Lee Kuan Yew was prime minister, Sir Alan Rose was chief justice, Sir George Oehlers was speaker of the Legislative Assembly and Yusof Ishak was head of the Public Service Commission.
105. Letter from W. Goode to W.I.J. Wallace, 12 October 1956, DO 35/9888, 6.
106. Ibid.
107. Ibid.
108. Note from W.I.J. Wallace to E. Melville, 19 November 1959, CO 1030/633, 9–10.
109. Letter from D.L. Pearson to T.J. Bligh, 18 November 1959, CO 1033/633, 90–92.
110. Petition from Tengku Muda Mohamed to Queen Elizabeth II, 10 February 1958, FCO 141/15022, 3A.
111. Minute by J.D. Hennings, 28 October 1959, CO 1030/633, 4.
112. *ST*, 7 November 1959, p. 2.
113. *BH*, 2 December 1959, p. 1; *Warta Negara*, 4 December 1959, p. 1.
114. Mohd Azhar Terimo, "UMNO and Malay Politics", p. 362.
115. *BH*, 18 November 1959, p. 1; *BH*, 28 November 1959, p. 5.
116. Quoted in Melanie Chew, *Leaders of Singapore* (Singapore: World Scientific, 1996), p. 183.
117. Ng, *The Singapore Lion*, pp. 301–30.
118. After independence, the PAP government has favoured a clearer "multiracial" approach in governance whereby the differences of racial communities were concretized, and their existence protected. The state also focuses on the building of a civic identity through "common spaces" for interracial

mingling. On a more critical assessment on Singapore's multiracialism, see Lai Ah Eng, *Meanings of Multiethnicity: A Case Study of Ethnicity and Ethnic Relations in Singapore* (Oxford: Oxford University Press, 1995).

119. *SLAD*, Vol. 11, Sitting No. 18, Col. 1092 (13 December 1959).

120. Ibid., Col. 1098–101.

121. Ibid.

122. *SLAD*, Vol. 11, Sitting No. 18, Col. 1104 (13 December 1959).

123. *BH*, 30 July 1960, p. 2. UMNO members hinted at the idea of using Malay culture as the basis of a Malayan culture a year earlier, see *SLAD*, Vol. 11, Sitting No. 5, Col. 243 (20 July 1959).

124. *SLAD*, Vol. 13, Sitting No. 2, Col. 75–76 (3 August 1960).

125. Ibid., Col 69–75 and *SLAD*, Vol. 13, Sitting No. 3, Col. 158 (4 August 1960).

126. *SLAD*, Vol. 11, Sitting No. 17, Col. 1086–1091 (13 December 1959).

127. Ibid., Col. 1101–103.

128. Ministry of Culture, *A Year of Construction* (Singapore: Government Printing Office, 1960), p. 18.

129. *SLAD*, Vol. 13, Sitting No. 2, Col. 65–77 (3 August 1960).

130. *ST*, 4 June 1960, p. 5.

131. *ST*, 21 September 1960, p. 4; *ST*, 24 September 1960, p. 16.

132. *ST*, 29 November 1960, p. 16.

133. Besides his swearing-in ceremony on 3 December 1959, see for instance the following occasions among others: Southern Islands visit, *ST*, 1 February 1960, p. 1; first Yang di-Pertuan Negara Address in the Assembly, *ST*, 21 July 1960, p. 1; visit to Brunei, *ST*, 24 September 1960, p. 16; awards ceremony in Brunei, *ST*, 29 November 1960, p. 16; 1961 National Day Banquet, *ST*, 3 June 1961, p. 4; 1961 National Day Parade, *ST*, 4 June 1961, p. 1. Bedlington also dwells on this point on "Malay" symbols, see Bedlington, "The Singapore Malay community", pp. 134–36.

134. Ali Salim, "A Pioneer of Malay Journalism", in *A. Samad Ismail: Journalism and Politics*, edited by Cheah Boon Kheng (Kuala Lumpur: Pustaka Budiman, 1985), p. 60.

135. Norshahril, *Yusof Ishak*, p. 17.

136. Amoroso, *Traditionalism*, pp. 73–78; Cannadine, *Ornamentalism*, pp. 105–14.

137. *ST*, 1 September 1961, p. 4.

138. For the dynamics of religion and Malayness, see the chapters by Anthony Reid and A.B. Shamsul in *Contesting Malayness: Malay Identity Across Boundaries*, edited by Timothy Barnard (Singapore: Singapore University Press, 2004). Also see Judith Nagata, "What is a Malay? Situational Selection of Ethnic Identity in a Plural Society", *American Ethnologist* 1, no. 2 (1974): 331–50 and Milner, *The Malays*, pp. 1–15.

139. Aljunied, *Colonialism, Violence and Muslims*, pp. 128–29.

140. The Women's Charter (implemented in 1960) exempts Muslim marriages, see *BH*, 30 April 1960, p. 1. Also see *SLAD*, Vol. 12, Sitting No. 1, Col. 29–44 (13 January 1960). The Administration of Muslim Law Bill also saw a hearty debate between Malay lawmakers and Muslim organizations: *ST*, 20 May 1961, p. 6.

141. *SLAD*, Vol. 14, Sitting No. 12, Col. 934–947 (11 January 1961).

142. Ibid.

143. *ST*, 17 November 1961, p. 1.

144. *BH*, 4 March 1960, p. 2 and *BH*, 22 April 1960, p. 2. The advocate-general clarified that the Yang di-Pertuan Negara needed to take cabinet advice for such appointments after PMIP demanded to have at least three of its representatives on the Board.

145. See for example *ST*, 5 December 1959, p. 10; *BH*, 6 June 1960, p. 5; *ST*, 19 March 1961, p. 11. Amongst the most prominent processions was a "giant" one held in 1960: *SFP*, 2 September 1960, p. 4.

146. *ST*, 26 February 1961, p. 5.

147. See for instance *ST*, 14 May 1961, p. 7; *ST*, 15 February 1961, p. 4.

148. Maidin, *Di Depan Api*, pp. 12–14.

149. For KMS's history and aims, see Roff, *Malay Nationalism*, pp. 190–97.

150. Maidin, *Di Depan Api*, pp. 16–17.

151. Aziz, *Mencari Bako*, p. 6.

152. Ibid.

153. Ibid., pp. 18–19.

154. Roff, *Malay Nationalism*, p. 177.

155. While the *Utusan* during the immediate years before the Second World War did challenge Malay stereotypes, both authors appear apologetic towards its attitudes towards immigrants, see Norshahril, *Yusof Ishak*, p. 80 and Zahairin, "Utusan Melayu", pp. 23–26.

156. Maier, "Abdul Rahim Kajai", pp. 75–76 and Latiff, *Kajai*, pp. 52–69.

157. Maier, "Abdul Rahim Kajai", pp. 77–81 and Roff, *Malay Nationalism*, pp. 169–72.

158. Roff, *Malay Nationalism*, p. 175 and Maidin, *Di Depan Api*, pp. 18–25.

159. Latiff, *Kajai*, pp. 105–12.

160. Ibid., pp. 194–206. Although Kajai did not draw the *Wak Ketok* cartoons in the *Utusan Zaman*, the *Utusan*'s co-publication, he was the author of its captions, see Samad, *Memoir*, pp. 110–12. For an analysis of the cartoons, see Muliyadi Mahamood, *The History of Malay Editorial Cartoons, 1930s–1993* (Kuala Lumpur: Utusan Publications, 2004), pp. 34–67.

161. Maier, "Abdul Rahim Kajai", pp. 90–98.

162. Latiff, *Kajai*, pp. 167–181, 207–48.

163. Samad, *Memoir*, p. 64.

164. Zubir Said called his group of friends "five musketeers". Aside from Zubir, the group included Yusof, Kajai, Rahim Tikus and Za'bha. See Zubir Said,

"Oral History Interviews, Reel 12, Accession Number 000293", National Archives of Singapore, 7 September 1984.

165. Ibid.
166. Chew, *President Yusof*, pp. 85–88, 97; Maidin, *Di Depan Api*, p. 29; Samad, *Memoir*, pp. 110–12.
167. Maidin, *Di Depan Api*, p. 41.
168. Ibid., pp. 48–63.
169. Ibid., pp. 66–89.
170. *ST*, 12 October 1960, p. 2. For the *Utusan*'s unpleasant experience dealing with Gerald Templer, see Maidin, *Di Depan Api*, pp. 71–73.
171. Maidin, *Di Depan Api*, p. 96.
172. Special Branch Dossier on Yusof Bin Ishak, undated, item MAL 53/312/1 (6), DO 35/9888.
173. Ibid., p. 90; Said Zahari, *Dark Clouds at Dawn* (Kuala Lumpur: Insan, 2001), pp. 83–87 and Zahairin, "Utusan Melayu", p. 76. Through his personal connections within the upper echelons of UMNO, Samad believed that the party leadership had not issued any instructions for his transfer, see Samad, *Memoir*, pp. 265–68.
174. Maidin, *Di Depan Api*, pp. 7–8.
175. Samad, *Memoir*, pp. 267–68.

EPILOGUE: HE WHO IS MADE LORD

On 3 December 1959, the recently elected government of Singapore successfully installed Yusof bin Ishak as the first Malayan-born Yang di-Pertuan Negara. After over a century of British colonialism and a brief interlude of Japanese rule, the island state entered a new era of self-government, even as it waited for an uncertain reunion with the Federation of Malaya. The gaudy rhetoric, visuals and styles that accompanied the representative of the British Crown produced an atmosphere of a nationalist revolution, a rupture from the colonial order. Singapore was on the precipice of the new and unknown, a threshold of change and transformation. The talismanic vigour of the Yang di-Pertuan Negara represented a "Malayan" nation emerging from the obsolete era of imperial domination.

But underneath the grand parading of national sovereignty, Singapore was still in limbo. The island remained trapped in a colonial purgatory, in a liminal zone where states were denied sovereign equality and kept in an imperial system under the enduring dominion of Britain. In this "new" Singapore, the Yang di-Pertuan Negara was also exalted as a symbol of social equality, and yet, the office generated a series of secret plots, surreptitious plans and public performances which revitalized the stratifying practices of class distinctions in colonial society—a few continued to be more equal than others.[1] With the coming of the

Malayan-born Yang di-Pertuan Negara, there was also a concurrent push towards the breaking down of the racial divisions entrenched during colonial rule. The office not only signified the erosion of the "Whites only" colour bar, but also served as a catalyst for a transcendental sense of "Malayan" identity between Singapore's different racial groups. The lumpiness of interracial relations, however, continued to taunt symbolic meanings of the Yang di-Pertuan Negara. Underneath the bold gesture of appointing a person of colour to the highest office in the land, uneasy contradictions persisted. Material disparities between different racial groups continued to threaten the promise of a post-racial and more equal social order.

An idealist among the PAP leaders, Minister S. Rajaratnam devolved the meaning of being "Malayan" to "the artists, the dramatists and the painters".[2] The same could be said for the multiple meanings of the Yang di-Pertuan Negara, the embodied representation of the "Malayan" nation in Singapore: the "artists" were the half-departed imperial overlords, the "dramatists" were the new nationalist rulers and the "painters" included anyone and everyone who had a stake in the island state. The canvass was Yusof Ishak. He was the man with a complex past who brought the Yang di-Pertuan Negara to life. The office triggered historical entanglements that linked Singapore with wider struggles and processes that transcended the space of the national unit. As a historical artefact, the Yang di-Pertuan Negara presents itself as an entryway to tunnel the many layers of Singapore's past—elements of which were creatively appropriated for the service of competing political projects during the era of decolonization. On 3 December 1959, Yusof Ishak was *made* lord of Singapore (among many other things) by different historical actors.

After many years of trepidation and negotiations, concrete passage for merger came with the signing of the Malaysia Agreement on 9 July 1963. The inauguration of the enlarged federation was initially set for "Malaysia Day" on 31 August 1963, the sixth-year anniversary of Malayan independence. But quagmires remained aplenty. Frenzied opposition from Indonesia and the Philippines against the incorporation of the Borneo territories led to a fact-finding mission from the UN to ascertain popular sentiment for Malaysia, forcing a postponement of the inauguration date to 16 September 1963.[3] At first, Prime Minister Lee assured the

British colonial secretary, Duncan Sandys, that he would drop any idea of declaring independence on 31 August, promising to "play it cool" to avoid infuriating the Alliance government in Kuala Lumpur, which was at this time settling the legal implications for delaying Malaysia Day.[4] Still, Lee backtracked on his assurance to Sandys. On 31 August 1963, at an event at the Padang, the Singaporean prime minister publicly declared de facto independence for the island, proclaiming a takeover of defence and foreign affairs, the two areas under British jurisdiction. He announced that "these powers will be invested in the Yang di-Pertuan Negara Inche Yusof bin Ishak ... We look upon ourselves as trustees for the Federal government in these 15 days. We will exercise these powers in the interests of Malaysia".[5] At least in the eyes of the PAP government, Yusof was now effectively sovereign of Singapore.

This move generated a whirlwind of reactions. Sandys called the Singaporean prime minister's actions a "typical piece of Lee trickery" and felt that the best response was no response. Any form of retort might sour relations with the people of Singapore and would lend credence to opponents of merger, particularly President Sukarno of Indonesia, who had denounced Malaysia as a neo-colonial plot.[6] Like Sandys, the Tunku was infuriated by Lee's hastiness. The Malayan prime minister immediately sent a letter of protest straight to his British counterpart, Harold MacMillan.[7] Indeed, Singapore's temporary "independence" was not stated in any part of the Malaysia Agreement. Lee's temerity was therefore seen a blatant incursion of the Federation government's initiative over the formation of the new nation-state. Lee, however, was on a different page from Kuala Lumpur. On 3 September, hoping to capitalize on the adrenaline following Singapore's declaration of independence, he advised the Yang di-Pertuan Negara to dissolve the Legislative Assembly and called for a snap election. But on that same day, following an emergency meeting between Alliance ministers and Sandys, an official joint statement between the Federation and British governments clarified that there was no effective change to Singapore's constitutional status.[8] The Alliance leaders put out another statement, stating equivocally that "... it is clear that the action of the Singapore government to assume powers over defence and external affairs in the State of Singapore has no legal or constitutional validity".[9]

These reactions reflected poorly on the PAP government and could severely embarrass the Singaporean prime minister if not managed appropriately. Defending his actions, Lee expressed "regret" that Federation government did not share his enthusiasm and assured Kuala Lumpur that the only people who should be concerned were the British, who chose not to formally castigate Lee's attempt to take over their responsibilities of defence and foreign affairs. Believing that "history will prove [the PAP government] right", the Singaporean premier placed blame for this uneasiness on ex-Chief Minister Lim Yew Hock, citing the latter's unscrupulous dealings in Kuala Lumpur.[10] On 11 September, Goh Keng Swee, the Singaporean minister of finance, subsequently signed a final agreement with Sandys and Federation leaders to placate all confusion and affirm Singapore's commitment to Malaysia's inauguration on 16 September.[11]

When the official date of Malaysia Day came to pass, Lee, who was in the midst of an election campaign, again made a declaration in a somewhat anti-climactic moment:

> Now I, Lee Kuan Yew, Prime Minister of Singapore, do hereby proclaim and declare on behalf of the people of Singapore that as from today, the sixteenth of September 1963, Singapore shall forever be part of the sovereign, democratic, and independent State of Malaysia, founded upon the principles of liberty and justice, and ever seeking welfare and happiness of her people in a more just and equal society.[12]

In an attempt to bury the hatchet with Kuala Lumpur, Lee further pledged the loyalty of the people of Singapore to "Malaysia, the central government and her leaders, the Tunku, Abdul Razak and his colleagues".[13] While relations between the PAP and Federation government had always been rocky, this debacle only aggravated tensions. Nevertheless, the PAP managed to ride on its success of delivering merger. Singapore's ruling party later secured a resounding electoral victory five days later, winning a two-thirds majority in the Legislative Assembly.[14]

The story of the Yang di-Pertuan Negara, however, did not end with Singapore's merger with the Federation. Under revised constitutional arrangements, the power to appoint the Yang di-Pertuan Negara was transferred from the Queen to the Yang di-Pertuan Agong, the supreme ruler of the Federation, who would consult the Singaporean prime minister before making the appointment.[15] The Yang di-Pertuan Negara, Singapore's last constitutional link to the British Crown, now became the connecting ligament between island state and the Malaysian sovereign. Throughout Singapore's time in the Federation, the Yang di-Pertuan Negara continued to reinscribe the rhythms and rituals of Malay(an) political culture, which Singaporean leaders were ever so keen to project, underscoring the nationalist destiny of the ex-colonial Malaysian state.

Yet history tells of Singapore's presence in Malaysia as a tempestuous time of conflicting political ideologies, unfulfilled promises and bloodshed.[16] The most visceral incident transpired in 1964. During an event at the Padang to celebrate the Prophet Muhammad's birthday in July that year, nameless and faceless racial extremists sullied the Yang di-Pertuan Negara, turning the most dignified figure of the island state into an emblem of racial betrayal—a stooge of the Chinese-dominated PAP.[17] Amid heightened racial sentiments, carnage broke out during the subsequent procession. Even in these ugly of times, however, Singapore's separation on 9 August 1965, like its merger with the Federation, was never a foregone conclusion. Just like the dealings, negotiations and squabbles that characterized Singapore's uncoupling from the British Empire, there is always a richer story that has yet to be told.

The story of the Yang di-Pertuan Negara during the period before and after merger is also in large part a story of Yusof Ishak. As the man who held the office for most of its constitutional life, Yusof cannot be extricated from any effort to make sense of the Yang di-Pertuan Negara. These pages contain a particular telling of office's story while also revealing segments of Yusof's life that has often been downplayed or forgotten. These biographical snapshots take nothing away from his contributions to the nation-state and his loyal service to Singaporeans— he was a man whose life many would say was well-lived. But the tale of his tribulations and the shifts in his character only humanize Yusof further, making him a much more relatable figure. Only with all his imperfections can Yusof truly be a man of the people.

At one point of time and in a distinct historical context, Yusof was the very personification of Singapore. Theorists of the nation have tried to come to grips with the temptation to link the mysterious concept of the "nation" with the idea of the individual.[18] Yusof's story exemplifies this urge. Human beings generally attempt to live their lives as autonomous individuals, making their own choices, trying to discern their sense of purpose and identifying their differences in relation to others. During the course of his life, Yusof had to come to terms with these human experiences too. He adapted to new circumstances and transformed himself in the face of new challenges. But even so, Yusof was a product of his past, shaped by his own historical, social and material realities. One thing was certain: he had prejudices, ambitions and convictions, just like any other human being who strives to achieve a meaningful life.

Besides speaking to the contested meanings of the Yang di-Pertuan Negara and the life of Yusof Ishak, this book is a monument to the idea that decolonization was a complicated, unpremeditated and ambivalent process which unfurled across many dimensions. In a decolonizing Singapore, there were dynamic negotiations to determine the character of the emerging postcolonial nation. The Yang di-Pertuan Negara represented the contesting ideologies and aspirations of the time. In trying to grasp their share of power, different historical actors, whether they were colonial masters or colonial elites, showed a sense of resilience. They amended their political projects and modified their ideas to strive for domination, reaching varying degrees of success. They found ways to overcome challenges in the concrete battles of party politics, constitutional negotiations as well as the symbolic struggles to project the values of the new socio-political order through the Yang di-Pertuan Negara. In a context of transition during the era of decolonization, elements of continuity and change were ambiguous, making them useful at different moments for the pursuit of power. Or to put it another way, the colonial and postcolonial are constitutive of the other.

Notions of the old and the new can be playful. In contemporary times and even all the way back to when Prime Minister Lee first welcomed Yusof to City Hall to be sworn-in as Yang di-Pertuan Negara, the PAP government has often conjoined the idea of novelty with the nation in Singapore, that the social collective must be able to reinvent itself and embrace constant change to "progress".[19] This impulse for renewal may also explain the longevity of the PAP regime, which still rule Singapore today. Existing structures that that persist—unequal relations of the global order, class distinctions and the entrenched category of race—did not disappear when Singapore underwent other moments of transition, whether it was the achievement of merger, separation from Malaysia or the decades' worth of crises since then. Structures of empire are indeed enduring, and the power struggles that animate decolonization did not end with self-government. The ruling elites of Singapore reinvigorated and consolidated these structures in new forms and under different circumstances. And this exercise is still ongoing. So long as these structures continue to hold value for the pursuit of power, they will continue to stay on. Underneath noble ambitions and symbolic efforts at meaning-making, there will be human concerns of pride, privileges and power.

Nothing is timeless, and change is ceaseless. The nation, along with other "objective" values attached to its character—like "freedom", "equality" and "multiracialism"—are concepts with no universal or eternal meaning, grounded on specific contexts and dynamic social relations. In their own time, attempts at meaning-making are always negotiable, and at times, however, individuals and organizations employ certain ideas and values to validate all sorts of causes, actions and policies. Such invocations, however, ought to be met with relentless scepticism and need to be put to task, especially when the ones speaking are the powerful.

Notes

1. This famous expression is of course adapted from George Orwell's *Animal Farm*, see George Orwell, *Animal Farm* (London: Penguin UK, 2004).
2. *SLAD*, Vol. 11, Sitting No. 18, Col. 1092 (13 December 1959).
3. Tan, *Creating 'Greater Malaysia'*, pp. 189–91.
4. Telegram from UK Commissioner in Singapore (on behalf of the colonial secretary) to Colonial Office, 1 September 1963, DO 187/31, 32.
5. *ST*, 1 September 1963, p. 1.
6. Telegram from UK Commissioner in Singapore (on behalf of the colonial secretary) to Colonial Office, 1 September 1963, DO 187/31, 31.
7. Letter from Ghazali Shafie to Sir Geofroy Tory, "Text of personal message from the honourable prime minister to the right honourable Harold Macmillan MP", 2 September 1963, DO 187/31, 33A.
8. Telegram from British High Commissioner in Kuala Lumpur to Secretary of State for Commonwealth Relations, 3 September 1963, DO 187/31, 42.

9. Ibid.
10. *ST*, 3 September 1963, p. 22.
11. *ST*, 12 September 1963, p. 1; Letter from UK Commissioner in Singapore to D.G.R. Bentliff, 14 September 1963, DO 187/31, 64.
12. Telegram from BDHC Singapore to Commonwealth Relations Office, 18 September 1963, DO 187/31, 65.
13. Ibid.
14. *ST*, 22 September 1963, p. 1.
15. Constitution of the State of Singapore, CO 1030/1475, 137.
16. See Albert Lau, *A Moment of Anguish: Singapore in Malaysia and the Politics of Disengagement* (Singapore: Times Academic Press, 1998).
17. See the scholarly appraisal of Othman Wok's account of the riots in Fairus Bin Jasmin, "Analyzing the Perceptions and Portrayals of the 1964 Racial Riot in Singapore", Unpublished Master's thesis (Singapore: Department of Malay Studies, National University of Singapore, 2013), pp. 48–49.
18. Calhoun, *Nationalism*, pp. 42–58.
19. Terence Chong, "Fluid Nation: The Perpetual 'Renovation' of Nation and National Identities in Singapore", in *Management of Success: Singapore Revisited*, edited by Terence Chong (Singapore: Institute of Southeast Asian Studies, 2010), pp. 504–20.

BIBLIOGRAPHY

Primary Sources

The National Archives (United Kingdom)

CO 1030. Colonial Office and Commonwealth Office: Far Eastern Department and successors: Registered Files (Far Eastern Department Series).

DO 35. Dominions Office and Commonwealth Relations Office: Original Correspondence.

DO 187. Commonwealth Relations Office and successors: High Commission, Federation of Malaya and Malaysia: Records.

FCO 141. Foreign and Commonwealth Office and predecessors: Records of Former Colonial Administrations: Migrated Archives.

FO 1091. Commissioner General for the United Kingdom in Southeast Asia, and United Kingdom Commissioner for Singapore and Southeast Asia: Registered Files.

National Archives of Singapore (Singapore)

Ministry of Information and the Arts Collection, courtesy of National Archives of Singapore.

Yusof Ishak Collection, courtesy of National Archives of Singapore.

Sahid Sahooman. 2007. Accession Number 003210. Singapore: National Archives of Singapore, August 2007.

Tan Sri Syed Esa Almenoar. 1984. Accession Number 000013. Singapore: National Archives of Singapore, January 1984.

Zubir Said. 1984. Accession Number 000293. Singapore: National Archives of Singapore, September 1984.

Newspapers

Berita Harian
Indian Daily Mail
Malaya Tribune
The Singapore Free Press
Singapore Standard
The Straits Budget
The Straits Times
Warta Negara

Party Publications

The People's Action Party, *Petir*.
——. 1959a. *The Tasks Ahead: PAP's Five-Year Plan 1959–1964 I.* Singapore: PETIR.
——. 1959b. *The Tasks Ahead: PAP's Five-Year Plan 1959–1964 II.* Singapore: PETIR.

Government Publications

Department of Information Services, Government of Singapore. 1959. *Singapore Constitution Exposition.* Singapore: Straits Times Press.
Government of Malaya. 1957a. *Federation of Malaya: Constitutional Proposals.* Kuala Lumpur: Government Press.
——. 1957b. *Chadangan-Chadangan Perlembagaan Persekutuan Tanah Melayu.* Kuala Lumpur: Jabatan Chetak Kerajaan.
Government of Singapore. 1958. Singapore (Constitution) Order in Council 1958. Singapore: Government Printing Office.
——. 1959. Towards a More Just Society. Singapore: Government Printing Press.
Ministry of Culture. 1959. *Minggu Kesetiaan Kebangsaan, Negara Singapura, 3-9/12/1959: Chendera-Mata.* Singapore: Government Printing Office.
——. 1960. *A Year of Construction.* Singapore: Government Printing Office.
——. 1961. *A Year of Decision.* Singapore: Government Printing Office.
Singapore Legislative Assembly Debates 1955–1963.
United Kingdom Colonial Office. 1957. *Constitutional Proposals for the Federation of Malaya.* London: H. M. Stationery Office.

Autobiographies

A. Samad Ismail. 1993. *Memoir A. Samad Ismail di Singapura.* Bangi: Penerbit Universiti Kebangsaan Malaysia.

Abdul Aziz Ishak. 1977. *Special Guest: The Detention in Malaysia of an Ex-Cabinet Minister.* Singapore: Oxford University Press.
——. 1983. Mencari Bako. Kuala Lumpur: Adabi.
Lee Kuan Yew. 2000. *From Third World to First.* New York: Harper Collins Publishers.
——. 2004. *The Singapore Story: Memoirs of Lee Kuan Yew.* Singapore: Marshall Cavendish.
Said Zahari. 2001. *Dark Clouds at Dawn: A Political Memoir.* Kuala Lumpur: INSAN.

Books and Chapters in Books

A. Samad Ahmad. 1984. *Sulalatus Salatin (Sejarah Melayu).* Kuala Lumpur: Dewan Bahasa dan Pustaka.
Abdul Aziz Bari. 2013. *The Monarchy and the Constitution of Malaya.* Kuala Lumpur: IDEAS.
Abdul Latiff Abu Bakar. 1984. *Abdul Rahim Kajai: Wartawan dan Sasterawan Melayu.* Kuala Lumpur: Dewan Bahasa dan Pustaka.
Abdullah, Elinah. 2006. "The Political Activities of the Singapore Malays, 1945–1959". In *Malays/Muslims in Singapore: Selected Readings in History 1819–1965*, edited by Kay Kim Khoo, Elinah Abdullah and Meng Hao Wan, pp. 315–54. Subang Jaya: Pelanduk Publications.
Ahmad Kassim, ed. 1965. *Hikayat Hang Tuah.* Kuala Lumpur: Dewan Bahasa dan Pustaka.
Ali Salim. 1985. "A Pioneer of Malay Journalism". In *A Samad Ismail: Journalism and Politics*, edited by Cheah Boon Kheng, pp. 52–74. Kuala Lumpur: Pustaka Budiman.
Aljunied, Syed Muhd Khairudin. 2009. *Colonialism, Violence and Muslims in Southeast Asia.* London and New York: Routledge.
——. 2015. *Radicals: Resistance and Protest in Colonial Malaya.* DeKalb: Northern Illinois University Press.
Amoroso, Donna J. 2014. *Traditionalism and the Ascendancy of the Malay Ruling Class in Colonial Malaya.* Singapore: NUS Press.
Amrith, Sunil S. 2008. "Internationalism and Political Pluralism in Singapore, 1950–1963". In *Paths Not Taken: Political Pluralism in Post-War Singapore*, edited by Michael Barr and Carl A. Trocki, pp. 37–56. Singapore: NUS Press.
Anderson, Benedict. 2006. *Imagined Communities: Reflections on the Origins and Spread of Nationalism.* Rev. ed. London and New York: Verso.
Banerjee, Milinda, Charlotte Backerra and Cathleen Sarti, ed. 2017. *Transnational Histories of the 'Royal Nation'.* Cham: Palgrave Macmillan.
Barnard, Timothy P. 2003. *Multiple Centres of Authority: Society, Environment and the Malay State in Siak, 1674–1827.* Leiden: KITLV.

Barnard, Timothy P. and Hendrik M.J. Maier. 2004. "Melayu, Malay, Maleis: Journeys Through the Identity of a Collection". In *Contesting Malayness: Malay Identity Across Boundaries*, edited by Timothy P. Barnard, pp. ix–xiii. Singapore: Singapore University Press.

Barnard, Timothy P. and Jan van der Putten. 2008. "Malay Cosmopolitan Activism in Post-War Singapore". In Paths Not Taken: Political Pluralism in Post-War Singapore, edited by Michael Barr and Carl A. Trocki, pp. 132–53. Singapore: NUS Press.

Barr, Michael D. 2018. Singapore: A Modern History. London: I.B. Tauris and Co. Ltd.

Barr, Michael D. and Zlatko Skrbis. 2008. *Constructing Singapore: Elitism, Ethnicity and the Nation-Building Project.* Copenhagen: NIAS Press.

Bayly, Christopher and Tim Harper. 2008. *Forgotten Wars: The End of Britain's Asian Empire.* London: Penguin Books.

Bender, Jill C. 2016. *The 1857 Uprising and the British Empire.* Cambridge: Cambridge University Press.

Bhabha, Homi K. 2004. *The Location of Culture.* London and New York: Routledge.

Boyce, D. George. 1999. *Decolonization and the British Empire, 1775–1997.* New York: St. Martin's Press.

Butler, David. 1991. "Introduction". In *Sovereigns and Surrogates: Constitutional Heads of State in the Commonwealth*, edited by David Butler and D.A. Low, pp. 1–9. London: Macmillan.

Calhoun, Craig. 1997. *Nationalism.* Buckingham: Open University Press.

Cannadine, David. 1983. "The Context, Performance and Meaning of Ritual: The British Monarchy and the 'Invention of Tradition', c. 1820–1977". In *The Invention of Tradition*, edited by Eric Hobsbawm and Terence Ranger, pp. 101–64. Cambridge: Cambridge University Press.

———. 2001. *Ornamentalism: How the British Saw Their Empire.* New York: Oxford University Press.

Cerulo, Karen A. 1995. *Identity Designs: The Sights and Sounds of a Nation.* New Jersey: Rutgers University Press.

Chakrabarty, Dipesh. 2000. *Provincializing Europe: Postcolonial Thought and Historical Difference.* Princeton and Oxford: Princeton University Press.

Chan, Heng Chee and Obaid ul Haq. 2007. *S. Rajaratnam: The Prophetic and the Political.* Singapore: Institute of Southeast Asian Studies.

Chatterjee, Partha. 1986. *Nationalist Thought and the Colonial World.* London: Zed Books.

———. 1993. *The Nation and Its Fragments.* Princeton: Princeton University Press.

Cheah, Boon Kheng. 1983. *Red Star Over Malaya: Resistance and Social Conflict During and After the Japanese Occupation, 1941–1946.* Singapore: Singapore University Press.

———. 1987. "Introduction". In *A. Samad Ismail: Journalism and Politics*, edited by Cheah Boon Kheng, pp. xv–xxvi. Kuala Lumpur: Singamal.

——. 2002. *Malaysia: The Making of a Nation*. Singapore: Institute of Southeast Asian Studies.

Chew, Melanie. 1996. *Leaders of Singapore*. Singapore: World Scientific.

——. 1999. *A Biography of President Yusof bin Ishak*. Singapore: Singapore National Printers for Board of Commissioners of Currency.

Chew, Soon Beng. 1991. *Trade Unionism in Singapore*. Singapore: McGraw-Hill.

Chin, C.C. 2008. "The United Front Strategy of the Malayan Communist Party in Singapore, 1950s–1960s". In *Paths Not Taken: Political Pluralism in Post-War Singapore*, edited by Michael Barr and Carl A. Trocki, pp. 58–77. Singapore: NUS Press.

Chin, Kin Wah. 1983. *The Defence of Malaysia and Singapore: The Transformation of Security System 1957–71*. Cambridge and New York: Cambridge University Press.

Chong, Terence. 2010. "Fluid Nation: The Perpetual 'Renovation' of Nation and National Identities in Singapore". In *Management of Success: Singapore Revisited*, edited by Terence Chong, pp. 504–20. Singapore: Institute of Southeast Asian Studies.

Chua, Ai Lin. 2008. "Imperial Subjects, Straits Citizens: Anglophone Asians in the Struggle for Political Rights in Inter-War Singapore". In *Paths Not Taken: Political Pluralism in Post-War Singapore*, edited by Michael Barr and Carl A. Trocki, pp. 16–36. Singapore: NUS Press.

Chua, Beng Huat. 1992. "Decoding the Political in Civic Spaces: An Interpretive Essay". In *Public Space: Design, Use and Management*, edited by Chua Beng Huat and Norman Edwards, pp. 55–68. Singapore: Singapore University Press.

Clutterbuck, Richard. 1984. *Conflict and Violence in Singapore and Malaysia, 1945–1983*. Singapore: Graham Brash.

Comber, Leon. 2012. *Singapore Correspondent: Political Dispatches from Singapore (1958–1962)*. Singapore: Marshall Cavendish.

Crowcroft, Barnaby. 2017. "The Problem of Protectorates in the Age of Decolonisation: Britain and West Africa, 1955–60". In *Protection and Empire: A Global History*, edited by Lauren Brenton, Adam Clulow and Bain Attwood, pp. 228–44. Cambridge: Cambridge University Press.

Darby, Philp. 1973. *British Defence Policy East of Suez 1947–1968*. London: Oxford University Press.

Darwin, John. 1988. *Britain and Decolonisation: The Retreat from Empire in the Post-War World*. Basingstoke and London: Macmillan Press.

——. 1999. "A Third British Empire? The Dominion Idea in Imperial Politics". In *The Oxford History of the British Empire: Volume IV: The Twentieth Century*, edited by Judith Brown and Wm. Roger Louis, pp. 64–87. Oxford: Oxford University Press.

——. 2009. *The Empire Project: The Rise and Fall of the British World System*. Cambridge: Cambridge University Press.

Department of Social Studies, University of Malaya. 1959. *Report on a Survey of Applications to the Singapore Labour Department Employment Exchange.* Singapore: University of Malaya.

Djamour, Judith. 1965. *Malay Kinship and Marriage in Singapore.* London: Athlone Press.

Drayton, Richard. 2020. "Commonwealth History from Below?: Caribbean National, Federal and Pan-African Renegotiations of the Empire Project, c. 1880–1950". In *Commonwealth History in the Twenty-First Century*, edited by Saul Dubow and Richard Drayton, pp. 41–60. Cham: Palgrave Macmillan.

Drysdale, John. 1984. *Singapore: Struggle for Success.* Singapore: Times Books International.

Duara, Prasenjit. 1995. *Rescuing History from the Nation: Questioning Narratives of Modern China.* Chicago and London: The University of Chicago Press.

Fanon, Frantz. 1963. *The Wretched of the Earth.* New York: Grove Press.

Fernandez, Michael and Loh Kah Seng. 2008. "The Left-Wing Trade Unions in Singapore, 1945–1970". In *Paths Not Taken: Political Pluralism in Post-War Singapore*, edited by Michael Barr and Carl A. Trocki, pp. 206–27. Singapore: NUS Press.

Fernando, Joseph. 2009. *The Alliance Road to Independence.* Kuala Lumpur: University of Malaya Press.

Firdaus Haji Abdullah. 1985. *Radical Malay Politics: Its Origins and Early Development.* Petaling Jaya: Pelanduk Publications.

Foucault, Michel. 1995. Discipline and Punish: The Birth of the Prison, translated by Alan Sheridan. New York: Vintage.

Gamba, Charles. 1962. *The Origins of Trade Unionism in Malaya: A Study in Colonial Labour Unrest.* Singapore: Eastern University Press.

Geertz, Clifford. 1980. *Negara: The Theatre State in Nineteenth-Century Bali.* New Jersey: Princeton University Press.

Geisler, Michael E., ed. 2005. *National Symbols, Fractured Identities: Contesting the National Narrative.* London: Middlebury College Press.

Gellner, Ernest. 2006. *Nations and Nationalism.* 2nd ed. Oxford: Wiley-Blackwell.

Getachew, Adom. 2019. *Worldmaking After Empire: The Rise and Fall of Self-Determination.* Princeton and Oxford: Princeton University Press.

Ghazali Shafie. 1998. *Ghazali Shafie's Memoir on the Formation of Malaysia.* Selangor: Penerbit Universiti Kebangsaan Malaysia.

Gill, Ranjit. 1990. *Of Political Bondage.* Singapore: Sterling Corporate.

Gillis, E. Kay. 2008. "Civil Society and the Malay Education Council". In *Paths Not Taken: Political Pluralism in Post-War Singapore*, edited by Michael Barr and Carl A. Trocki, pp. 154–69. Singapore: NUS Press.

Goh, Keng Swee. 1958. *Urban Incomes & Housing: A Report on the Social Survey of Singapore, 1953–54.* Singapore: Government Printing Office.

——. 1976. "A Socialist Economy that Works". In *Socialism that Works: the Singapore Way*, edited by C.V. Devan Nair, pp. 77–85. Singapore: Federal Publications.

Gordon, Colin. 1991. "Governmental Rationality: An Introduction". In *The Foucault Effect*, pp. 1–52. Chicago: University of Chicago Press.

Gorski, Philip S. 2013. "Nation-ization Struggles: S Bourdieusian Theory of Nationalism". In *Bourdieu and Historical Analysis*, edited by Philip S. Gorski, pp. 242–65. Durham and London: Duke University Press.

Gullick, J.M. 1992. *Rulers and Residents: Influence and Power in the Malay State: 1870–1920*. Singapore: Oxford University Press.

Hack, Karl. 2001. *Defence and Decolonisation in Southeast Asia*. Surrey: Curzon.

———. 2003. "Theories and Approaches to British Decolonization in Southeast Asia". In *The Transformation of Southeast Asia: International Perspectives on Decolonization*, edited by Marc Frey, Ronald Pruessen and Tan Tai Yong, pp. 105–26. London and New York: Routledge.

———. 2010. "The Malayan Trajectory in Singapore's History". In *Singapore from Temasek to 21st Century: Reinventing the Global City*, edited by Karl Hack, Jean-Louis Margolin and Karine Delaye, pp. 243–91. Singapore: NUS Press.

———. 2019. "We Meet Again: Britain and Singapore, 1945–1946". In *200 Years of Singapore and the United Kingdom*, edited by Tommy Koh and Scott Wightman, pp. 118–25. Singapore: Straits Times Press.

Harper, T.N. 1999. *The End of Empire and the Making of Malaya*. Cambridge: Cambridge University Press.

Headrick, Daniel. 1981. *The Tools of Empire: Technology and European Imperialism in the Nineteenth Century*. Oxford and New York: Oxford University Press.

Hendershot, Vernon and W.G. Shellabear. 1945. *A Dictionary of Standard Malay*. Mountain View: Pacific Press Publishing Association.

Hickling, Hugh. 1991. "Malaysia". In *Sovereigns and Surrogates: Constitutional Heads of States in the Commonwealth*, edited by David Butler and D.A. Low, pp. 203–32. London: Macmillan.

Hill, Michael and Kwen Fee Lian. 1995. *The Politics of Nation-Building and Citizenship in Singapore*. London and New York: Routledge.

Hobsbawm, Eric. 1983a. "Introduction: Inventing Traditions". In *The Invention of Tradition*, edited by Eric Hobsbawm and Terence Ranger, pp. 1–14. Cambridge: Cambridge University Press.

———. 1983b. "Mass Producing Traditions: Europe, 1870–1914". In *The Invention of Tradition*, by Eric Hobsbawm and Terence Ranger, pp. 263–308. Cambridge: Cambridge University Press.

Holden, Philip. 2008. *Autobiography and Decolonization: Modernity, Masculinity, and the Nation-State*. Madison: University of Wisconsin Press.

Hong Lysa. 2008. "Apothesis: The Lee Kuan Yew Story as Singapore's History". In *The Scripting of a National History: Singapore and Its Pasts*, edited by Lysa Hong and Huang Jianli. Singapore: NUS Press.

Huang, Jianli. 2008. "The Young Pathfinders: Portrayal of Student Political Activism". In *Paths Not Taken: Political Pluralism in Post-War Singapore*, edited by Michael Barr and Carl A. Trocki, pp. 188–205. Singapore: NUS Press.

Huxley, Tim. 2000. *Defending the Lion City: The Armed Forces of Singapore.* St Leonards: Tim Huxley.

Hyam, Ronald and Wm. Roger Louis. 2000. *The Conservative Government and the End of Empire 1957–1964.* London: Stationery Office.

Jansen, Jan and Jürgen Osterhammel. 2017. *Decolonization: A Short History,* translated by Jeremiah Riemer. Princeton: Princeton University Press.

Jones, Matthew. 2001. *Conflict and Confrontation in Southeast Asia 1961–1965: Britain, the United States and the Creation of Malaysia.* Cambridge: Cambridge University Press.

Kelly, John D. and Martha Kaplan. 2001. *Represented Communities: Fiji and World Decolonization.* Chicago and London: University of Chicago Press.

Knapman, Gareth. 2019. "The Liberal Security Experiment in Southeast Asia". In *Liberalism and the British Empire in Southeast Asia,* edited by Gareth Knapman, Anthony Milner and Mary Quilty, pp. 192–214. London and New York: Routledge.

Kratoska, Paul H. 2018. *The Japanese Occupation of Malaya and Singapore, 1941–45.* 2nd ed. Singapore: NUS Press.

Van der Kroef, Justus M. 1967. *Communism in Malaysia and Singapore: A Contemporary Survey.* The Hague: Martinus Nijhoff.

Kumarasingham H. 2020. "Viceregalism". In *Viceregalism: The Crown as Head of State in Political Crises in the Postwar Commonwealth,* edited by H. Kumarasingham, pp. 15–35. Cham: Palgrave Macmillan.

Kwa, Chong Guan. 2006. "Why did Tengku Hussein Sign the 1819 Treaty with Stamford Raffles". In *Malays/Muslims in Singapore: Selected Readings in History 1819–1965,* edited by Khoo Kay Kim, Elinah Abdullah and Wan Meng Hao, pp. 1–36. Subang Jaya: Pelanduk Publications.

Lai, Ah Eng. 1995. *Meanings of Multiethnicity: A Case Study of Ethnicity and Ethnic Relations in Singapore.* Oxford: Oxford University Press.

Lau, Albert. 1991. *The Malayan Union Controversy.* Singapore: Oxford University Press.

——. 1998. *A Moment of Anguish: Singapore in Malaysia and the Politics of Disengagement.* Singapore: Times Academic Press.

——. 2003. "'Nationalism' in the Decolonization of Singapore". In *The Transformation of Southeast Asia: International Perspectives on Decolonization,* edited by Marc Frey, Ronald Pruessen and Tan Tai Yong, pp. 180–96. London and New York: Routledge.

——. 2005. "Nation-Building and the Singapore Story: Some Issues in the Study of Contemporary Singapore History". In *Nation-building: Five Southeast Asian Histories,* edited by Wang Gungwu, pp. 221–50. Singapore: Institute of Southeast Asian Studies.

——. 2009. "The Politics of Becoming 'Malaysian' and 'Singaporean'". In *Across the Causeway: A Multi-dimensional Study of Malaysia-Singapore Relations,* edited by Takashi Shiraishi, pp. 92–124. Singapore: Institute of Southeast Asian Studies.

——. 2012. "Decolonization and the Cold War in Singapore, 1955–9". In *Southeast Asia and the Cold War*, edited by Albert Lau, pp. 43–66. Oxon and New York: Routledge.

——. 2019. "Political Developments in Singapore, 1945–1963". In *200 Years of Singapore and the United Kingdom*, edited by Tommy Koh and Scott Wightman, pp. 136–43. Singapore: Straits Times Press.

Lee, Christopher J., ed. 2010. *Making a World After Empire: The Bandung Moment and Its Political Afterlives*. Athens: Ohio University Press.

Lee, Edwin. 2008. *Singapore: The Unexpected Nation*. Singapore: Institute of Southeast Asian Studies.

Lee, Koon Choy. 2013. *Golden Dragon and Purple Phoenix: The Chinese and Their Multi-Ethnic Descendents in Southeast Asia*. Singapore: World Scientific.

Lee Kuan Yew. 2014. The Battle for Merger. Singapore: Straits Times Press.

Lee Ting Hui. 1996. The Open United Front: The Communist Struggle in Singapore 1954–1966. Singapore: South Seas Society. Li, Tania. 1989. *Malays in Singapore: Culture, Economy and Ideology*. Singapore: Oxford University Press.

Lily Zubaidah Rahim. 2008. "Winning and Losing Malay Support: PAP-Malay Community Relations, 1950s and 1960s". In *Paths Not Taken: Political Pluralism in Post-War Singapore*, pp. 95–115. Singapore: NUS Press.

——. 2009. *Singapore in the Malay World: Building and Breaching Regional Bridges*. Milton Park, Abingdon, Oxon, New York: Routledge.

Lim, Edmund. 2017. *Yusof Ishak*. Singapore: Straits Times Press.

Lim, Yew Hock. 1986. *Reflections*. Kuala Lumpur: Pustaka Antara.

Llyod, Lorna. 2007. *Diplomacy with a Difference: The Commonwealth Office of High Commissioner, 1880–2006*. Leiden and Boston: Martinus Nijhoff.

Loh, Kah Seng. 2013. Squatters into Citizens: The 1961 Bukit Ho Swee Fire and the Making of Modern Singapore. Singapore: NUS Press.

Loh, Kah Seng, Edgar Liao, Cheng Tju Lim and Guo-Quan Seng. 2012. *The University Socialist Club and the Contest for Malaya: Tangled Strands of Modernity*. Amsterdam: Amsterdam University Press.

Long, S.R. Joey. 2011. "Bringing the International and Transnational Back In: Singapore, Decolonisation, and the Cold War". In *Singapore in Global History*, pp. 215–33. Amsterdam: Amsterdam University Press.

Louis, Wm. Roger. 2006. *Ends of British Imperialism: The Scramble for Empire, Suez and Decolonization*. London and New York: I.B. Tauris.

Lyon, Peter. 1991. "The Commonwealth and the Suez Crisis". In *Suez 1956: The Crisis and its Consequences,* edited by Wm. Roger Louis and Roger Owen, pp. 257–74. New York: Oxford University Press.

Macmillan, Harold. 1973. *Memoirs: At the End of the Day, 1961–1963*. London: Macmillan Press.

Maidin, Zainuddin. 2013. *Di Depan Api, di Belakang Duri*. Kuala Lumpur: Utusan Publication.

Majelis Pemusyawaratan Rakyat Republik Indonesia. 2011. *Undang-Undang Dasar Negara Republik Indonesia Tahun 1945*. Jakarta: Sekretariat Jenderal MPR RI.

Majumdar, Raachona. 2010. *Writing Postcolonial History.* London and New York: Bloomsbury Academic.

Margolin, Jean-Louis. 2010. "The People's Action Party Blueprint for Singapore, 1959–1965". In *Singapore from Temasek to 21st Century: Reinventing the Global City*, edited by Karl Hack, Jean-Louis Margolin and Karine Delaye, pp. 292–322. Singapore: NUS Press.

McIntyre, W. David. 1966. *Colonies into Commonwealth.* London: Blandford Press.

———. 1977. *The Commonwealth of Nations: Origins and Impact, 1869–1971.* Minneapolis: University of Minnesota Press.

McLean, Gavin. 2004. "From Cocked Hats to Designer Frocks—The 'Queen in Drag' in Twentieth-Century New Zealand". In *Exploring the British World: Identity, Cultural Production, Institutions*, edited by Kate Darian-Smith, pp. 979–1002. Melbourne: RMIT Publishing.

Milner, Anthony. 1982. *Kerajaan: Malay Political Culture on the Eve of Colonial Rule.* Tucson: University of Arizona Press.

———. 1994. *The Invention of Politics in Colonial Malaya: Contesting Nationalism and the Expansion of the Public Sphere.* Cambridge: Cambridge University Press.

———. 2008. *The Malays.* West Sussex: Wiley-Blackwell.

———. 2016. Kerajaan: Malay Political Culture on the Eve of Colonial Rule. 2nd ed. Petaling Jaya: SIRD.

Mohamed Noordin Sopiee. 2005. *From Malayan Union to Separation: Political Unification in the Malaysia Region 1945–1965.* Kuala Lumpur: University of Malaya Press.

Mohd Azhar Terimo. 2006. "From Self-Government to Independence: UMNO and Malay Politics in Singapore, 1959–1965". In *Malays/Muslims in Singapore: Selected Readings in History 1819–1965*, edited by Khoo Kay Kim, Elinah Abdullah and Wan Meng Hao, pp. 355–86. Subang Jaya: Pelanduk.

Morris, Jan. 1982. The Spectacle of Empire. London: Faber and Faber.

Morris, Jan and Robert Fermor-Hesketh. 1986. *Architecture of the British Empire.* London: Weidenfeld and Nicolson.

Mrázek, Rudolf. 2002. *Engineers of Happy Land: Technology and Nationalism in a Colony.* Princeton: Princeton University Press.

Muliyadi Mahamood. 2004. *The History of Malay Editorial Cartoons, 1930s–1993.* Kuala Lumpur: Utusan Publications.

Murphy, Philip. 2019. *Monarchy and the End of Empire: The House of Windsor, the British Government and the Postwar Commonwealth.* Oxford: Oxford University Press.

Nietzsche, Friedrich. 1997. "On the Uses and Disadvantages of History for Life". In *Untimely Meditations*, edited by Daniel Breazeale, translated by R.J. Hollingdale, pp. 59–123. Cambridge: Cambridge University Press.

Ng, Irene. 2010. *The Singapore Lion: A Biography of S. Rajaratnam.* Singapore: Institute of Southeast Asian Studies.

Norshahril Saat. 2015. *Yusof Ishak: Singapore's First President.* Singapore: Institute of Southeast Asian Studies.

——. 2016. "Progressive Malay/Muslim Singaporeans—The Thoughts of Yusof Ishak". In *Majulah! 50 Years of Malay/Muslim Community in Singapore*, edited by Zainul Abideen Rasheed and Norshahril Saat, pp. 3–18. Singapore: World Scientific.

Omar, Ariffin. 2015. *Bangsa Melayu: Malay Concepts of Democracy and Community, 1945–1950*. Petaling Jaya: SIRD.

Ongkili, James P. 1985. *Nation-Building in Malaysia 1946–1974*. Singapore: Oxford University Press.

Ooi Kee Beng. 2006. *The Reluctant Politician: Tun Dr Ismail and His Time*. Singapore: Institute of Southeast Asian Studies.

——. 2017. *Yusof Ishak: A Man of Many Firsts*. Singapore: Institute of Southeast Asian Studies.

Orwell, George. 2004. *Animal Farm*. London: Penguin UK.

Osterhammel, Jürgen. 1997. *Colonialism: A Theoretical Overview*, translated by Shelley Frisch. Princeton: Markus Wiener Publishers.

Özkirimli, Umut. 2010. *Theories of Nationalism: A Critical Introduction*. Basingstoke: Palgrave Macmillan.

Pang, Cheng Lian. 1971. Singapore's People's Action Party. Singapore and Kuala Lumpur: Oxford University Press.

Patel, Ian Sanjay. 2021. *We Are Here Because You Were There: Immigration and the End of Empire*. London and New York: Verso.

Peleggi, Maurizio. 2002. *Lord of Things: The Fashioning of the Siamese Monarchy's Modern Image*. Honolulu: University of Hawaii Press.

Perpustakaan Negara Malaysia. 1980. *Senarai Gelaran Melayu*. Kuala Lumpur: Perpustakaan Negara.

Poh, Soo Kai, Kok Fang Tan, and Hong Lysa. 2013. *The 1963 Operation Coldstore in Singapore: Commemorating 50 Years*. Kuala Lumpur: SIRD.

Poh, Soo Kai, Quee Jing Tan, and Yew Kay Koh. 2010. *The Fajar Generation: The University Socialist Club and the Politics of Postwar Malaya and Singapore*. Petaling Jaya: SIRD.

Porter, A.N. and A.J. Stockwell. 1987. *British Imperial Policy and Decolonization, 1938–64*. London: Macmillan Press.

Pugh, Peter. 2000. *Rolls-Royce: The Magic of a Name*. London: Icon.

Puthucheary, J.J. 1979. *Ownership and Control in the Malayan Economy*. Kuala Lumpur: University of Malaya Co-operative Bookshop.

Ramakrishna, Kumar. 2002. *Emergency Propaganda: The Winning of Malayan Hearts and Minds 1948–1958*. Surrey: Curzon.

——. 2015. 'Original Sin'? Revising the Revisionist Critique of the 1963 Operation Coldstore in Singapore. Singapore: Institute of Southeast Asian Studies.

Reid, Anthony. 2000. "Negeri: The Culture of Malay-Speaking City-States of the Fifteenth and Sixteenth Century". In *A Comparative Study of Thirty City-State Cultures: An Investigation*, edited by Morgan Herman Hansen, pp. 417–30. Copanhagen: The Royal Danish Academy of Science and Letters.

——. 2004. "Understanding Melayu (Malay) as a Source of Diverse Modern Identities". In *Contesting Malayness: Malay Identity Across Boundaries*, edited by Timothy P. Barnard, pp. 1–24. Singapore: Singapore University Press.

——. 2016. *Imperial Alchemy: Nationalism and Political Identity in Southeast Asia*. Cambridge: Cambridge University Press.

Roff, William R. 1967. *The Origins of Malay Nationalism*. Kuala Lumpur: University of Malaya Press.

Rozeman Abu Hassan. 2015. *Dasar British Terhadap Hubungan Singapura-Malaysia 1959–1969*. Bangi: UKM Press.

Sadka, Emily. 1968. *The Protected Malay States 1874–1895*. Kuala Lumpur: University of Malaya Press.

Sandhu, K.S. and Paul Wheatley, eds. 1989. *Management of Success: The Moulding of Modern Singapore*. Singapore: Institute of Southeast Asian Studies.

Saunders, Graham. 2002. *A History of Brunei*. London: RoutledgeCurzon.

Scott, David. 1999. *Refashioning Futures: Criticism After Postcoloniality*. Princeton University Press.

Shamsul, A.B. 2004. "A History of Identity, an Identity of a History: The Idea and Practice of 'Malayness' in Malaysia Reconsidered". In *Contesting Malayness: Malay Identity across Boundaries*, edited by Timothy Barnard, pp. 135–48. Singapore: Singapore University Press.

Sheppard, Mubbin. 1983. *Papers Relating to Trengganu*. Kuala Lumpur: MBRAS.

Sheridan, L.A. and Harry Groves. 1967. *The Constitution of Malaysia*. New York: Oceana Publications.

Shipway, Martin. 2008. *Decolonization and Its Impact: A Comparative Approach to the End of Colonial Empires*. Oxford: Blackwell.

Siddique, Sharon. 1986. "The Administration of Islam in Singapore". In *Islam and Society in Southeast Asia*, edited by Taufik Abdullah and Sharon Siddique, pp. 315–31. Singapore: Institute of Southeast Asian Studies.

Simorangkir, J.C.T. and B. Mang Reng Say. 1980. *Around and About the Indonesian Constitution of 1945*. Jakarta: Djambata.

Singh, Bilveer. 2014. *Quest for Political Power: Communist Subversion and Militancy in Singapore*. Singapore: Marshall Cavendish Asia.

Sivasundaram, Sujit. 2013. *Islanded: Britain, Sri Lanka, and the Bounds of an Indian Ocean Colony*. Chicago: University of Chicago Press.

Smith, Simon C. 1995. *British Relations with the Malay Rulers from Decentralization to Malayan Indpendence 1953–1957*. London: Oxford University Press.

Spencer, Stephen. 2014. *Race and Ethnicity: Culture, Identity and Representation*. 2nd ed. London and New York: Routledge.

Spivak, Gayatri Chakravorty. 1994. "Can the Subaltern Speak?". In *Colonial Discourse and Post-Colonial Theory: A Reader*, edited by Patrick Williams and Laura Chrisman, pp. 66–111. New York: Columbia University Press.

Stenson, Michael. 1980. *Class, Race, and Colonialism in West Malaysia: The Indian Case*. St. Lucia: University of Queensland Press.

Stockwell, A.J., ed. 1995. *British Documents on the End of Empire*. Series B, vol. 3: Malaya. London: HMSO.

——. ed. 2004. *British Documents on the End of Empire.* Series B, vol. 8: Malaysia. London: HMSO.

——. 2019. "The British Role in the Formation of Malaysia". In *200 Years of Singapore and the United Kingdom*, edited by Tommy Koh and Scott Wightman, pp. 136–43. Singapore: Straits Times Press.

Straits Times, The. 1957. *Buku Merdeka: Tanah Melayu Menjadi Negara*. Singapore: The Straits Times Press.

Strange, Carolyn, ed. 1996. *Qualities of Mercy: Justice, Punishment, and Discretion.* Vancouver: UBC Press.

Summers, Julie. 2016. *The Colonel of Tamarkan: Philip Toosey and the Bridge on the River Kwai.* New York: Simon and Schuster.

Sundaram, Jomo Kwame. 1986. *A Question of Class: Capital, the State and Uneven Development in Malaysia.* Singapore: Oxford University Press.

Suwannathat-Pian, Kobkua. 2011. *Palace, Political Party and Power: A Story of the Socio-Political Development of Malay Kingship.* Singapore: NUS Press.

Sweeney, Amin. 1987. *A Full Hearing: Orality and Literacy in the Malay World.* Berkeley: University of California Press.

Syed Husin Ali, Ariffin Omar, Jeyakumar Devaraj, and Fahmi Reza. 2017. *The People's Constitutional Proposals for Malaya.* Petaling Jaya: SIRD.

Tan, Jing Quee, Kok Chiang Tan, and Hong Lysa. 2011. *The May 13 Generation: The Chinese Middle School Student Movement and Singapore Politics in the 1950s.* Petaling Jaya: SIRD.

Tan, Jing Quee and K.S. Jomo. 2001. *Comet in Our Sky: Lim Chin Siong in History.* Kuala Lumpur: Insan.

Tan, Kevin Y.L. 2008. *Marshall of Singapore: A Biography.* Singapore: Institute of Southeast Asian Studies.

——. 2015. *The Constitution of Singapore: A Contextual Analysis.* Oxford: Bloomsbury.

——. 2017. *Puan Noor Aishah: Singapore's First Lady.* Singapore: Straits Times Press.

Tan, Kevin Y.L. and Peng Er Lam. 1997. *Managing Political Change in Singapore: The Elected Presidency.* London: Routledge.

——. 2018. Lee's Lieutenants: Singapore's Old Guard. Rev. ed. Singapore: Straits Times Press.

Tan Tai Yong. 2008. *Creating 'Greater Malaysia': Decolonisation and the Politics of Merger.* Singapore: Institute of Southeast Asian Studies.

——. 2019. "The Rise of Nationalism and the Anti-Colonial Movement in Singapore". In *200 Years of Singapore and the United Kingdom*, edited by Tommy Koh and Scott Wightman, pp. 126–35. Singapore: Straits Times Press.

Tarling, Nicholas. 2001. *A Sudden Rampage: The Japanese Occupation of Southeast Asia, 1941–1945.* London: Hurst and Company.

Taylor, James. 2016. *British Luxury Cars of the 1950s and '60s*. Oxford: Bloomsbury.

Tosh, John. 2022. *The Pursuit of History: Aims, Methods and New Directions in the Study of History*. 7th ed. London and New York: Routledge.

Trocki, Carl. 2007. *Prince of Pirates: The Temenggongs and the Development of Johor and Singapore 1784–1885*. Singapore: NUS Press.

———. 2008. "David Marshall and the Struggle for Civil Rights in Singapore". In *Paths Not Taken: Political Pluralism in Post-War Singapore*, edited by Michael Barr and Carl A. Trocki, pp. 116–30. Singapore: NUS Press.

Trocki, Carl and Michael D. Barr. 2008. "Introduction". In *Paths Not Taken: Political Pluralism in Post-War Singapore*, edited by Michael Barr and Carl A. Trocki, pp. 1–15. Singapore: NUS Press.

Tunku Abdul Rahman. 1977. *Looking Back—Monday Musings and Memories*. Kuala Lumpur: Pustaka Antara.

Turnbull, C.M. 2020. *A History of Modern Singapore, 1819–2005*. New ed. Singapore: NUS Press.

United Nations Food and Agriculture Organisation. 1957. *Report of Malaya Constitutional Commision*. Kuala Lumpur: Government Press.

Utusan Melayu. 1949. *Utusan Melayu 10 tahun*. Singapore: Utusan Melayu Press Limited.

———. 1964. *Utusan Melayu 25 Tahun*. Kuala Lumpur: Utusan Melayu Press Limited.

van Voss, Lex Heerma. 2002. "Introduction". In *Petitions in Social History*, edited by Lex Heerma van Voss, pp. 1–10. Cambridge: Cambridge University Press.

Ward, W.E.F. 1967. *A History of Ghana*. 4th ed. London: George Allen and Unwin.

White, Hayden. 1978. *Tropics of Discourse: Essays in Cultural Criticism*. Baltimore and London: John Hopkins University Press.

Wilson, H.E. 1978. *Social Engineering in Singapore: Educational Policies and Social Change 1819–1972*. Singapore: Singapore University Press.

Winstedt, Richard. 1957. *Dictionary of Colloquial Malay*. Singapore: Marican & Sons.

Yap, Sonny, Richard Lim and Leong Weng Kam. 2009. *Men in White: The Untold Story of Singapore's Ruling Political Party*. Singapore: Straits Times Press.

Yau, Sochou. 2008. "All Quiet on Jurong Road: Nanyang University and Radical Vision in Singapore". In *Paths Not Taken: Political Pluralism in Post-War Singapore*, edited by Michael Barr and Carl A. Trocki, pp. 170–87. Singapore: NUS Press.

Yeo, Kim Wah. 1973. *Political Development in Singapore*. Singapore: Singapore University Press.

Yeo, Kim Wah and Albert Lau. 1991. "From Colonialism to Independence, 1945–1965". In *A History of Singapore*, edited by Ernest C.T. and Edwin Lee, pp. 117–53. Singapore: Oxford University Press.

Yong, C.F. 1997. *The Origins of Malayan Communism*. Singapore: South Seas Society.

Zhou, Taomo. 2019. *Migration in the Time of Revolution: China, Indonesia, and the Cold War*. Ithaca and London: Cornell University Press.

Articles in Journals

Arnold, David. 2005. "Europe, Technology and Colonialism in the 20th Century". *History and Technology* 21, no. 1: 85–106.

Ball, Simon J. 1999. "Selkirk in Singapore". *Twentieth Century British History* 10, no. 1: 162–91.

Barr, Michael D. 2021. "Singapore Comes to Terms with its Malay Past: The Politics of Crafting a National History". *Asian Studies Review*: 1–19.

Bradley, C. Paul. 1964. "The Formation of Malaysia". *Current History* (February): 89–116.

Broich, John. 2007. "Engineering the Empire: British Water Supply Systems and Colonial Societies, 1850–1900". *Journal of British Studies* 46, no. 2: 346–65.

Cheah Boon Kheng. 1988. "The Erosion of Ideological Hegemony and Royal Power and the Rise of Postwar Malay Nationalism, 1945–46". *Journal of Southeast Asian Studies* 19, no. 1: 1–26.

Dartford, Gerald P. 1962. "Plan of Malaysian Federation". *Current History* (November): 278–313.

Derichs, Claudia and Thomas Heberer. 2006. "Introduction: Diversity and Nation-Building in East and Southeast Asia". *European Journal of East Asian Studies* 5, no. 1: 1–13.

Emmanuel, Mark. 2010. "Viewspapers: The Malay Press of the 1930s". *Journal of Southeast Asian Studies* 41, no. 1: 1–20.

Finlayson, Alan. 1998. "Ideology, Discourse and Nationalism". *Journal of Political Ideologies* 3, no. 1: 99–118.

Hack, Karl. 2019. "Unfinished Decolonisation and Globalisation". *The Journal of Imperial and Commonwealth History* 47, no. 5: 818–50.

Hirschmann, Charles. 1986. "The Making of Race in Colonial Malaya: Political Economy and Racial Ideology". *Sociological Forum* 1, no. 2: 330–61.

Hussin, Iza. 2014. "Textual Trajectories: Re-Reading the Constitution and Majalah in 1890s Johor". *Indonesia and the Malay World* 41, no. 120: 255–72.

Huzzy, Richard and Henry Miller. 2021. "Colonial Petitions, and the Imperial Parliament, ca. 1780–1918". *Journal of British Studies*: 1–29.

Jones, Matthew. 2000. "Creating Malaysia: Singapore Security, the Borneo Territories and the Contours of British Policy, 1961–63". *Journal of Imperial and Commonwealth History* 28, no. 2: 85–109.

Khoo, Kay Kim. 1981. "Sino-Malay Relations in Peninsular Malaysia before 1942". *Journal of Southeast Asian Studies* 12, no. 1: 93–107.

Krivine, J.D. 1948. "Malta and Self-Government". *World Affairs* 111, no. 2: 111–13.

Kumar, Krishnan. 2021. "Colony and Empire, Colonialism and Imperialism: A Meaningful Distinction?". *Comparative Studies in Society and History* 63, no. 2: 280–309.

Kumarasingham, H. 2013. "The 'Tropical Dominions': The Appeal of Dominion Status in the Decolonisation of India, Pakistan and Ceylon". *Transactions of the Royal Historical Society* 23: 223–45.

Lau, Albert. 1994. "The Colonial Office and the Singapore Merdeka Mission, 23 April to 15 May 1956". *Journal of the South Seas Society* 49: 104–22.

Leong, Stephen. 1977. "The Chinese in Malaya and China's Politics, 1895–1911". *Journal of the Malaysian Branch of the Royal Asiatic Society* 50, no. 2: 7–24.

Lipsker, S. 1963. "Formation of Malaysia". *Current Notes on International Affairs* (October): 5–27.

Low, James. 2004. "Kept in Position: The Labour Front-Alliance Government of Chief Minister David Marshall in Singapore, April 1955–June 1956". *Journal of Southeast Asian Studies* 35, no. 1: 41–64.

Maier, Henk. 2010. "The Writings of Abdul Rahim Kajai: Malay Nostalgia in a Crystal". *Journal of Southeast Asian Studies* 41, no. 1: 71–100.

Malhi, Amrita. 2021. "Race, Space, and the Malayan Emergency: Expelling Malay Muslim Communism and Reconstituting Malaya's Racial State, 1945–1954". *Itinerario* (November): 1–25.

Manickam, Sandra Khor. 2009. "Race and the Colonial Universe in British Malaya". *Journal of Southeast Asian Studies* 40, no. 3: 593–612.

Marshall, David. 1970. "Singapore's Struggle for Nationhood 1945–1959". Journal of Southeast Asian Studies 1, no. 2: 99–104.

Matheson, Virginia. 1986. "Strategies of Survival: The Malay Royal Line of Lingga-Riau". *Journal of Southeast Asian Studies* 17, no. 1: 5–38.

McIntyre, W.D. 1999. "The Strange Death of Dominion Status". *The Journal of Imperial and Commonwealth History* 27, no. 2: 193–212.

Means, Gordon. 1963. "Malaysia—A New Federation in Southeas". *Pacific Affairs* 36, no. 2: 138–59.

Milne, R.S. 1963. "Malaysia: A New Federation in the Making". *Asian Survey* 3, no. 2 (February): 76–82.

Mohamed Noordin Sopiee. 1973. "The Advocacy of Malaysia Before 1961". *Modern Asian Studies* 7, no. 4: 717–32.

Nagata, Judith. 1974. "What is a Malay? Situational Selection of Ethnic Identity in a Plural Society". *American Ethnologist* 1, no. 2: 331–50.

Ong, Chit Chung. 1975. "The 1959 Singapore General Election". *Journal of Southeast Asian Studies* 6, no. 1: 175–84.

Pluvier, J.M. 1968. "Malayan Nationalism: A Myth". *Journal of the Historical Society* 6: 26–40.

Sai, Siew-Min. 2013. "Educating Multicultural Citizens: Colonial Nationalism, Imperial Citizenship and Education in Late Colonial Singapore". *Journal of Southeast Asian Studies* 44, no. 1: 49–73.

———. 2019. "Dressing Up Subjecthood: Straits Chinese, the Queue, and Contested Citizenship in Colonial Singapore". *The Journal of Imperial and Commonwealth History* 47, no. 3: 446–73.

Scott, David. 1995. "Colonial Governmentality". *Social Text*, no. 43: 191–220.

Smith, T.E. 1962. "Proposals for Malaysia". *The World Today* 18, no. 5 (May).

Srinivasan, Krishnan. 2006. "Nobody's Commonwealth? The Commonwealth in Britain's Post-Imperial adjustment". *Commonwealth & Comparative Politics* 44, no. 2 (July): 257–69.

Stockwell, A.J. 1977. "The Formation and First Years of the United Malays National Organization (U.M.N.O.) 1946–1948". *Modern Asian Studies* 11, no. 4: 481–513.

———. 1982. "The White Man's Burden and Brown Humanity: Colonialism and Ethnicity in British Malaya". *Southeast Asian Journal of Social Science* 10, no. 1: 44–68.

———. 1984. "British Imperial Policy and Decolonization in Malaya 1942–52". *Journal of Imperial and Commonwealth History* 13, no. 1: 68–87.

———. 1998. "Malaysia: The Making of a Neo-Colony". *Journal of Imperial and Commonwealth History* 26: 138–56.

———. 2003. "Malaysia: The Making of a Grand Design". *Asian Affairs* 34, no. 3 (November): 227–42.

Van der Straeten, Jonan and Ute Hasenöhrl. 2016. "Connecting the Empire: New Research Perspectives on Infrastructures and the Environment in the (Post) Colonial World". *NTM Journal of the History of Science, Technology and Medicine* 24, no. 35: 355–91.

Thum, Ping Tjin. 2013. "The Fundamental Issue is Anti-Colonialism, Not Merger". *Asia Research Institute Working Paper Series*, no. 211: 1–25.

Tilman, Robert O. 1963. "Malaysia: The Problems of Federation". *The Western Political Quaterly* (December): 897–911.

Tregonning, K.G. 1979. "Tan Cheng Lock: A Malayan Nationalist". *Journal of Southeast Asian Studies* 10, no. 1 (March): 25–76.

Visscher, Sikko. 2008. "Chinese Merchants in Politics: The Democratic Party in the 1955 Legislative Assembly Election". In *Paths Not Taken: Political Pluralism in Post-War Singapore*, edited by Michael Barr and Carl A. Trocki, pp. 78–94. Singapore: NUS Press.

Wang, Gungwu. 1962. "Malayan Nationalism". *Journal of the Royal Central Asian Society* 49: 317–28.

Wicks, Peter. 1980. "Education, British Colonialism, and a Plural Society in West Malaysia: The Development of Education in the British Settlements Along the Straits of Malacca, 1786–1874". *History of Education Quarterly* 20, no. 2: 163–87.

Yeo Kim Wah. 1973. "The Anti-Federation Movement in Malaya, 1946–1948". *Journal of Southeast Asian Studies* 4, no. 1: 31–51.

Yoji, Akashi. 1969. "Japanese Military Administration in Malaya: Its Formation and Evolution in Reference to the Sultans, the Islamic Religion and the Moslem-Malays, 1941–1945". Asian Studies 7, no. 1: 61–89.

Yong, C.F. 1994. "Singapore Politics in Late Colonial Era". Journal of the South Seas Society 49: 1–9.

Yong, C.F. and R.B. McKenna. 1984. "The Kuomintang Movement in Malaya and Singapore, 1925–30". *Journal of Southeast Asian Studies* 15, no. 1 (March): 91–107.

Unpublished Theses

Bedlington, Stanley Sanders. 1974. "The Singapore Malay Community: The Politics of State Integration". PhD dissertation, Faculty of the Graduate School of Cornell University.

Fairus Bin Jasmin. 2013. "Analyzing the Perceptions and Portrayals of the 1964 Racial Riot in Singapore". Master's dissertation, Department of Malay Studies, National University of Singapore.

Ho Chi Tim. 2016. "The Origins, Building and Impact of the Social Welfare State in Late Colonial Singapore". PhD dissertation, University of Hawai'i Mānoa.

Lopez, Bruno. 1987. "Yusof Bin Ishak: Journalist and Head of State". Academic exercise, Department of History, National University of Singapore.

Noor Fadilah Yusof. 2009. "'Malayans First and Last': The Cultural Battle for Merger, from 1959 to 1963". Academic exercise, Department of History, National University of Singapore.

Pillay, Chandrasekaran. 1977. "Some Dominant Concepts and Dissenting Ideas on Malay Rule and the Malay Society from the Malacca to the Colonial and the Merdeka Periods". PhD dissertation, University of Singapore.

Sukmawati Haji Sirat. 1995. "Trends in Malay Political Leadership: The People's Action Party Malay Political Leaders and the Integration of the Singapore Malays". PhD dissertation, Department of Government and International Studies, University of South Carolina.

Zahairin Abdul Rahman. 1988. "Utusan Melayu: Origin and History, 1939–1959". Academic exercise, Department of History, National University of Singapore.

Zheng, Liren. 1997. "Overseas Chinese Nationalism in British Malaya, 1894–1941". PhD dissertation, Cornell University.

Websites

Ilse, Jess. 2022. "Milestones of a Monarch: Barbados Becomes a Republic". *Royal Central*, 30 March 2022. https://royalcentral.co.uk/uk/milestones-of-a-monarch-barbados-becomes-a-republic-174721/ (accessed 24 April 2022).

Perdana Leadership Foundation. Undated. "Biography of Tunku Abdul Rahman (English)". http://www.perdana.org.my/index.php/pms-of-malaysia/tunku-abdul-rahman/tunku-abdul-rahman (accessed 24 April 2022).

President's Office. 2022. "Istana Open House", last updated 21 April 2022. https://www.istana.gov.sg/Visit-And-Explore/Istana-Open-House (accessed 24 April 2022).

Tan, Kevin. 2022. "A History of the Padang". *Biblioasia* 18, no. 1 (April to June). https://biblioasia.nlb.gov.sg/vol-18/issue-1/apr-to-jun-2022/history-padang (accessed 7 November 2022).

Zaain Zin. 2018. "Tunku Abdul Rahman Pada Mata Puterinya". *Utusan Online*, 6 September 2018. https://www.utusan.com.my/mega/rona/video-tunku-abdul-rahman-pada-mata-puterinya-1.743081 (accessed 8 June 2019).

INDEX

ABOUT THE AUTHOR

Muhammad Suhail Mohamed Yazid is a PhD candidate in History at Trinity College, University of Cambridge. He is the college's Prince of Wales Student, having been awarded one of its named doctoral studentships. Suhail concurrently serves as Senior Tutor at the Department of Malay Studies in the National University of Singapore (NUS).

Previously, he was a Research Associate at the Institute of Southeast Asian Studies (ISEAS – Yusof Ishak Institute) and was the institute's Tan Cheng-Lock scholar. He received his Bachelor of Arts with Honours (Highest Distinction) in History and a Master of Arts in Malay Studies from NUS. A Singaporean historian, Suhail has research interests that cover the broader history of decolonization in the Malay World, the Commonwealth of Nations, and the Global South.

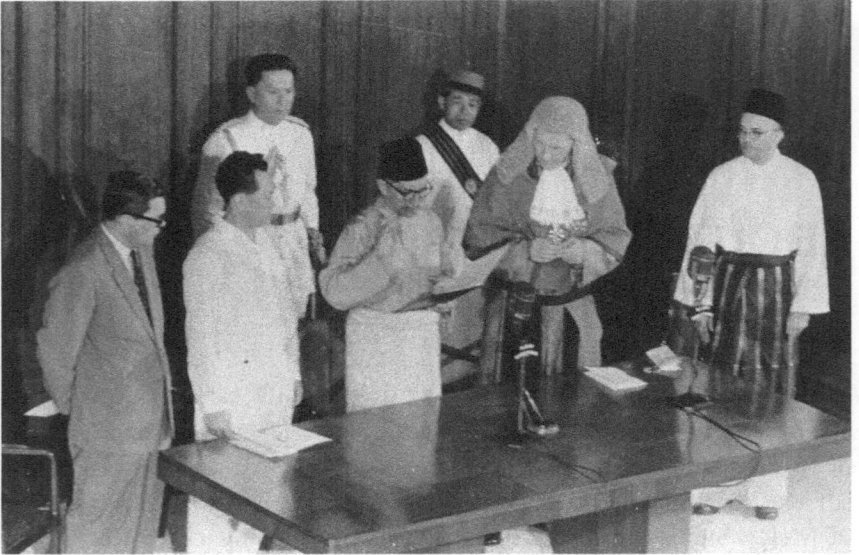

Yusof Ishak (centre) takes his oath as the first Malayan-born Yang di-Pertuan Negara on 3 December 1959, while Prime Minister Lee Kuan Yew (Yusof's right) and Chief Justice Sir Alan Rose (Yusof's left) look on. *Photo credit*: Ministry of Information and the Arts Collection, courtesy of National Archives of Singapore

The singing of *Majulah Singapura* and the raising of the new state flag, with politicians, dignitaries and the freshly installed Yang di-Pertuan Negara standing on the steps of City Hall. *Photo credit*: Yusof Ishak Collection, courtesy of National Archives of Singapore

The Yang di-Pertuan Negara delivers his address to the crowd at the Padang following his swearing-in ceremony. *Photo credit*: Ministry of Information and the Arts Collection, courtesy of National Archives of Singapore

The Yang di-Pertuan Negara receives salute from marching contingents after his first public address. *Photo credit*: Ministry of Information and the Arts Collection, courtesy of National Archives of Singapore

Sir William Goode, the last governor of Singapore, dresses in full ceremonial attire to welcome the Duke of Edinburgh during the latter's visit to the island in February 1959. Note the cock-hat with white plumes. *Photo credit*: Ministry of Information and the Arts Collection, courtesy of National Archives of Singapore

Yang di-Pertuan Negara Sir William Goode (in lounge suit) inspects the guard of honour during the opening of the first legislative session following the 1959 general elections. *Photo credit*: Ministry of Information and the Arts Collection, courtesy of National Archives of Singapore

The Yang di-Pertuan Negara, Yusof Ishak (centre), in the company of village headmen from Pulau Bukhom Kechil during his tour of the Southern Islands in January 1960. *Photo credit*: Yusof Ishak Collection, courtesy of National Archives of Singapore

The Yang di-Pertuan Negara addresses the islanders of Pulau Semakau during a separate leg of his Southern Islands tour. *Photo credit*: Yusof Ishak Collection, courtesy of National Archives of Singapore

Village headmen and islanders of Pulau Seking patiently line up to greet the Yang di-Pertuan Negara as he arrives on the island as part of his January 1960 Southern Islands tour. *Photo credit*: Yusof Ishak Collection, courtesy of National Archives of Singapore

The Yang di-Pertuan Negara speaks to residents of Pulau Brani, one of the many islands that form Singapore's Southern Islands, in February 1960. Labour and Law Minister K.M. Byrne sits on his right. *Photo credit*: Yusof Ishak Collection, courtesy of National Archives of Singapore

The Yang di-Pertuan Negara and the rulers of the Federation of Malaya (left elevated platform) witness the coronation of the new Yang di-Pertuan Agong in January 1961. *Photo credit*: Yusof Ishak Collection, courtesy of National Archives of Singapore

The Yang di-Pertuan Negara (left) and his wife, Puan Noor Aishah (right), leave the Hall of Audience after the coronation ceremony of the Yang di-Pertuan Agong in January 1961. *Photo credit*: Yusof Ishak Collection, courtesy of National Archives of Singapore

The Yang di-Pertuan Negara (left), who also serves as Singapore's Chief Scout, interacts with troops at Jubilee Camp in July 1960. *Photo credit*: Yusof Ishak Collection, courtesy of National Archives of Singapore

Members of the Carnival Management Committee welcome the Yang di-Pertuan Negara as he officiates the 1960 National Day Carnival at Raffles Institution to celebrate Singapore's first National Day. *Photo credit*: Ministry of Information and the Arts Collection, courtesy of National Archives of Singapore

Yusof Ishak inspects the guard of honour consisting of servicemen from the First Battalion, Singapore Infantry Regiment, prior to his first Yang di-Pertuan Negara Address to mark the opening of the legislative session in July 1960. *Photo credit*: Ministry of Information and the Arts Collection, courtesy of National Archives of Singapore

The Yang di-Pertuan Negara chats with Field Marshal Gerald Templer, the "Tiger of Malaya", at the Istana Negara in October 1960. Both men had a long history of dealing with each other. *Photo credit*: Yusof Ishak Collection, courtesy of National Archives of Singapore

Hoe Puay Choo (right), assemblywoman for Bras Basah, accompanies the Yang di-Pertuan Negara (left) in the state car during the latter's visit to her constituency in April 1961. *Photo credit*: Yusof Ishak Collection, courtesy of National Archives of Singapore

The Yang di-Pertuan Negara in the company of Mandai Village residents during his tour of Bukit Panjang in May 1961. Lee Khoon Choy, Parliamentary Secretary at the Ministry of Culture and assemblyman of the constituency, sits with him while enjoying a cigarette. *Photo credit*: Yusof Ishak Collection, courtesy of National Archives of Singapore

The Yang di-Pertuan Negara (centre) and his wife, Noor Aishah, welcome the British Commissioner in Singapore, Lord Selkirk, and his wife to a garden party at the Istana Negara to celebrate Singapore's National Day in June 1961. *Photo credit*: Ministry of Information and the Arts Collection, courtesy of National Archives of Singapore

A PAP rally at City Hall in June 1959 to celebrate the party's handsome electoral victory during the general elections. Note the Chinese-language banners that adorn the City Hall building. *Photo credit*: Ministry of Information and the Arts Collection, courtesy of National Archives of Singapore

The Yang di-Pertuan Negara officiating the 1961 Quranic Reading Competition organized by the Muslim Advisory Board. *Photo credit*: Yusof Ishak Collection, courtesy of National Archives of Singapore

The Yang di-Pertuan Negara sends off Muslim pilgrims in February 1961 as they embark on their long journey via sea to Mecca. *Photo credit*: Yusof Ishak Collection, courtesy of National Archives of Singapore

The Yang di-Pertuan Negara (centre) entertains state guests during a dinner at the Istana Negara to commemorate Singapore's National Day in June 1962. On his right is Dr Ismail Abdul Rahman, the Malayan Minister for Home Affairs and the Federation representative to Singapore's Internal Security Council. *Photo credit*: Yusof Ishak Collection, courtesy of National Archives of Singapore

The Yang di-Pertuan Negara, now head of state of an ex-colonial Singapore, reviews a parade at City Hall to usher the official formation of Malaysia on 16 September 1963. *Photo credit*: Ministry of Information and the Arts Collection, courtesy of National Archives of Singapore